EDGAR ALLAN POE'S
SNIFTER of DEATH

AHOY
COMICS

EDGAR ALLAN POE'S

SNIFTER OF DEATH

COMICSAHOY.COM @AHOYCOMICMAGS

HART SEELY - PUBLISHER
TOM PEYER - EDITOR-IN-CHIEF
FRANK CAMMUSO - CHIEF CREATIVE OFFICER
STUART MOORE - OPS
SARAH LITT - EDITOR-AT-LARGE
CORY SEDLMEIER - COLLECTIONS EDITOR

DAVID HYDE - PUBLICITY
DERON BENNETT - PRODUCTION COORDINATOR
KIT CAOAGAS - MARKETING ASSOCIATE
HANNA BAHEDRY - PUBLICITY COORDINATOR
LILLIAN LASERSON - LEGAL
RUSSELL NATHERSON SR. - BUSINESS

EDGAR ALLAN POE'S SNIFTER OF DEATH VOL. 1 - Published AHOY Comics LLC, PO Box 189, DeWitt, NY 13214.

PRINTED IN THE U.S.A. - FIRST PRINTING - SEPTEMBER 2022 - ISBN: 978-1-952090-19-6

RICHARD WILLIAMS | COVER ARTIST
TODD KLEIN | ORIGINAL LOGO
JOHN J. HILL | DESIGN
DERON BENNETT | ASSOCIATE EDITOR
TOM PEYER | EDITOR
CORY SEDLMEIER | COLLECTION EDITOR

INTRODUCTION

When you're a bartender, you interact with all kinds. That's the main part of the job. Some people are great to be around, others not so much. But I never had a worse customer than Edgar Allan Poe.

First of all, it's well-known what a pathetic drunk he was—broke, self-destructive, always carrying a torch for some corpse in a nightgown—so half the time you're dealing with him you're just sad. But the other half you're not sad at all, owing to the fact that he was an asshole.

He'd show up around 11 A.M. and when you'd see him walking in you felt like the day was already shot. Because Poe needed so much attention. Always something to complain about, or some involved story about money coming in and could I advance him some drinks now. Maybe he wrote a poem and needed to recite it, right then, no matter how long it was or how many customers I had waiting.

It didn't matter who you were, if you had ears he'd fill them up. So people would say, "Isn't it nice, a famous guy like that, gets his name in the paper all the time, but he talks to everyone the same." Well, it wasn't nice. He didn't talk to everyone the same because he thought we were all important. He talked to everyone the same because we were *unimportant.* I don't think he could distinguish between any two people on Earth, unless one of them was a dying girl with a name like Eulalie or Jacinta. Then he wouldn't be talking. He'd be kissing her arm all the way up and back down and she'd be shooting me a look like, "Help!" So I'd run him out and then he'd be afraid to show up for a week. It made for a nice break, but he'd always come back.

So anyway, he'd come in like I said around 11, and he'd be quiet, hung over. But get him halfway into his second gin-and-oysters and the floodgates would come crashing down. This son-of-a-so-and-so editor didn't pay him, or some bastard critic was too stupid to understand his masterpiece, or his rotten landlord expected rent. On and on and on. I don't know how he wrote stories with characters in them, because off the page he couldn't see anybody's point of view but his own.

I make it sound like it was all bad, but there were good times. He'd mouth off to the wrong Irishman and get the shit beat out of him. We'd all laugh.

We didn't have a lot to entertain us back then, so to pass the time, my customers would sing songs, or play the piano, or do recitations. But not so much when Poe was around. Anytime a singer or reciter was getting all the attention, he would be enraged. He'd start breathing heavy through his nose, like a horse about to charge, and I'd tell him to watch himself or he's out for good, so he'd calm down a little. But then he'd blow his nose real loud right over the reciter's punchline or the singer's high note and they'd stomp away mad. So most of the time, the customers and I would sit around bored, because Poe wouldn't let you do anything. You couldn't even carry on a conversation without him butting in.

Sometimes I'd put an extra something in his drink, just so he'd pass out and we could get a little peace. But even then he'd snore so loud it scared the horses. And the knockout drops gave him terrible gas. I had to stop using them.

One night, I got so fed up with his constant horseshit that I said to him, "Poe, I want you to check out this new wine we got downstairs. Come with me." There wasn't any new wine, but there were a whole lot of bricks, because we were remodeling. So we're down there and I go, "Hey, look over there," and when he looks I slap these manacles on him. Every bar kept manacles, but that's not the point. The point is, I take the bricks and some mortar and I start building a wall. And he's screaming, but if anyone heard him they wouldn't come running, because it's Poe and they hate him. So I wall him in.

I guess I have a tender heart because a couple days later I felt so bad I knocked the new wall down and let him out. I bought him a nice meal, stood him a whole night of drinks. Next thing I know, he's sold this story about a guy who walls a guy in. So I tell him it was my idea, I should get a cut of the money, and he got up and walked out.

He never came back after that. I don't know how much money we were arguing about, but whatever it was, it was worth every cent.

Erasmus Monroe
Baltimore, MD
July 2022

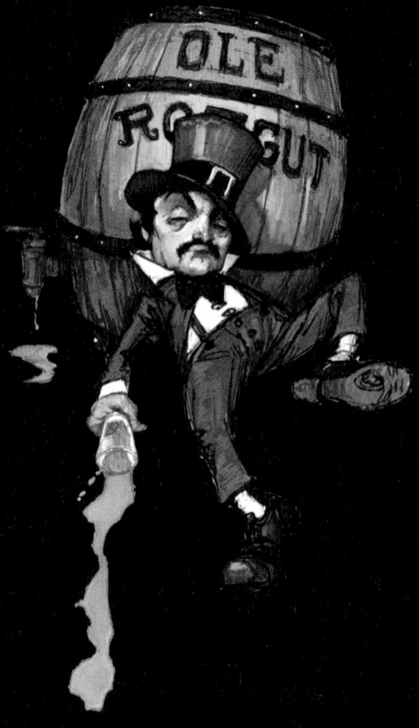
OLE

Erasmus Monroe tended bar at The Crab Tavern in Baltimore, MD, from 1822-1855.

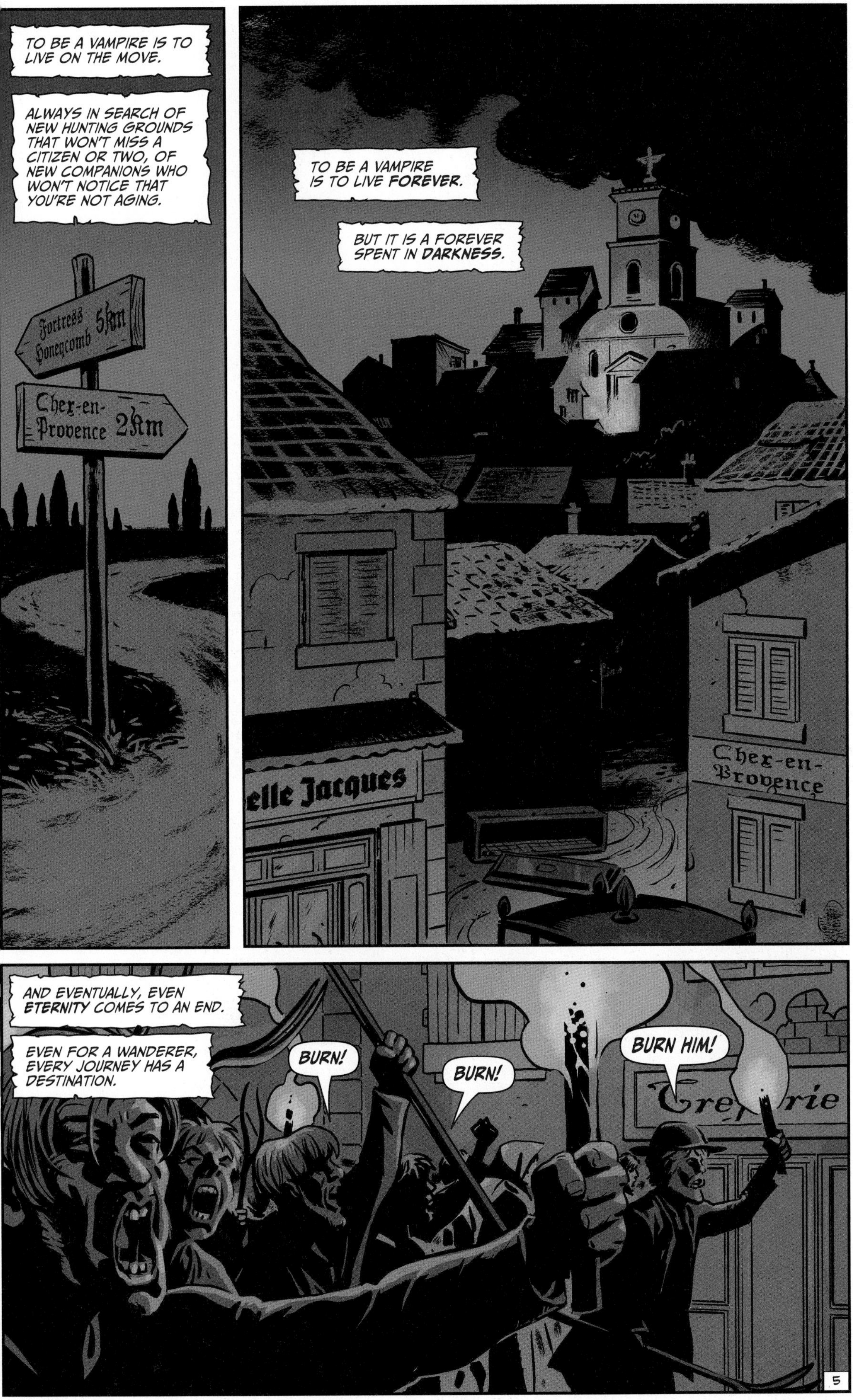
TO BE A VAMPIRE IS TO LIVE ON THE MOVE.
ALWAYS IN SEARCH OF NEW HUNTING GROUNDS THAT WON'T MISS A CITIZEN OR TWO, OF NEW COMPANIONS WHO WON'T NOTICE THAT YOU'RE NOT AGING.
Fortress Honeycomb 5km
Chez-en-Provence 2km
TO BE A VAMPIRE IS TO LIVE FOREVER.
BUT IT IS A FOREVER SPENT IN DARKNESS.
Chez-en-Provence
AND EVENTUALLY, EVEN ETERNITY COMES TO AN END.
EVEN FOR A WANDERER, EVERY JOURNEY HAS A DESTINATION.
BURN!
BURN!
BURN HIM!

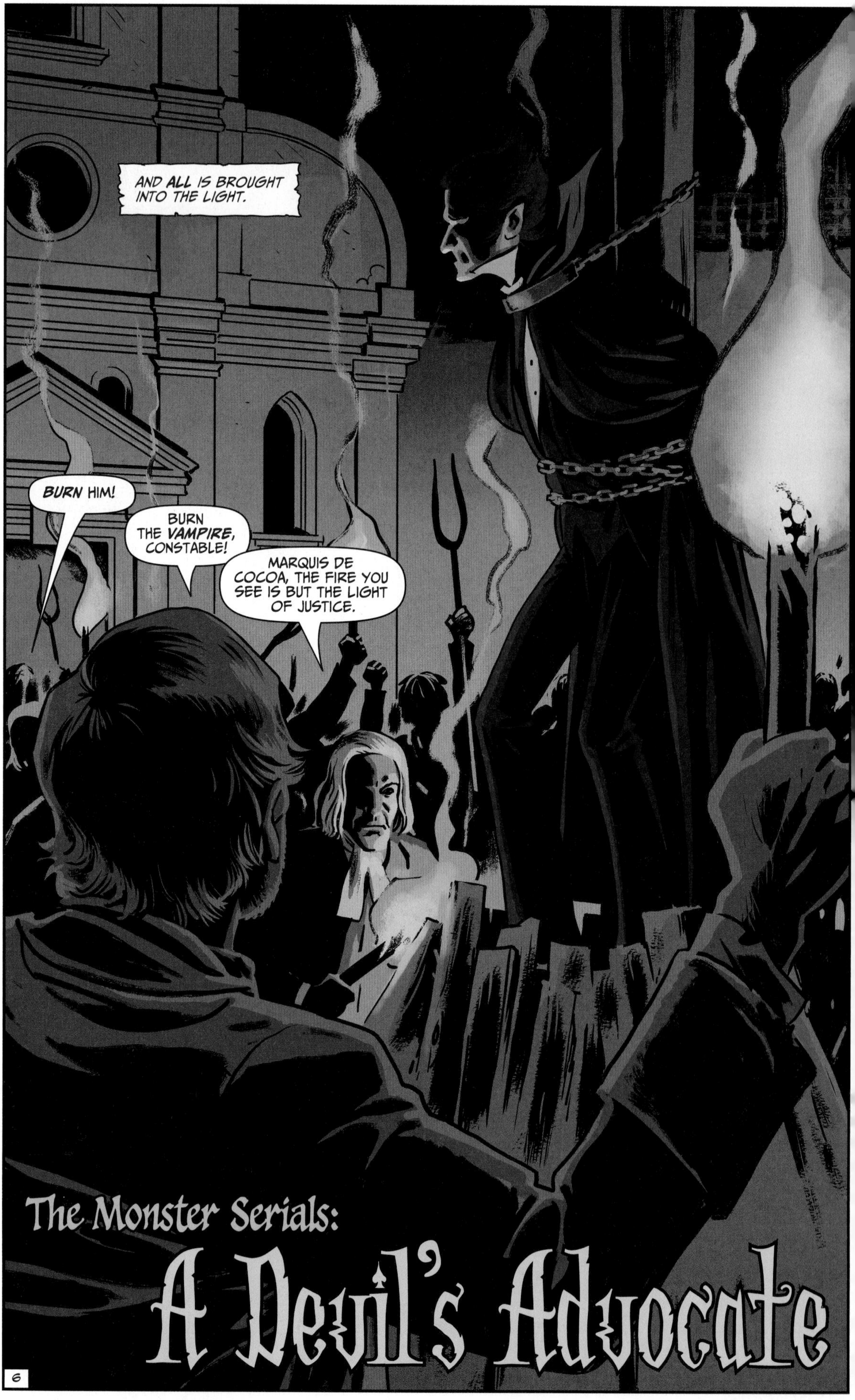
AND ALL IS BROUGHT INTO THE LIGHT.
BURN HIM!
BURN THE VAMPIRE, CONSTABLE!
MARQUIS DE COCOA, THE FIRE YOU SEE IS BUT THE LIGHT OF JUSTICE.
The Monster Serials:
A Devil's Advocate

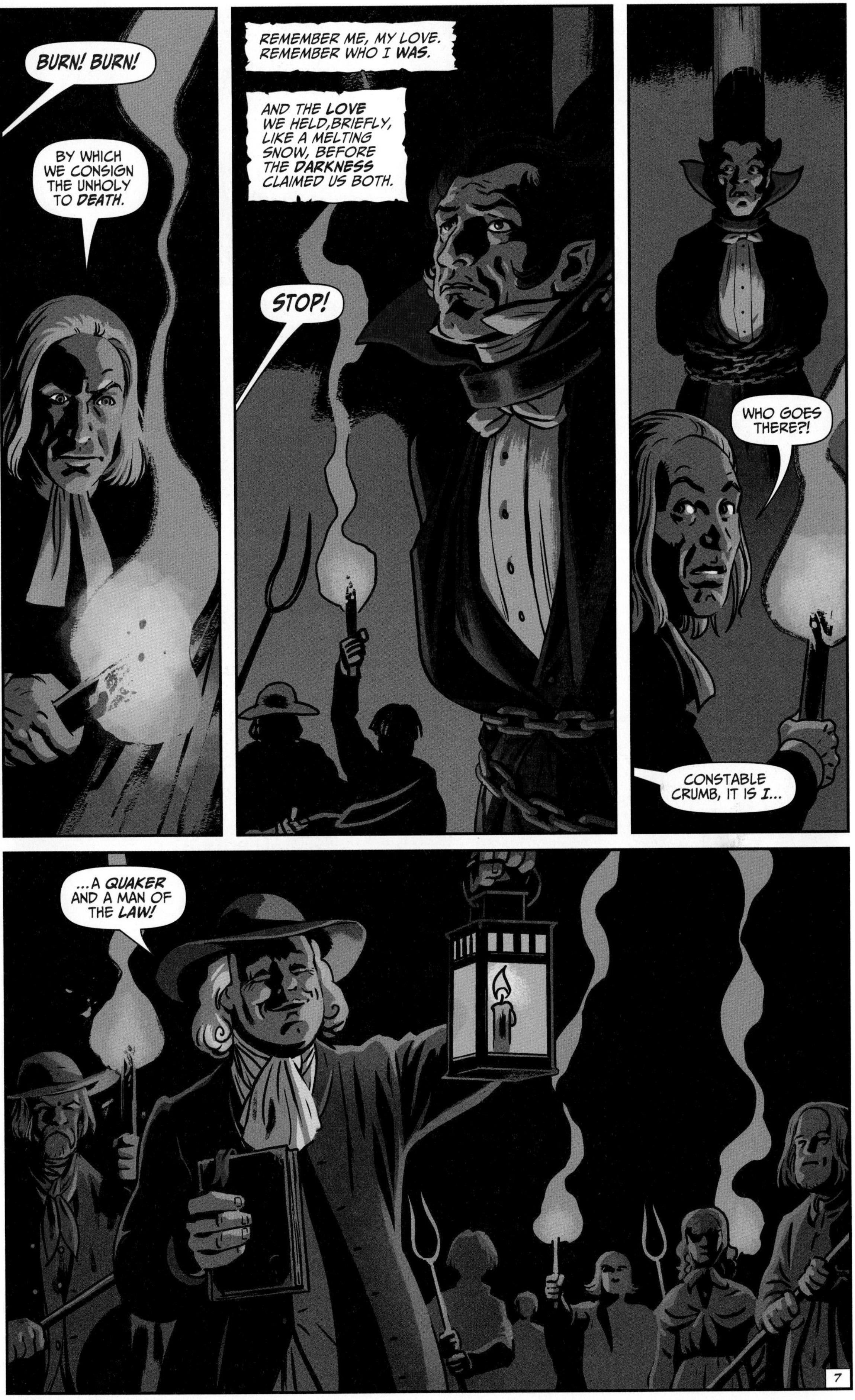
BURN! BURN!
BY WHICH WE CONSIGN THE UNHOLY TO DEATH.
REMEMBER ME, MY LOVE. REMEMBER WHO I WAS.
AND THE LOVE WE HELD, BRIEFLY, LIKE A MELTING SNOW, BEFORE THE DARKNESS CLAIMED US BOTH.
STOP!
WHO GOES THERE?!
CONSTABLE CRUMB, IT IS I...
...A QUAKER AND A MAN OF THE LAW!

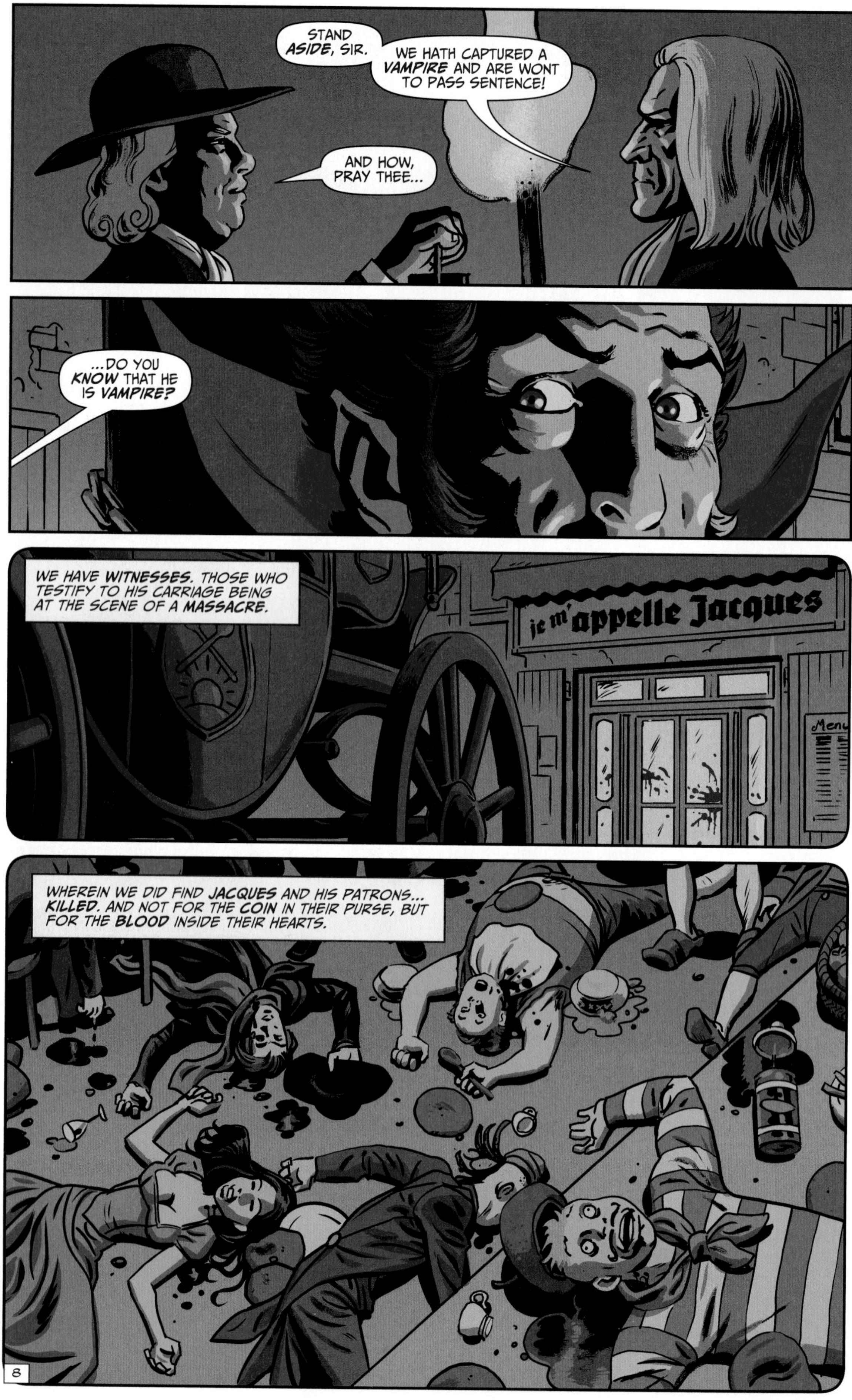
STAND ASIDE, SIR.
WE HATH CAPTURED A VAMPIRE AND ARE WONT TO PASS SENTENCE!
AND HOW, PRAY THEE...
...DO YOU KNOW THAT HE IS VAMPIRE?
WE HAVE WITNESSES. THOSE WHO TESTIFY TO HIS CARRIAGE BEING AT THE SCENE OF A MASSACRE.
je m'appelle Jacques
Menu
WHEREIN WE DID FIND JACQUES AND HIS PATRONS... KILLED. AND NOT FOR THE COIN IN THEIR PURSE, BUT FOR THE BLOOD INSIDE THEIR HEARTS.

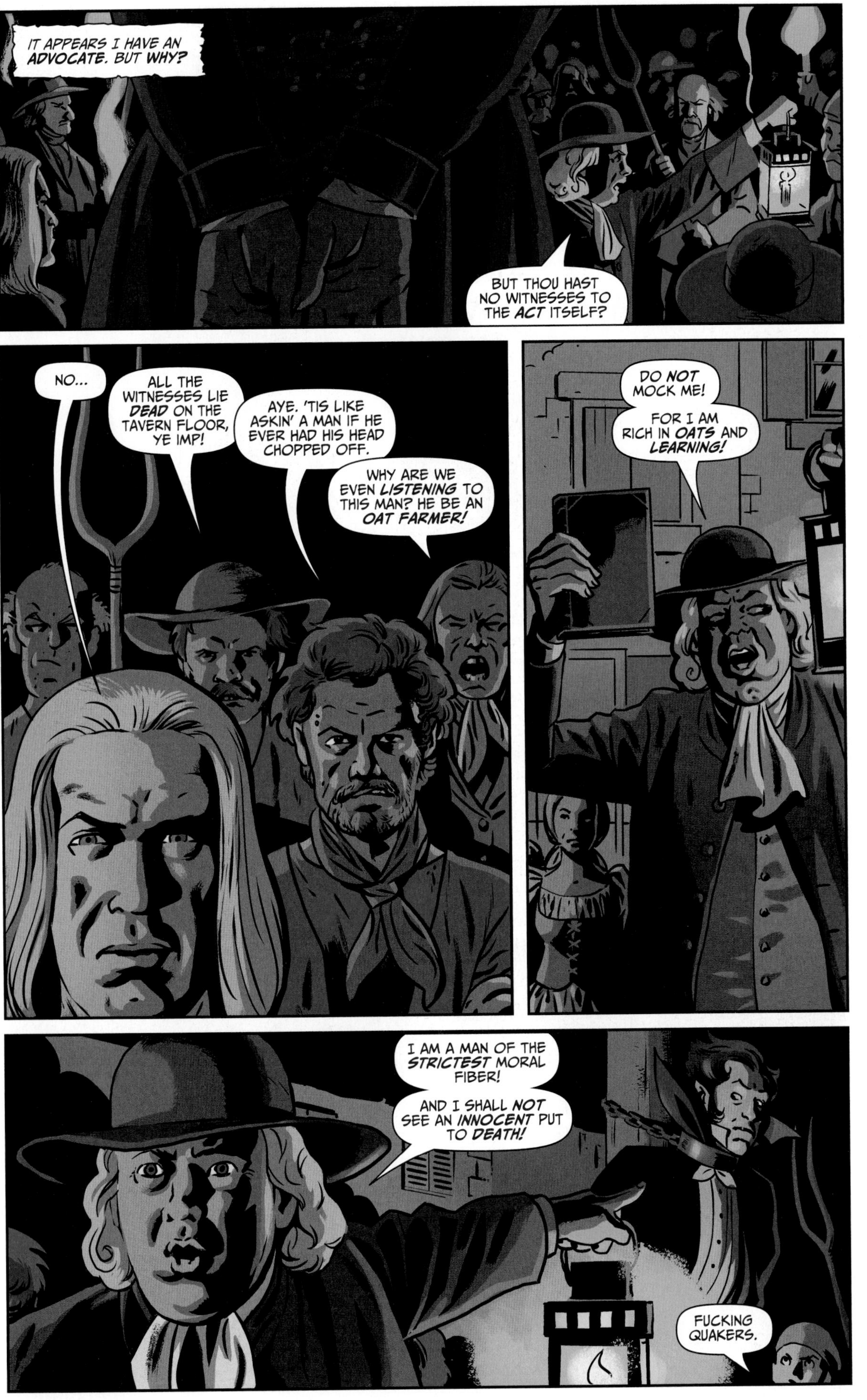

IT APPEARS I HAVE AN ADVOCATE. BUT WHY?
BUT THOU HAST NO WITNESSES TO THE ACT ITSELF?
NO...
ALL THE WITNESSES LIE DEAD ON THE TAVERN FLOOR, YE IMP!
AYE. 'TIS LIKE ASKIN' A MAN IF HE EVER HAD HIS HEAD CHOPPED OFF.
WHY ARE WE EVEN LISTENING TO THIS MAN? HE BE AN OAT FARMER!
DO NOT MOCK ME!
FOR I AM RICH IN OATS AND LEARNING!
I AM A MAN OF THE STRICTEST MORAL FIBER!
AND I SHALL NOT SEE AN INNOCENT PUT TO DEATH!
FUCKING QUAKERS.

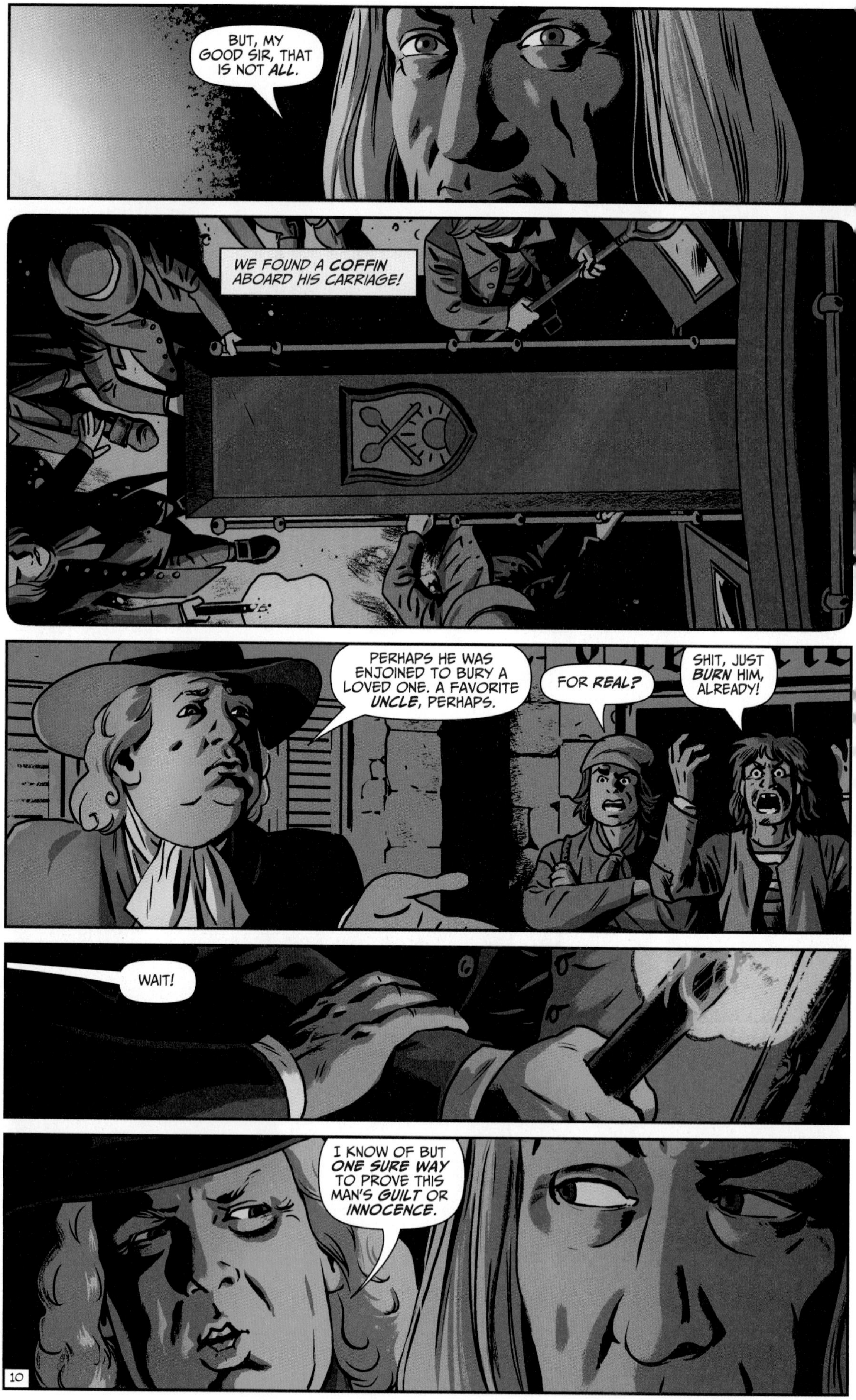
BUT, MY GOOD SIR, THAT IS NOT ALL.
WE FOUND A COFFIN ABOARD HIS CARRIAGE!
PERHAPS HE WAS ENJOINED TO BURY A LOVED ONE. A FAVORITE UNCLE, PERHAPS.
FOR REAL?
SHIT, JUST BURN HIM, ALREADY!
WAIT!
I KNOW OF BUT ONE SURE WAY TO PROVE THIS MAN'S GUILT OR INNOCENCE.

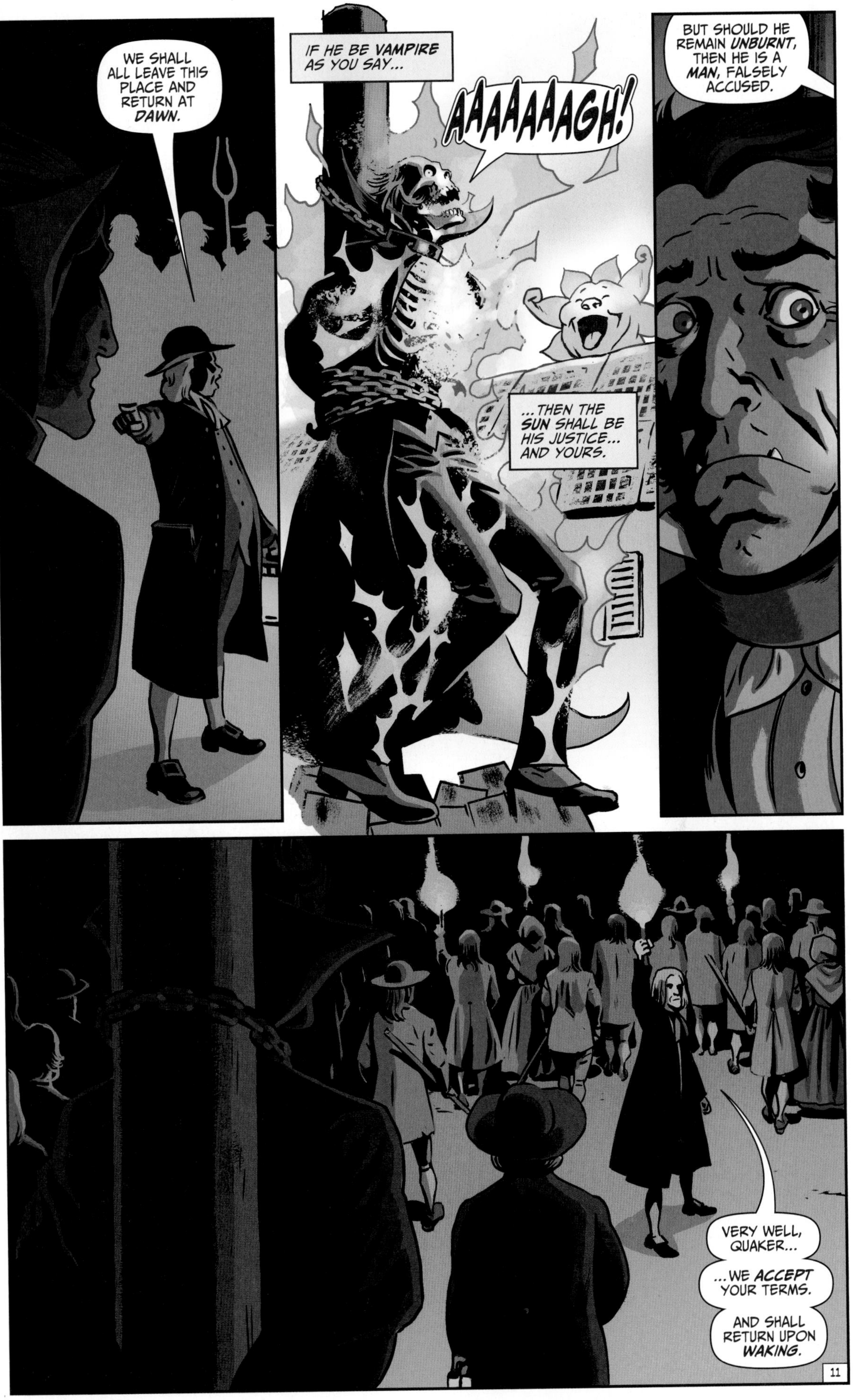

WE SHALL ALL LEAVE THIS PLACE AND RETURN AT DAWN.
IF HE BE VAMPIRE AS YOU SAY...
AAAAAAAGH!
...THEN THE SUN SHALL BE HIS JUSTICE... AND YOURS.
BUT SHOULD HE REMAIN UNBURNT, THEN HE IS A MAN, FALSELY ACCUSED.
VERY WELL, QUAKER...
...WE ACCEPT YOUR TERMS.
AND SHALL RETURN UPON WAKING.

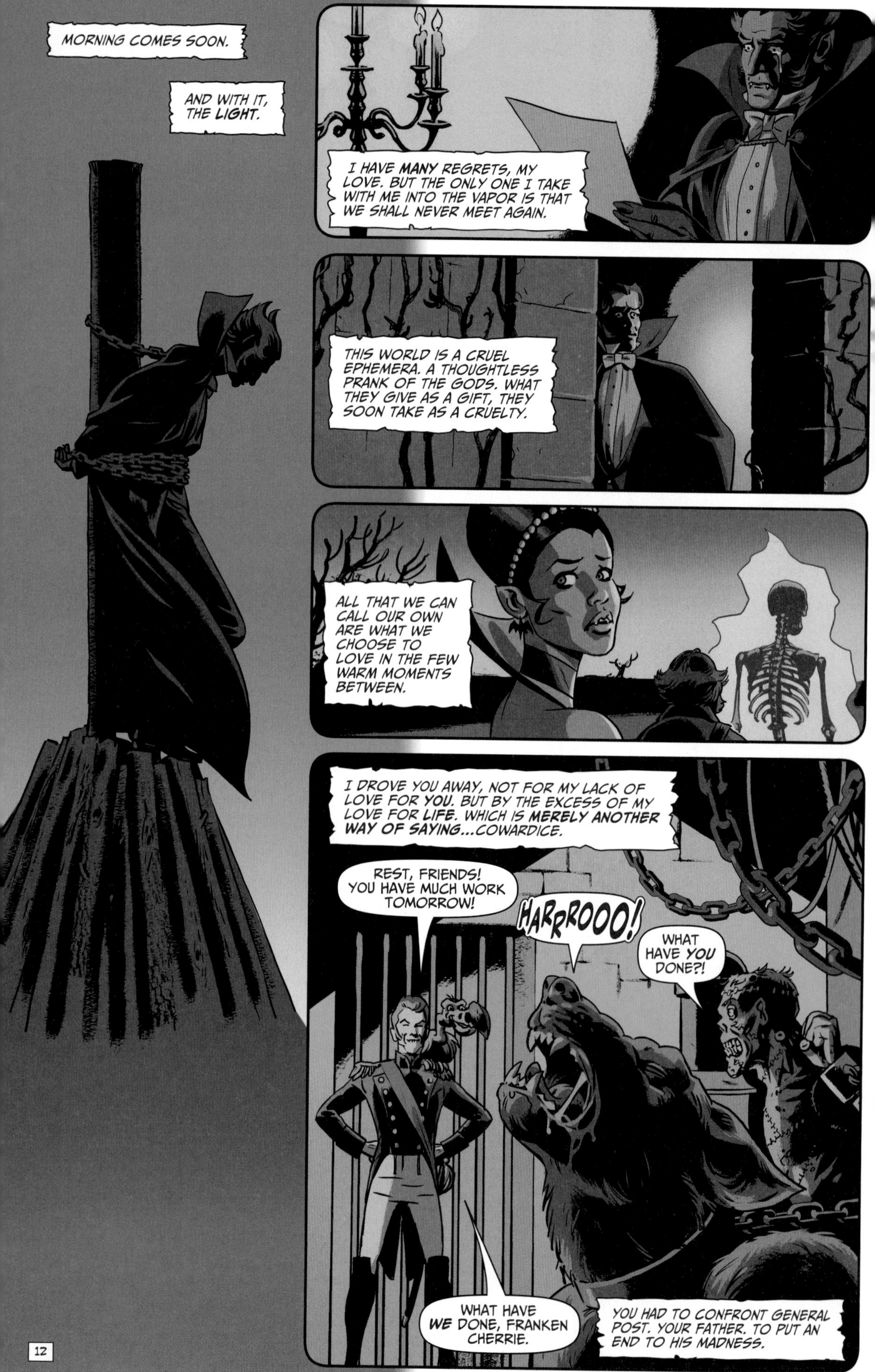

MORNING COMES SOON.
AND WITH IT, THE LIGHT.
I HAVE MANY REGRETS, MY LOVE. BUT THE ONLY ONE I TAKE WITH ME INTO THE VAPOR IS THAT WE SHALL NEVER MEET AGAIN.
THIS WORLD IS A CRUEL EPHEMERA. A THOUGHTLESS PRANK OF THE GODS. WHAT THEY GIVE AS A GIFT, THEY SOON TAKE AS A CRUELTY.
ALL THAT WE CAN CALL OUR OWN ARE WHAT WE CHOOSE TO LOVE IN THE FEW WARM MOMENTS BETWEEN.
I DROVE YOU AWAY, NOT FOR MY LACK OF LOVE FOR YOU. BUT BY THE EXCESS OF MY LOVE FOR LIFE. WHICH IS MERELY ANOTHER WAY OF SAYING...COWARDICE.
REST, FRIENDS! YOU HAVE MUCH WORK TOMORROW!
HARRROOO!
WHAT HAVE YOU DONE?!
WHAT HAVE WE DONE, FRANKEN CHERRIE.
YOU HAD TO CONFRONT GENERAL POST. YOUR FATHER. TO PUT AN END TO HIS MADNESS.

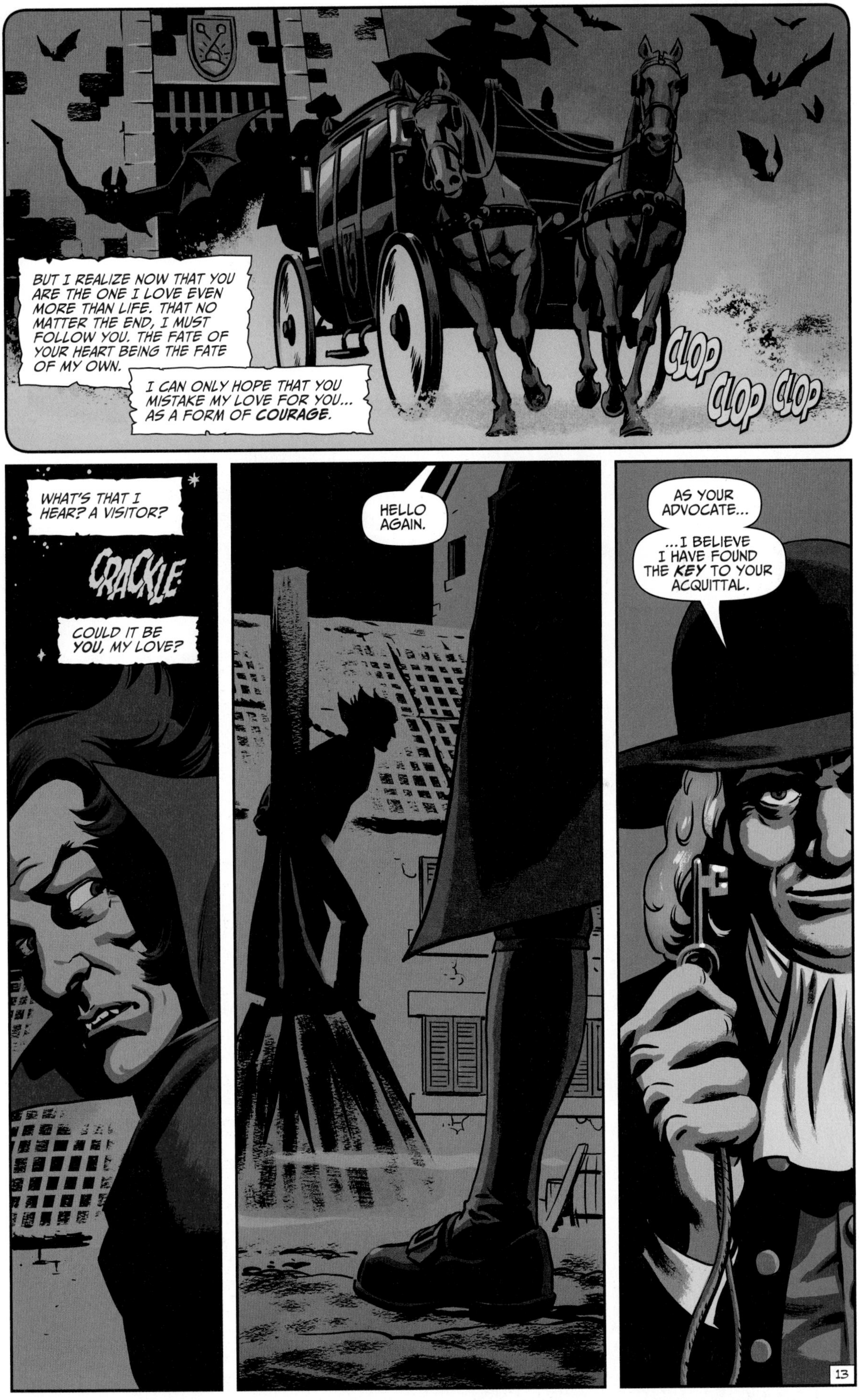
BUT I REALIZE NOW THAT YOU ARE THE ONE I LOVE EVEN MORE THAN LIFE. THAT NO MATTER THE END, I MUST FOLLOW YOU. THE FATE OF YOUR HEART BEING THE FATE OF MY OWN.
I CAN ONLY HOPE THAT YOU MISTAKE MY LOVE FOR YOU... AS A FORM OF COURAGE.
CLOP CLOP CLOP
WHAT'S THAT I HEAR? A VISITOR?
CRACKLE
COULD IT BE YOU, MY LOVE?
HELLO AGAIN.
AS YOUR ADVOCATE...
...I BELIEVE I HAVE FOUND THE KEY TO YOUR ACQUITTAL.

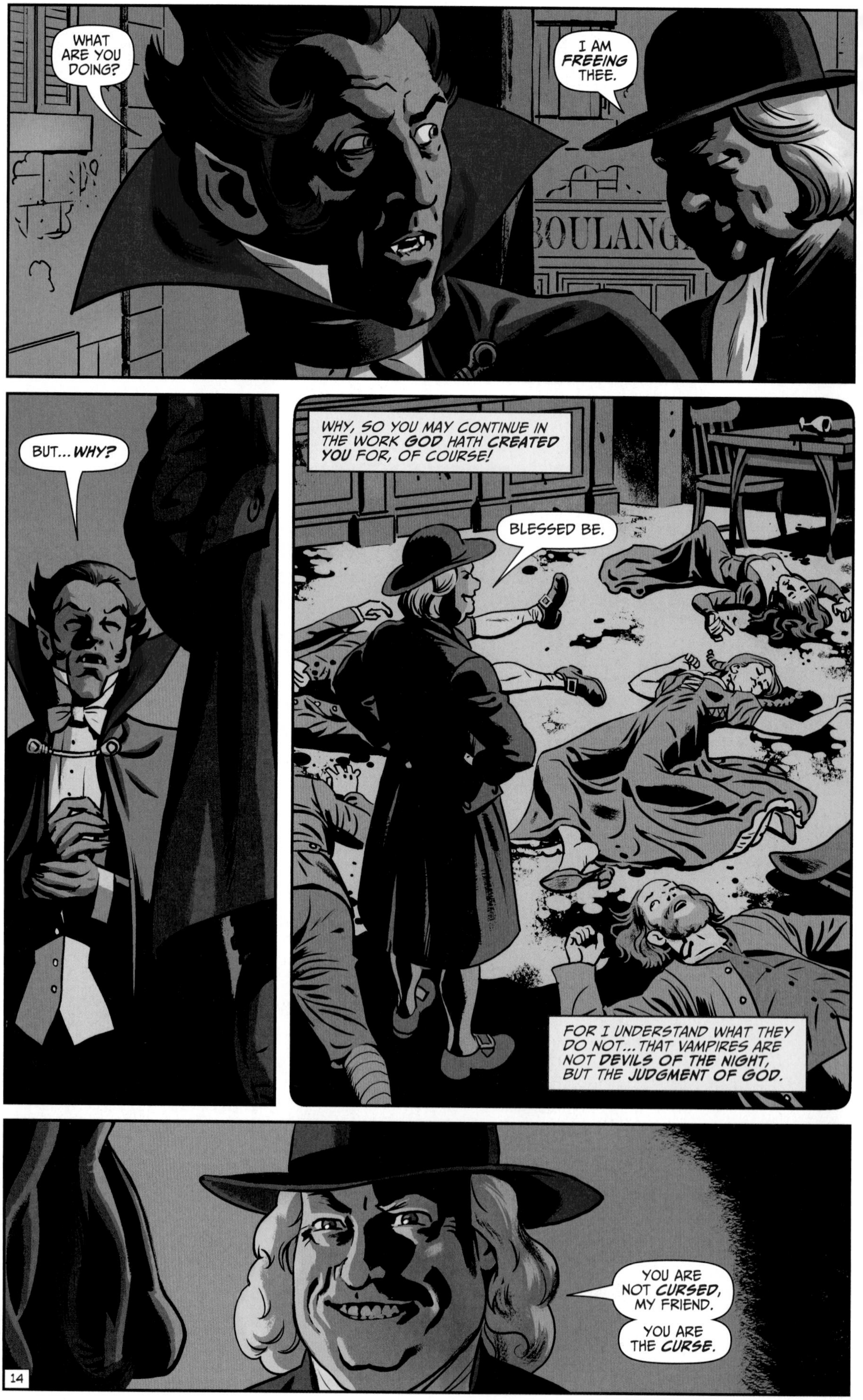
WHAT ARE YOU DOING?
I AM FREEING THEE.
BOULANG
BUT... WHY?
WHY, SO YOU MAY CONTINUE IN THE WORK GOD HATH CREATED YOU FOR, OF COURSE!
BLESSED BE.
FOR I UNDERSTAND WHAT THEY DO NOT... THAT VAMPIRES ARE NOT DEVILS OF THE NIGHT, BUT THE JUDGMENT OF GOD.
YOU ARE NOT CURSED, MY FRIEND.
YOU ARE THE CURSE.

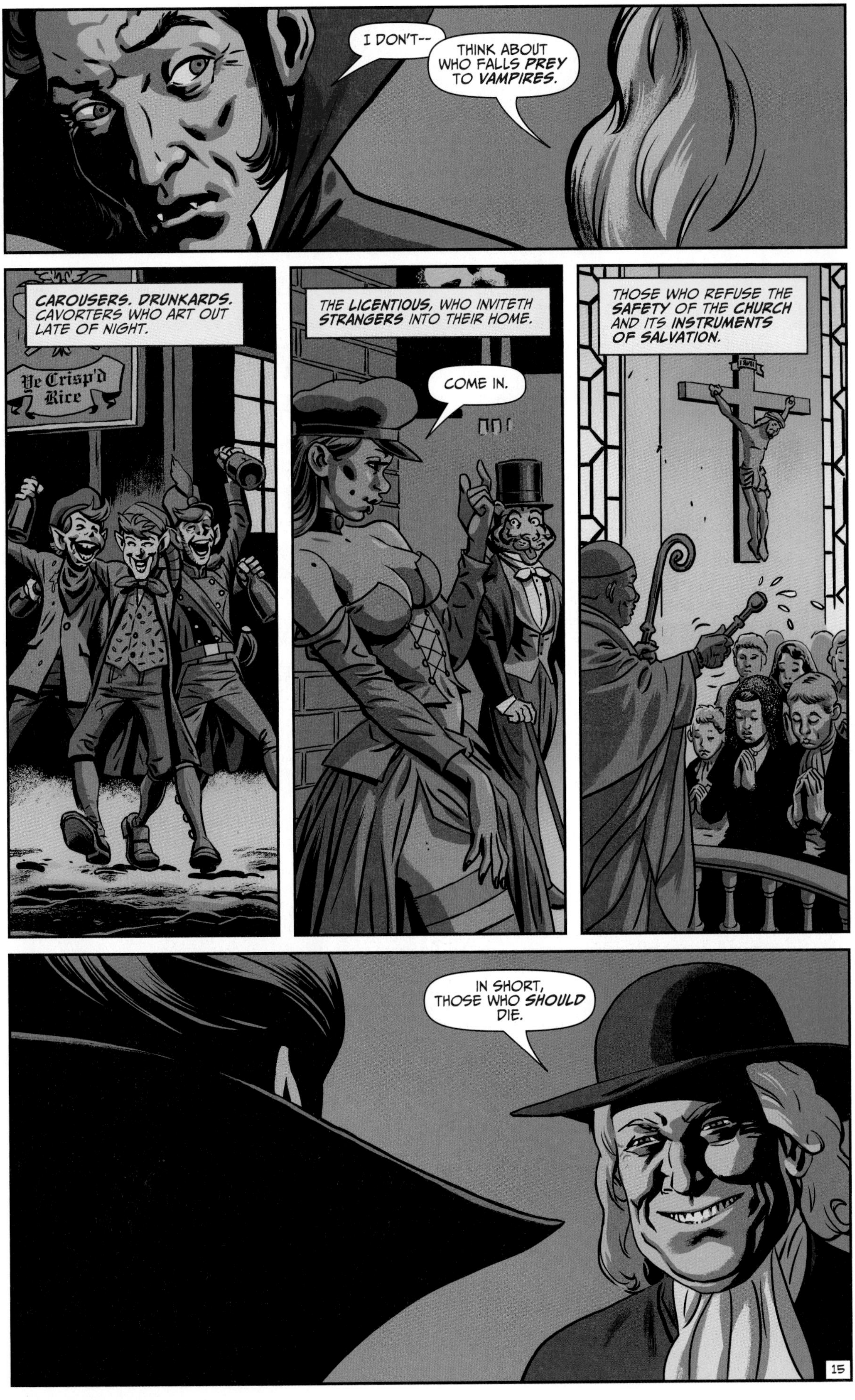
I DON'T--
THINK ABOUT WHO FALLS PREY TO VAMPIRES.
CAROUSERS. DRUNKARDS. CAVORTERS WHO ART OUT LATE OF NIGHT.
Ye Crisp'd Rice
THE LICENTIOUS, WHO INVITETH STRANGERS INTO THEIR HOME.
COME IN.
THOSE WHO REFUSE THE SAFETY OF THE CHURCH AND ITS INSTRUMENTS OF SALVATION.
IN SHORT, THOSE WHO SHOULD DIE.

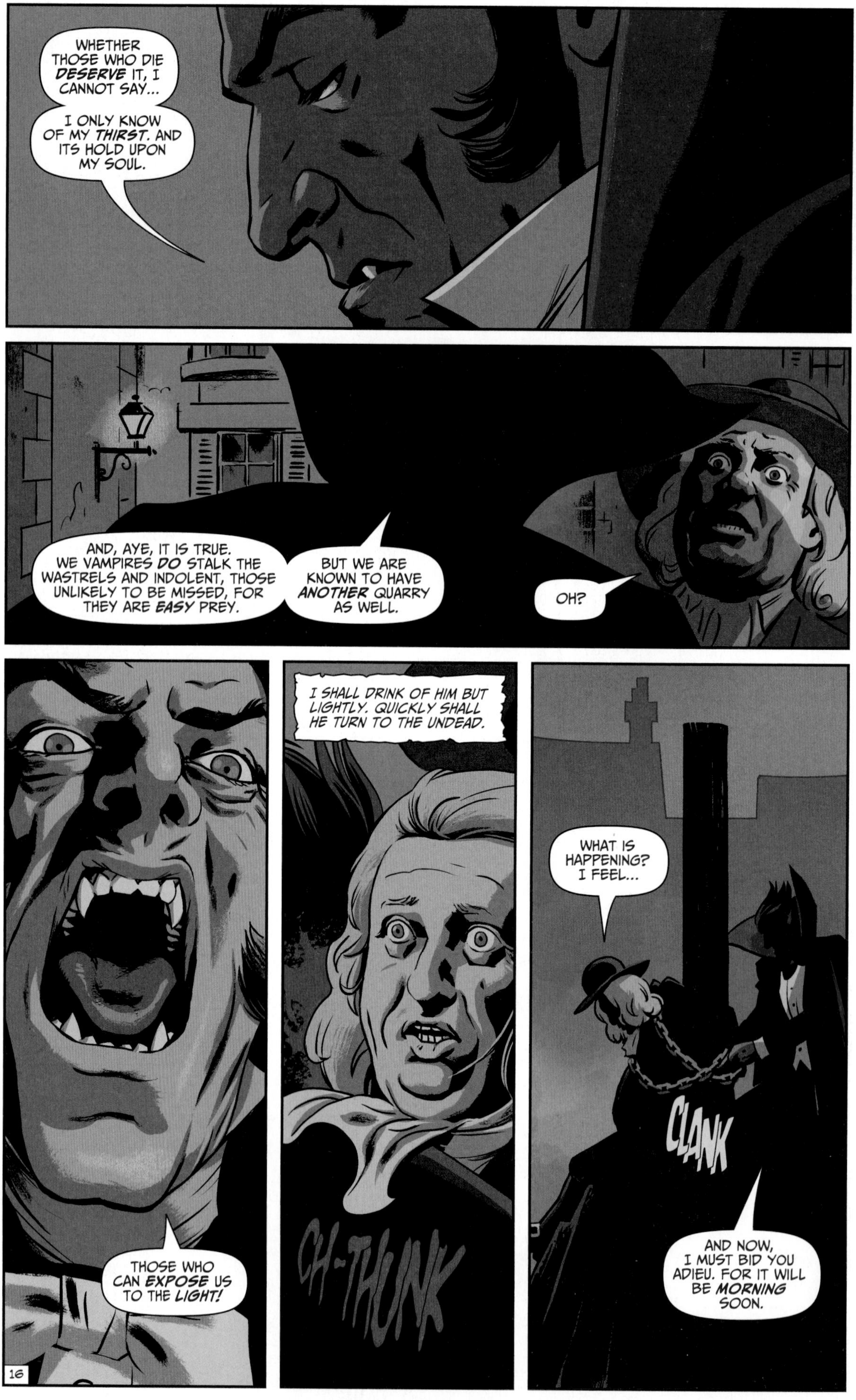
WHETHER THOSE WHO DIE DESERVE IT, I CANNOT SAY...
I ONLY KNOW OF MY THIRST. AND ITS HOLD UPON MY SOUL.
AND, AYE, IT IS TRUE. WE VAMPIRES DO STALK THE WASTRELS AND INDOLENT, THOSE UNLIKELY TO BE MISSED, FOR THEY ARE EASY PREY.
BUT WE ARE KNOWN TO HAVE ANOTHER QUARRY AS WELL.
OH?
THOSE WHO CAN EXPOSE US TO THE LIGHT!
I SHALL DRINK OF HIM BUT LIGHTLY. QUICKLY SHALL HE TURN TO THE UNDEAD.
CH-THUNK
WHAT IS HAPPENING? I FEEL...
CLANK
AND NOW, I MUST BID YOU ADIEU. FOR IT WILL BE MORNING SOON.

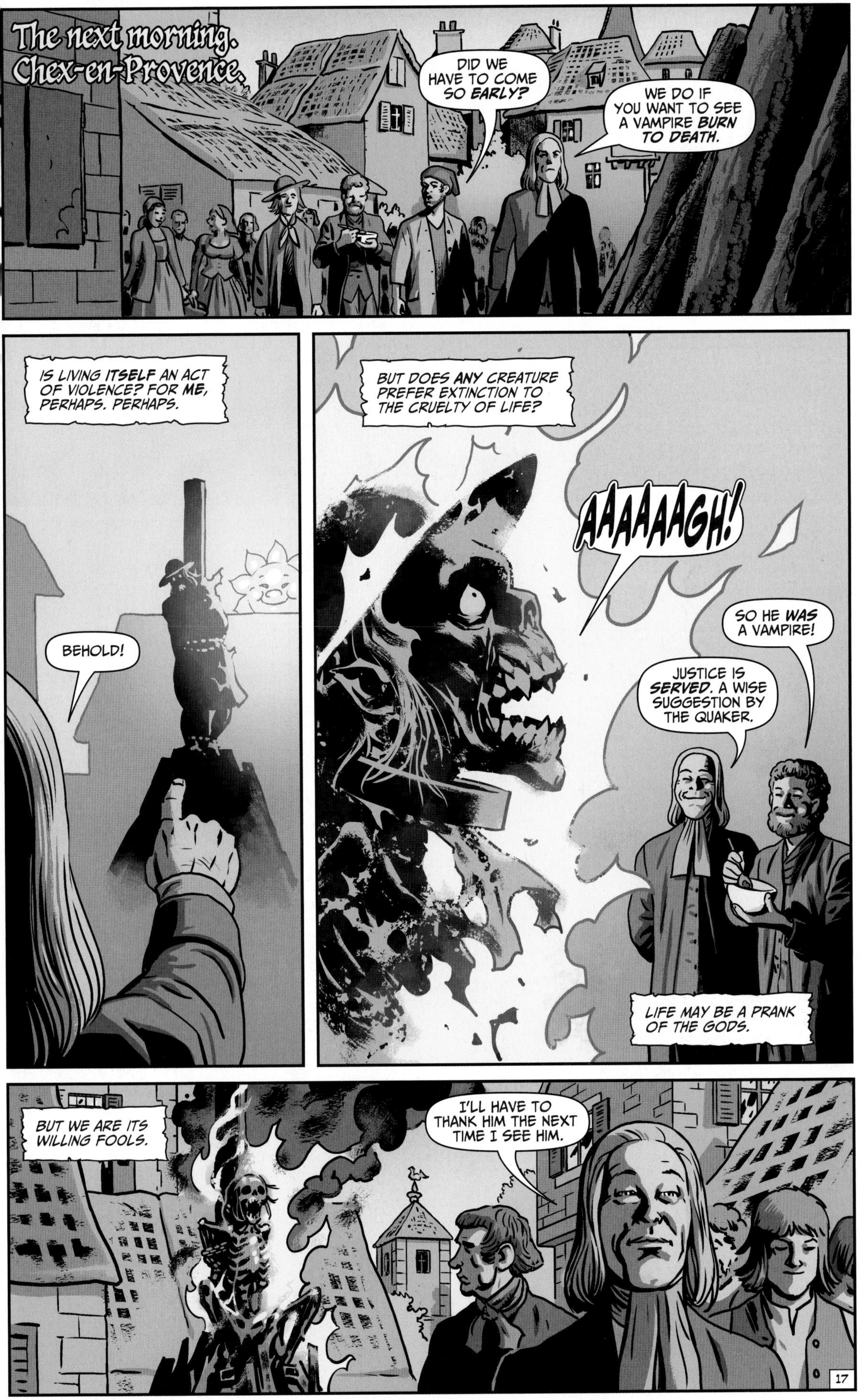
The next morning. Chex-en-Provence.
DID WE HAVE TO COME SO EARLY?
WE DO IF YOU WANT TO SEE A VAMPIRE BURN TO DEATH.
IS LIVING ITSELF AN ACT OF VIOLENCE? FOR ME, PERHAPS. PERHAPS.
BEHOLD!
BUT DOES ANY CREATURE PREFER EXTINCTION TO THE CRUELTY OF LIFE?
AAAAAAGH!
SO HE WAS A VAMPIRE!
JUSTICE IS SERVED. A WISE SUGGESTION BY THE QUAKER.
LIFE MAY BE A PRANK OF THE GODS.
BUT WE ARE ITS WILLING FOOLS.
I'LL HAVE TO THANK HIM THE NEXT TIME I SEE HIM.

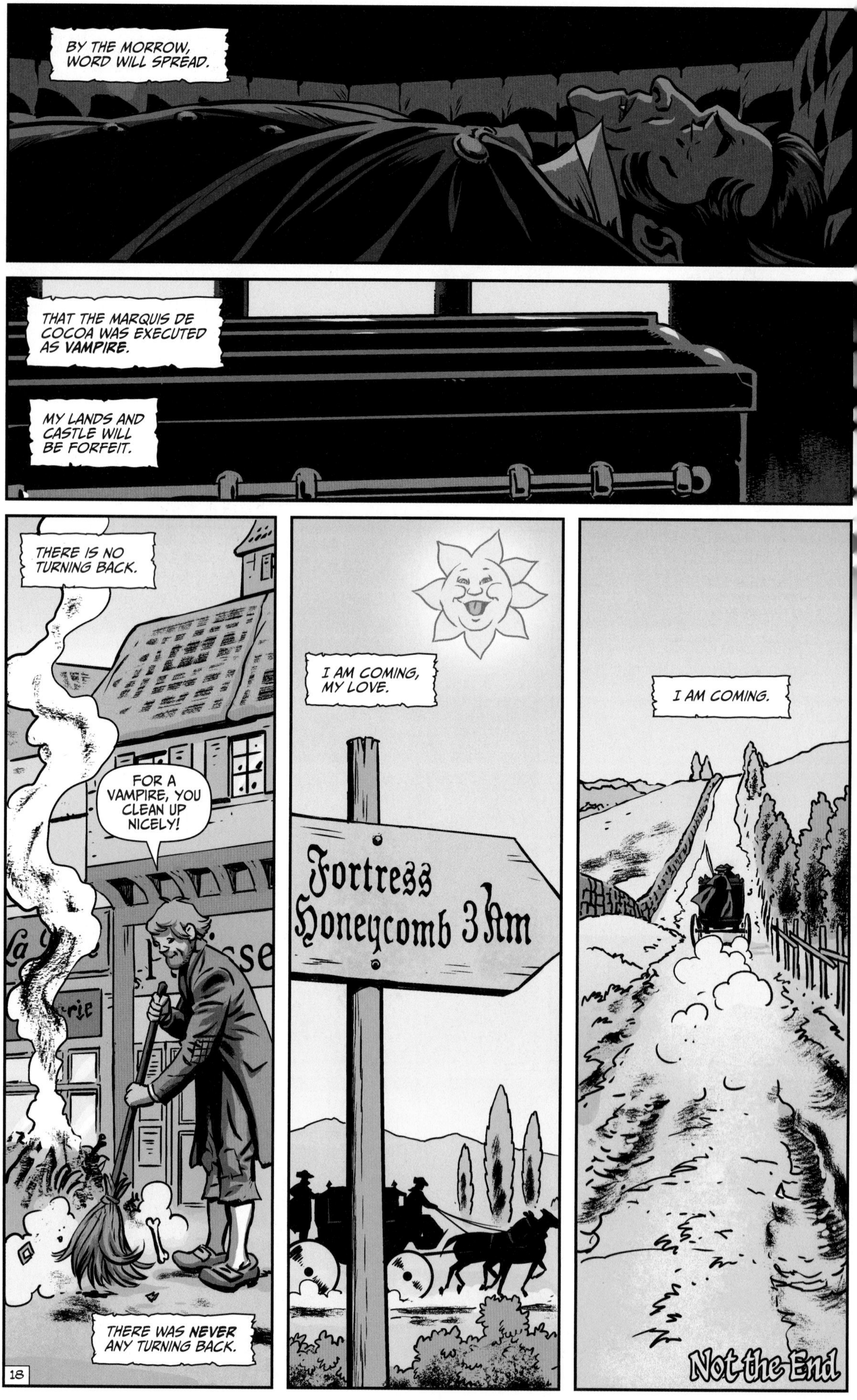

BY THE MORROW, WORD WILL SPREAD.
THAT THE MARQUIS DE COCOA WAS EXECUTED AS VAMPIRE.
MY LANDS AND CASTLE WILL BE FORFEIT.
THERE IS NO TURNING BACK.
FOR A VAMPIRE, YOU CLEAN UP NICELY!
THERE WAS NEVER ANY TURNING BACK.
I AM COMING, MY LOVE.
Fortress Honeycomb 3 Km
I AM COMING.
Not the End

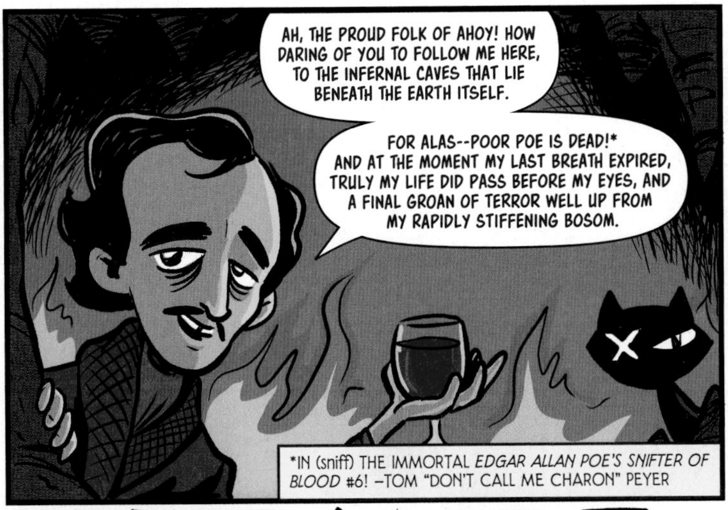
AH, THE PROUD FOLK OF AHOY! HOW DARING OF YOU TO FOLLOW ME HERE, TO THE INFERNAL CAVES THAT LIE BENEATH THE EARTH ITSELF.
FOR ALAS--POOR POE IS DEAD!* AND AT THE MOMENT MY LAST BREATH EXPIRED, TRULY MY LIFE DID PASS BEFORE MY EYES, AND A FINAL GROAN OF TERROR WELL UP FROM MY RAPIDLY STIFFENING BOSOM.
*IN (sniff) THE IMMORTAL *EDGAR ALLAN POE'S SNIFTER OF BLOOD* #6! –TOM "DON'T CALL ME CHARON" PEYER

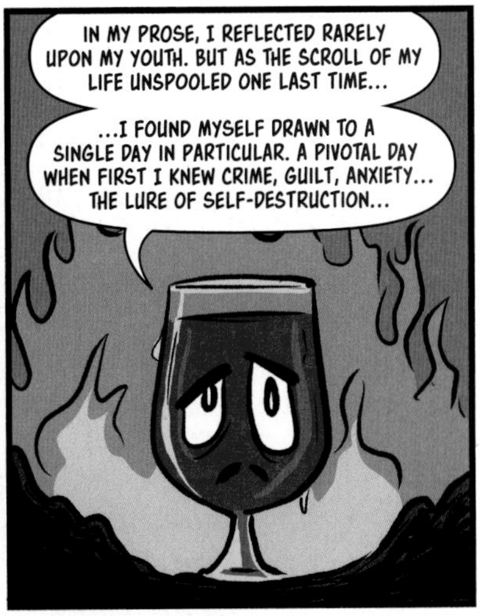
IN MY PROSE, I REFLECTED RARELY UPON MY YOUTH. BUT AS THE SCROLL OF MY LIFE UNSPOOLED ONE LAST TIME...
...I FOUND MYSELF DRAWN TO A SINGLE DAY IN PARTICULAR. A PIVOTAL DAY WHEN FIRST I KNEW CRIME, GUILT, ANXIETY... THE LURE OF SELF-DESTRUCTION...

EVERMORE

THE ADVENTURES OF

EDGAR ALLAN POE

WHEN HE WAS A BOY

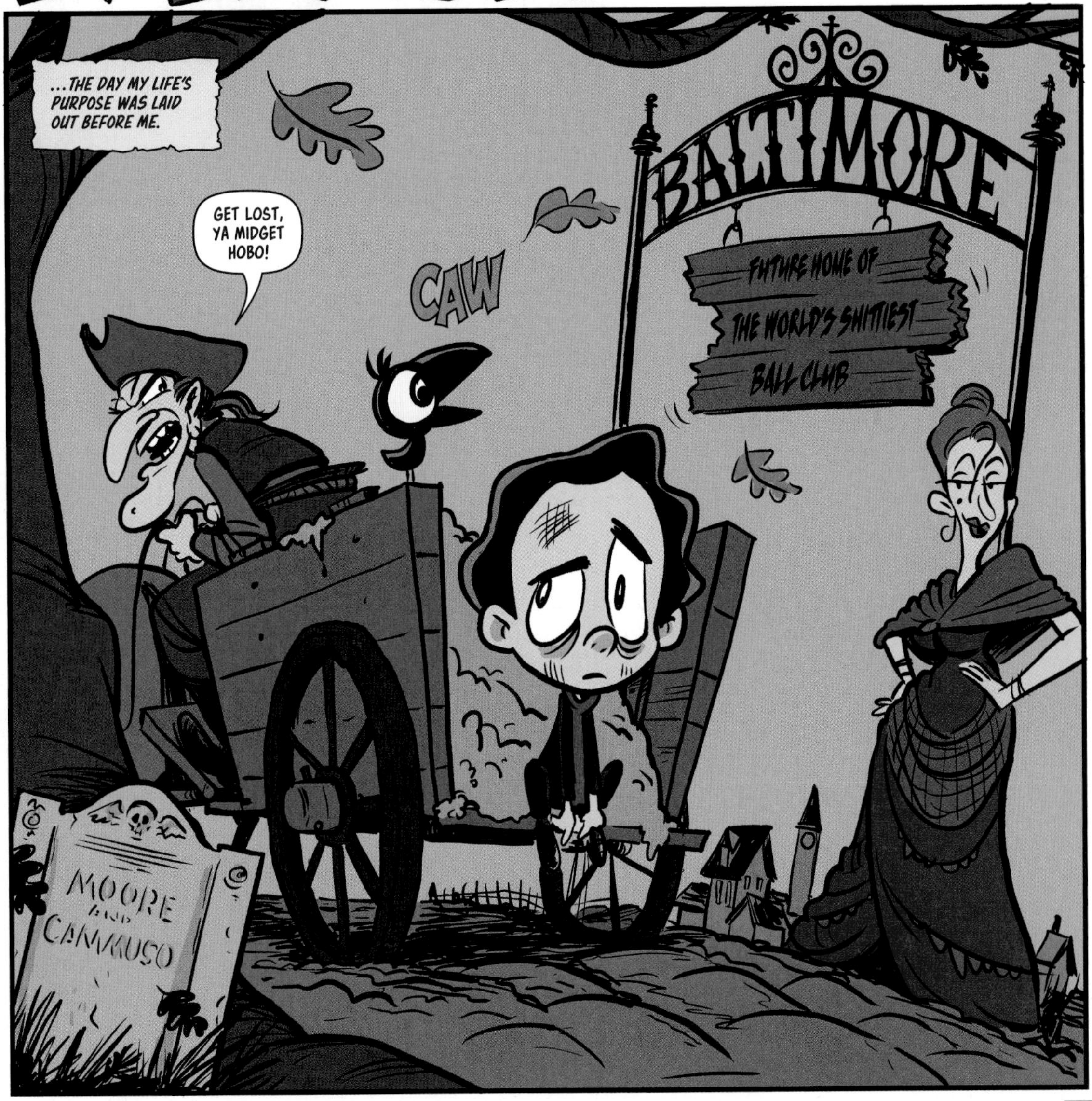
...THE DAY MY LIFE'S PURPOSE WAS LAID OUT BEFORE ME.
BALTIMORE
GET LOST, YA MIDGET HOBO!
CAW
FUTURE HOME OF THE WORLD'S SHITTIEST BALL CLUB
MOORE AND CAMMUSO

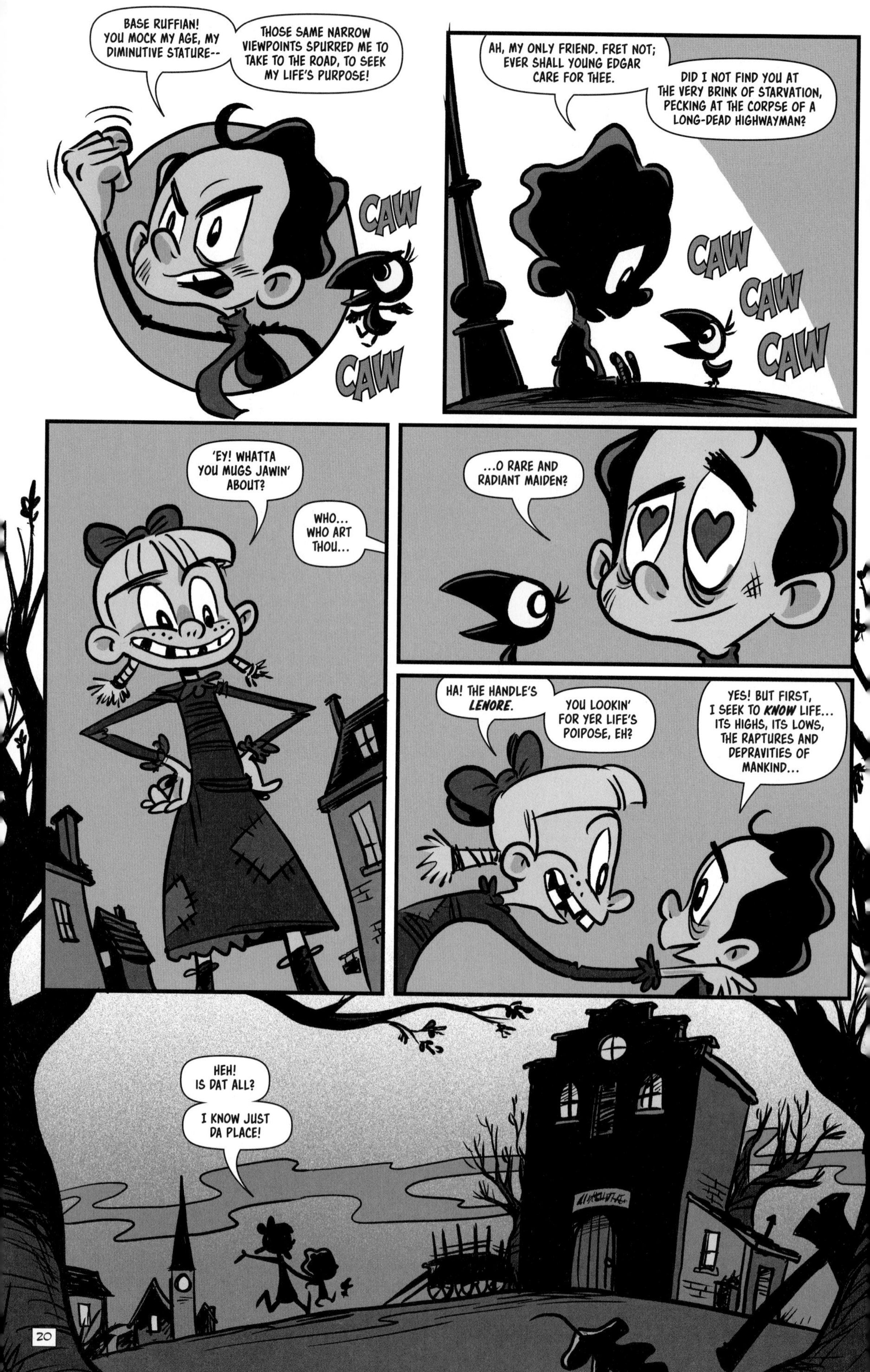
BASE RUFFIAN! YOU MOCK MY AGE, MY DIMINUTIVE STATURE--
THOSE SAME NARROW VIEWPOINTS SPURRED ME TO TAKE TO THE ROAD, TO SEEK MY LIFE'S PURPOSE!
CAW
CAW
AH, MY ONLY FRIEND. FRET NOT; EVER SHALL YOUNG EDGAR CARE FOR THEE.
DID I NOT FIND YOU AT THE VERY BRINK OF STARVATION, PECKING AT THE CORPSE OF A LONG-DEAD HIGHWAYMAN?
CAW
CAW
CAW
'EY! WHATTA YOU MUGS JAWIN' ABOUT?
WHO... WHO ART THOU...
...O RARE AND RADIANT MAIDEN?
HA! THE HANDLE'S *LENORE*.
YOU LOOKIN' FOR YER LIFE'S POIPOSE, EH?
YES! BUT FIRST, I SEEK TO *KNOW* LIFE... ITS HIGHS, ITS LOWS, THE RAPTURES AND DEPRAVITIES OF MANKIND...
HEH! IS DAT ALL?
I KNOW JUST DA PLACE!

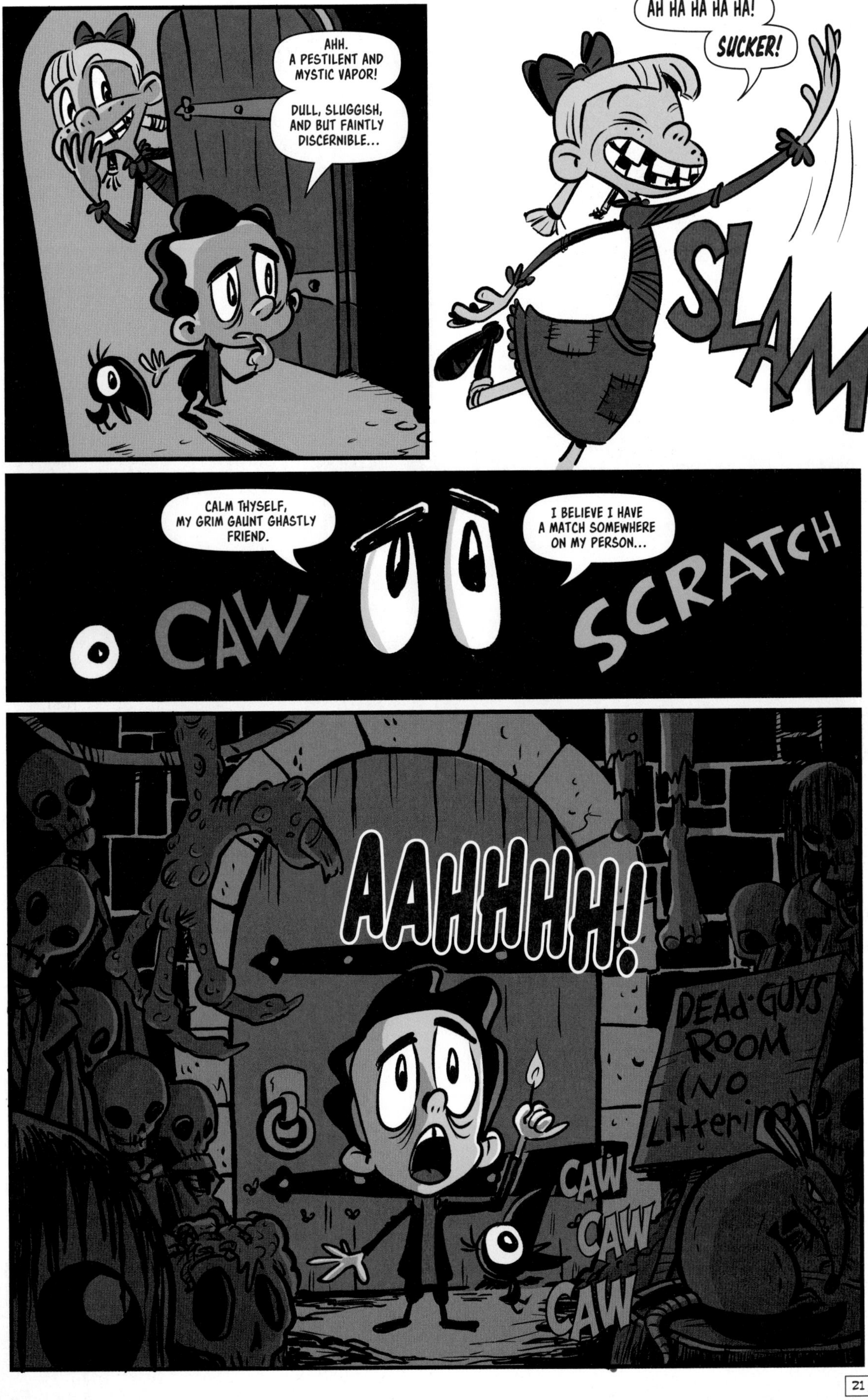
AHH.
A PESTILENT AND MYSTIC VAPOR!
DULL, SLUGGISH, AND BUT FAINTLY DISCERNIBLE...
AH HA HA HA HA!
SUCKER!
SLAM
CALM THYSELF, MY GRIM GAUNT GHASTLY FRIEND.
CAW
I BELIEVE I HAVE A MATCH SOMEWHERE ON MY PERSON...
SCRATCH
AAHHHHH!
DEAd·GUYS ROOM (NO Litterin
CAW
CAW
CAW

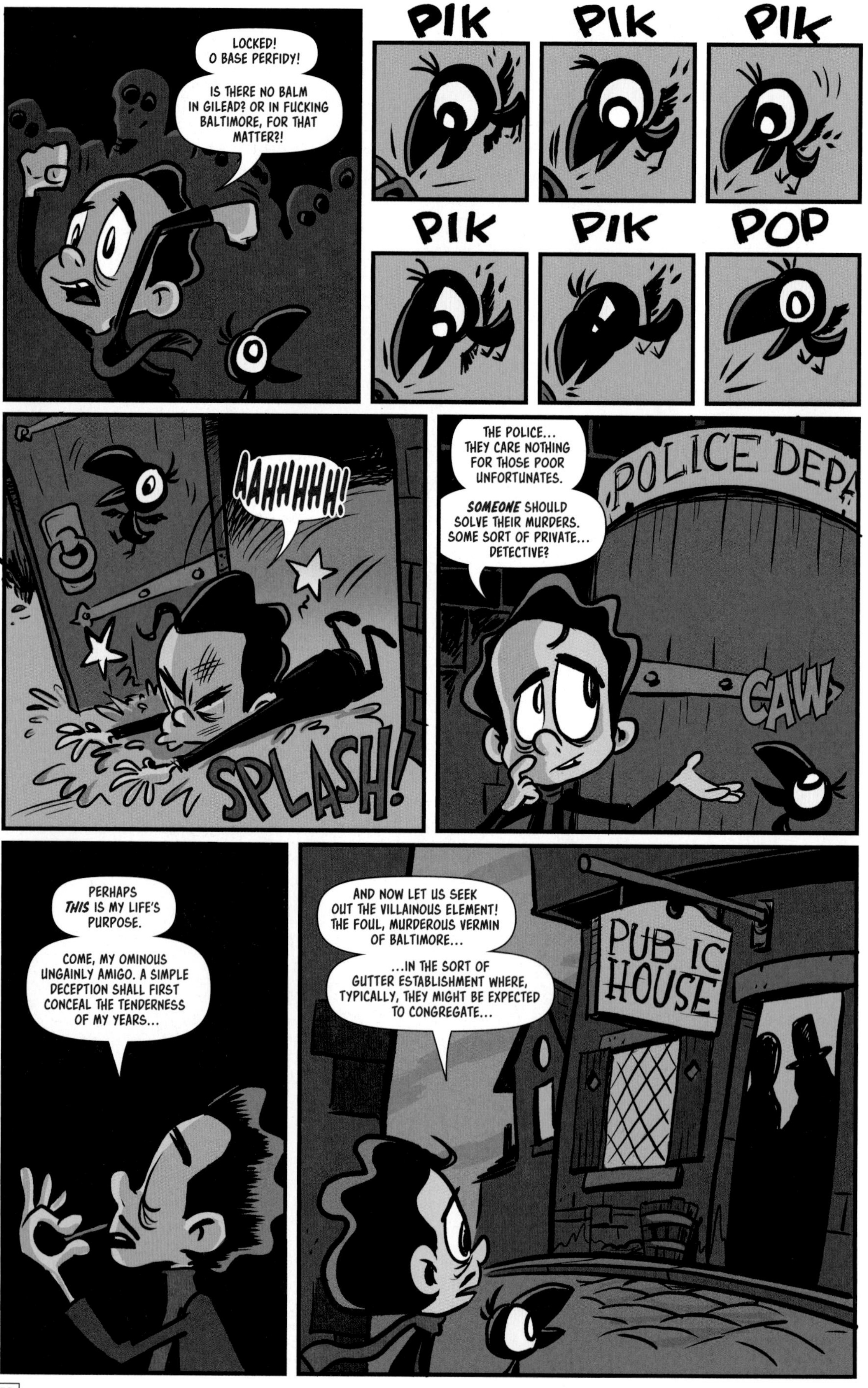
LOCKED!
O BASE PERFIDY!
IS THERE NO BALM IN GILEAD? OR IN FUCKING BALTIMORE, FOR THAT MATTER?!
PIK
PIK
PIK
PIK
PIK
POP
AAHHHHH!
SPLASH!
THE POLICE... THEY CARE NOTHING FOR THOSE POOR UNFORTUNATES.
SOMEONE SHOULD SOLVE THEIR MURDERS. SOME SORT OF PRIVATE... DETECTIVE?
POLICE DEPA
CAW
PERHAPS *THIS* IS MY LIFE'S PURPOSE.
COME, MY OMINOUS UNGAINLY AMIGO. A SIMPLE DECEPTION SHALL FIRST CONCEAL THE TENDERNESS OF MY YEARS...
AND NOW LET US SEEK OUT THE VILLAINOUS ELEMENT! THE FOUL, MURDEROUS VERMIN OF BALTIMORE...
...IN THE SORT OF GUTTER ESTABLISHMENT WHERE, TYPICALLY, THEY MIGHT BE EXPECTED TO CONGREGATE...
PUB IC HOUSE

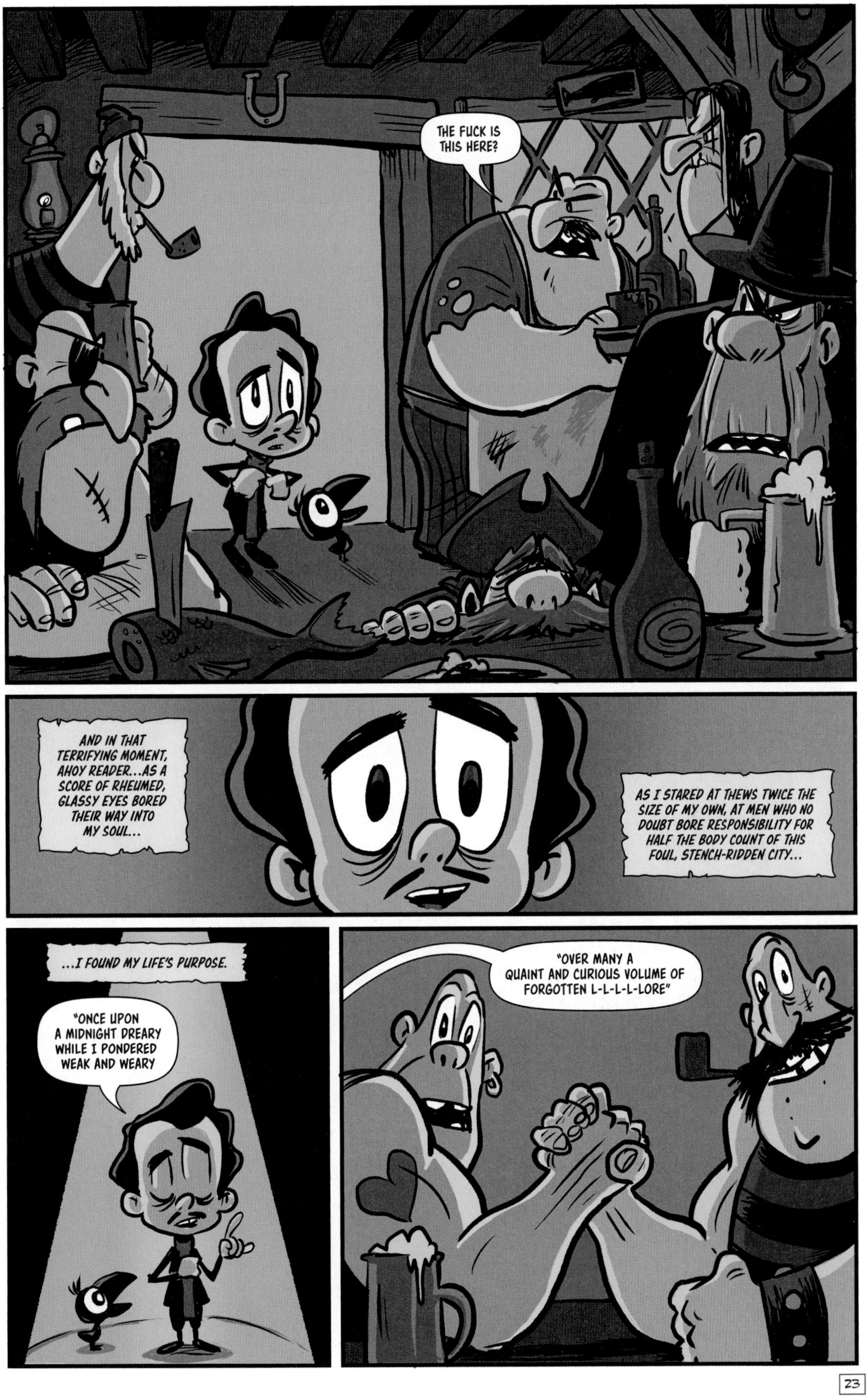
THE FUCK IS
THIS HERE?
AND IN THAT TERRIFYING MOMENT, AHOY READER...AS A SCORE OF RHEUMED, GLASSY EYES BORED THEIR WAY INTO MY SOUL...
AS I STARED AT THEWS TWICE THE SIZE OF MY OWN, AT MEN WHO NO DOUBT BORE RESPONSIBILITY FOR HALF THE BODY COUNT OF THIS FOUL, STENCH-RIDDEN CITY...
...I FOUND MY LIFE'S PURPOSE.
"ONCE UPON A MIDNIGHT DREARY WHILE I PONDERED WEAK AND WEARY
"OVER MANY A QUAINT AND CURIOUS VOLUME OF FORGOTTEN L-L-L-L-LORE"

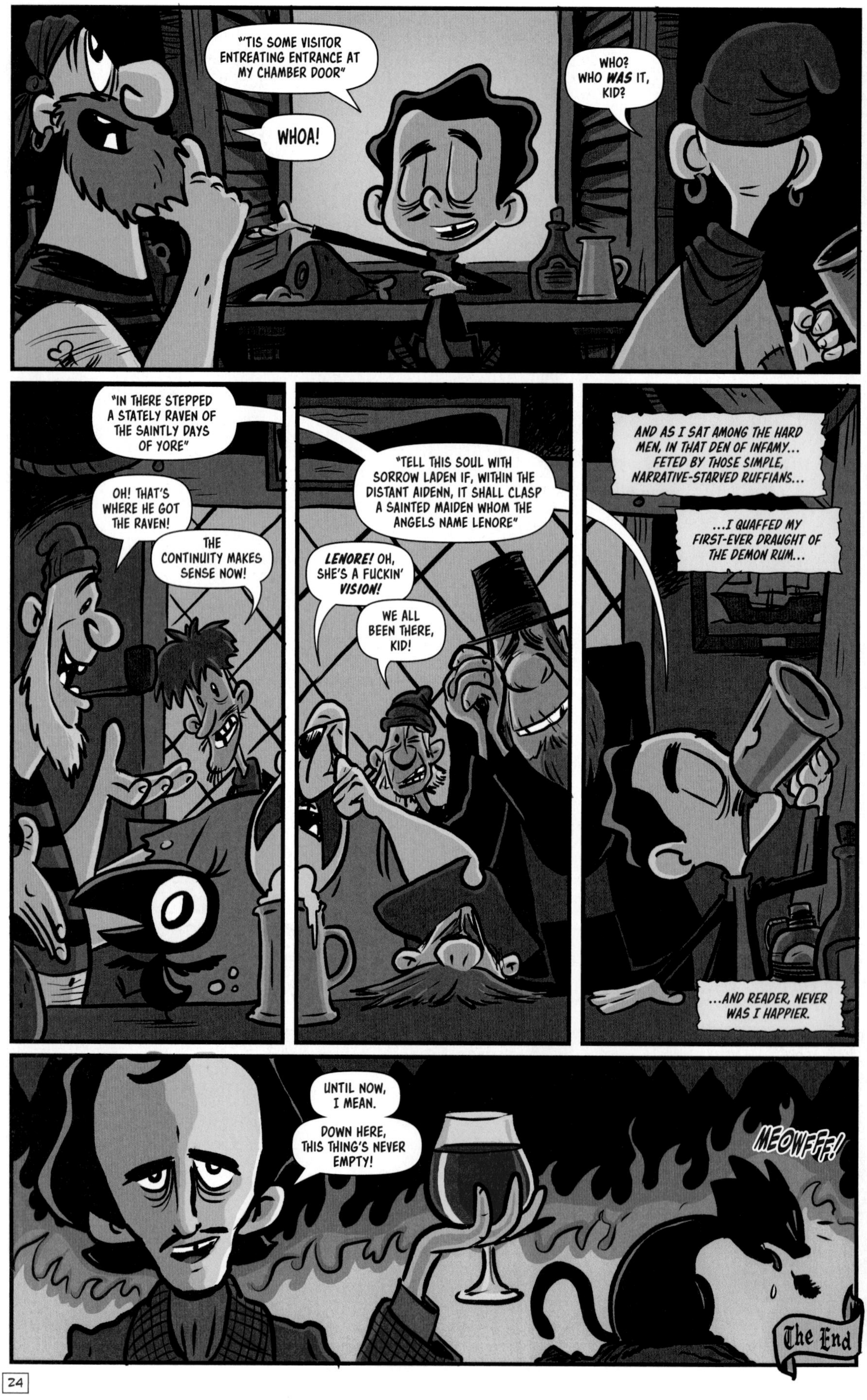
"TIS SOME VISITOR ENTREATING ENTRANCE AT MY CHAMBER DOOR"
WHOA!
WHO? WHO *WAS* IT, KID?
"IN THERE STEPPED A STATELY RAVEN OF THE SAINTLY DAYS OF YORE"
OH! THAT'S WHERE HE GOT THE RAVEN!
THE CONTINUITY MAKES SENSE NOW!
"TELL THIS SOUL WITH SORROW LADEN IF, WITHIN THE DISTANT AIDENN, IT SHALL CLASP A SAINTED MAIDEN WHOM THE ANGELS NAME LENORE"
LENORE! OH, SHE'S A FUCKIN' *VISION!*
WE ALL BEEN THERE, KID!
AND AS I SAT AMONG THE HARD MEN, IN THAT DEN OF INFAMY... FETED BY THOSE SIMPLE, NARRATIVE-STARVED RUFFIANS...
...I QUAFFED MY FIRST-EVER DRAUGHT OF THE DEMON RUM...
...AND READER, NEVER WAS I HAPPIER.
UNTIL NOW, I MEAN.
DOWN HERE, THIS THING'S NEVER EMPTY!
MEOWFFF!
The End

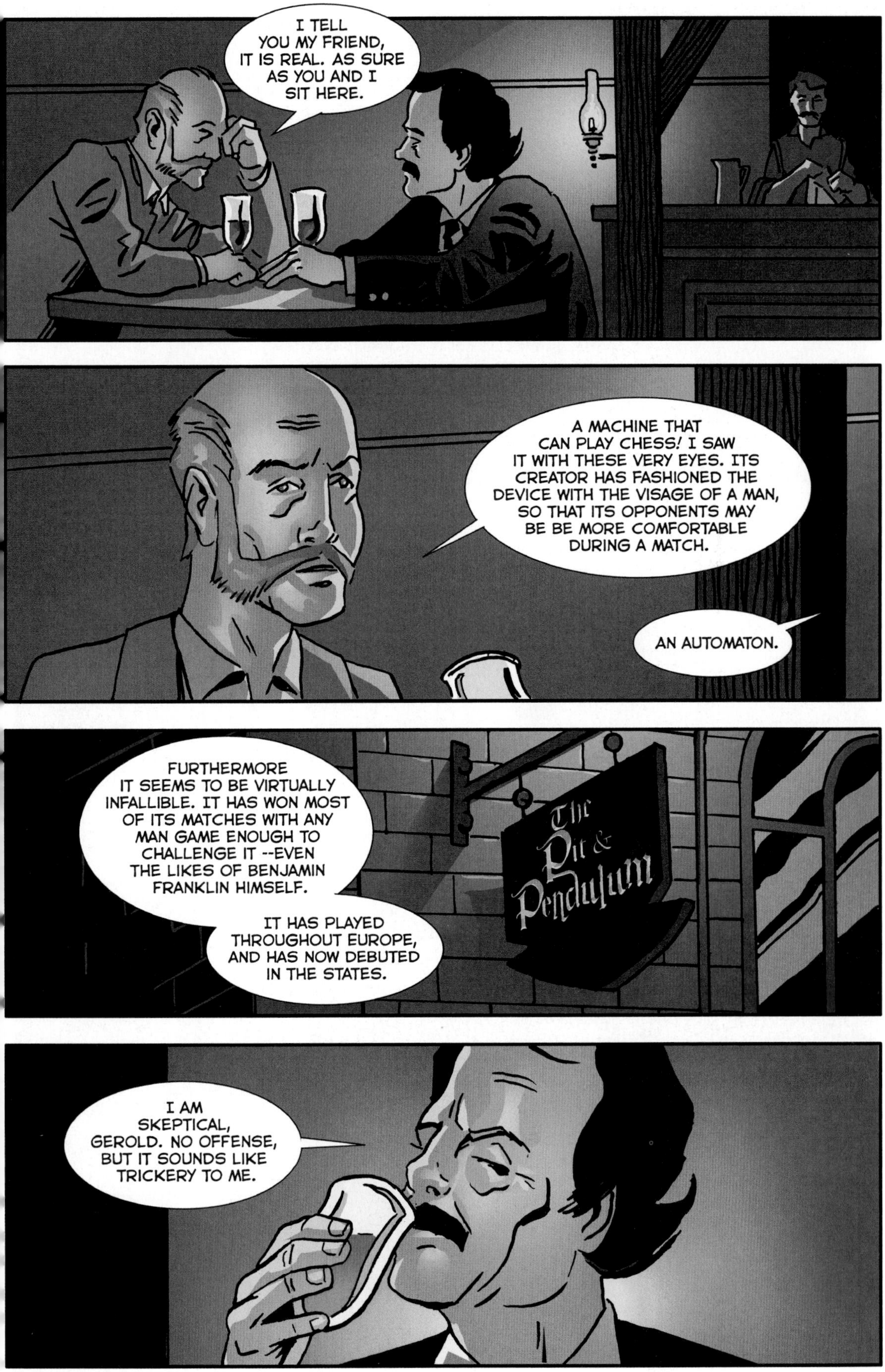
I TELL YOU MY FRIEND, IT IS REAL. AS SURE AS YOU AND I SIT HERE.
A MACHINE THAT CAN PLAY CHESS! I SAW IT WITH THESE VERY EYES. ITS CREATOR HAS FASHIONED THE DEVICE WITH THE VISAGE OF A MAN, SO THAT ITS OPPONENTS MAY BE BE MORE COMFORTABLE DURING A MATCH.
AN AUTOMATON.
FURTHERMORE IT SEEMS TO BE VIRTUALLY INFALLIBLE. IT HAS WON MOST OF ITS MATCHES WITH ANY MAN GAME ENOUGH TO CHALLENGE IT --EVEN THE LIKES OF BENJAMIN FRANKLIN HIMSELF.
The Pit & Pendulum
IT HAS PLAYED THROUGHOUT EUROPE, AND HAS NOW DEBUTED IN THE STATES.
I AM SKEPTICAL, GEROLD. NO OFFENSE, BUT IT SOUNDS LIKE TRICKERY TO ME.

"I TOO, WAS SKEPTICAL, MY DEAR EDGAR. AND I AM A DISCERNING MAN. THERE WAS NO EVIDENCE OF TRICKERY. IT'S OWNER LAID BARE THE INNER WORKINGS OF..."

MAELZEL'S CHESS PLAYER

"I WATCHED WITH RAPT INTEREST AS THE CHESS MASTER KOPOV ZELINSKY TOOK ON THE MACHINE THAT BORE THE NAME, THE TURK.

"ITS MOVEMENTS WERE SLOW, DELIBERATE. MECHANICAL. BUT THEY WERE DECISIVE.

"I DON'T KNOW HOW LONG THE MATCH LASTED, I WAS SO FASCINATED BY THE CONTEST."

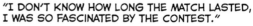

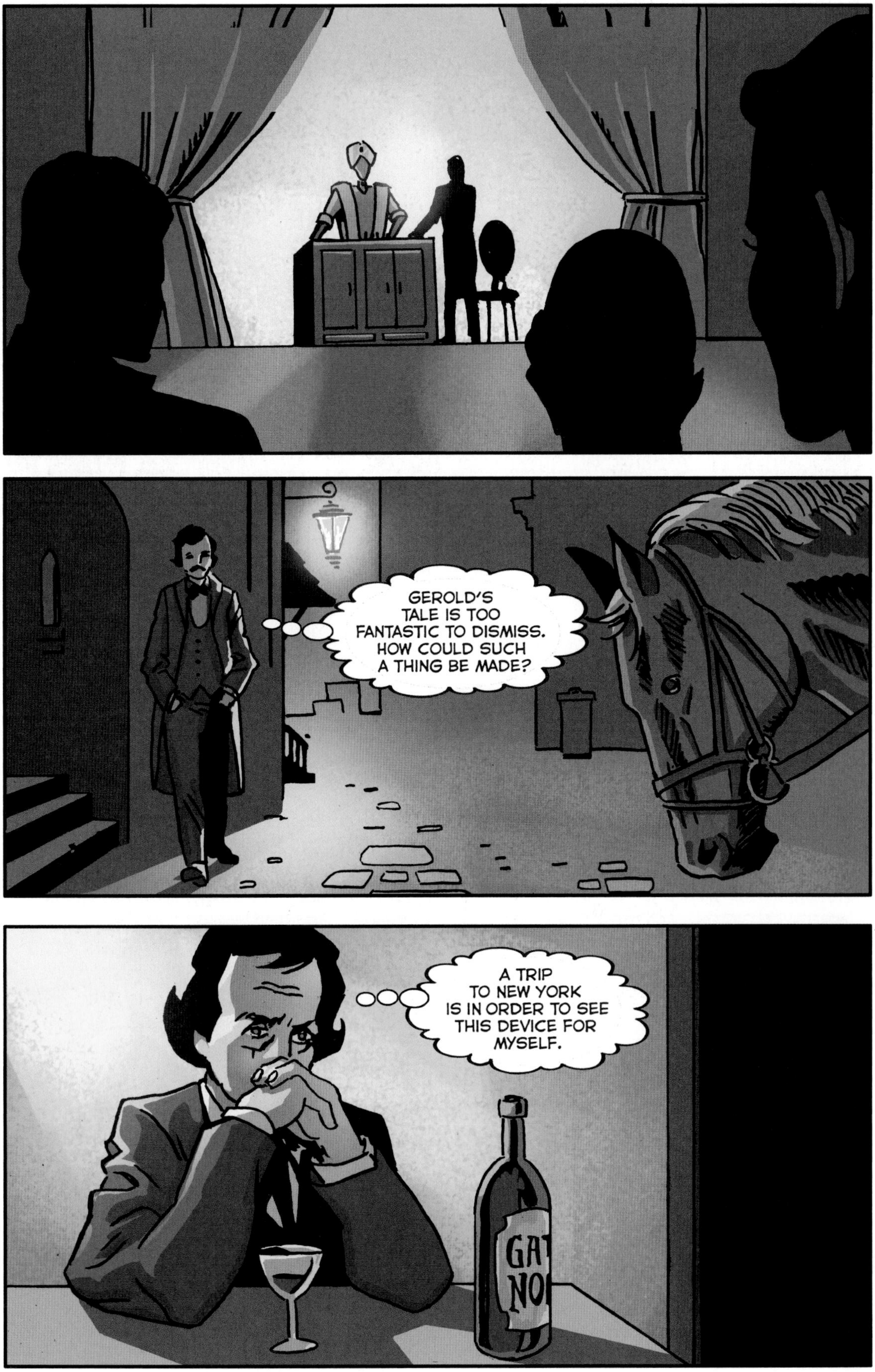
GEROLD'S TALE IS TOO FANTASTIC TO DISMISS. HOW COULD SUCH A THING BE MADE?
A TRIP TO NEW YORK IS IN ORDER TO SEE THIS DEVICE FOR MYSELF.

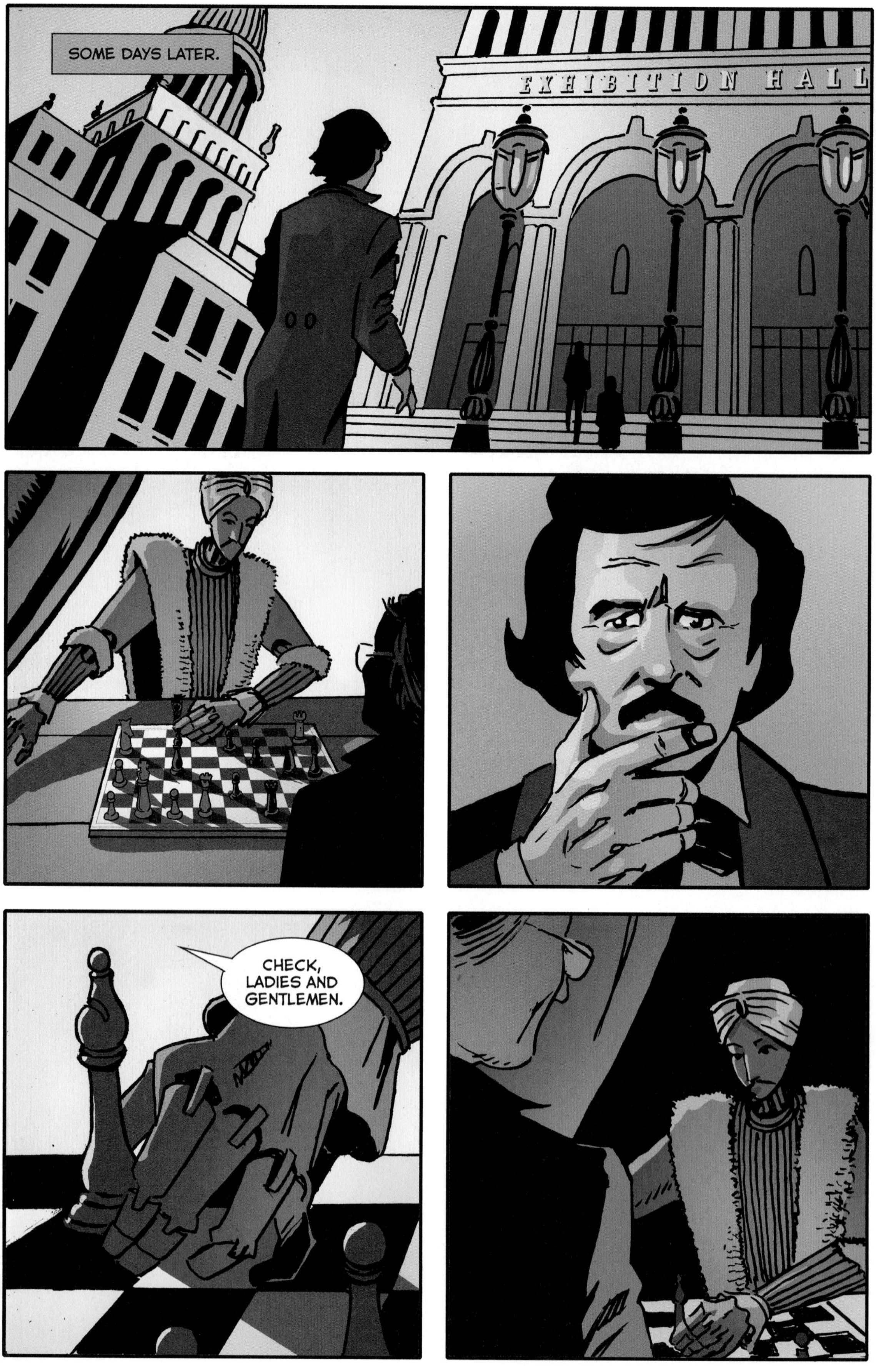
SOME DAYS LATER.
EXHIBITION HALL
CHECK, LADIES AND GENTLEMEN.

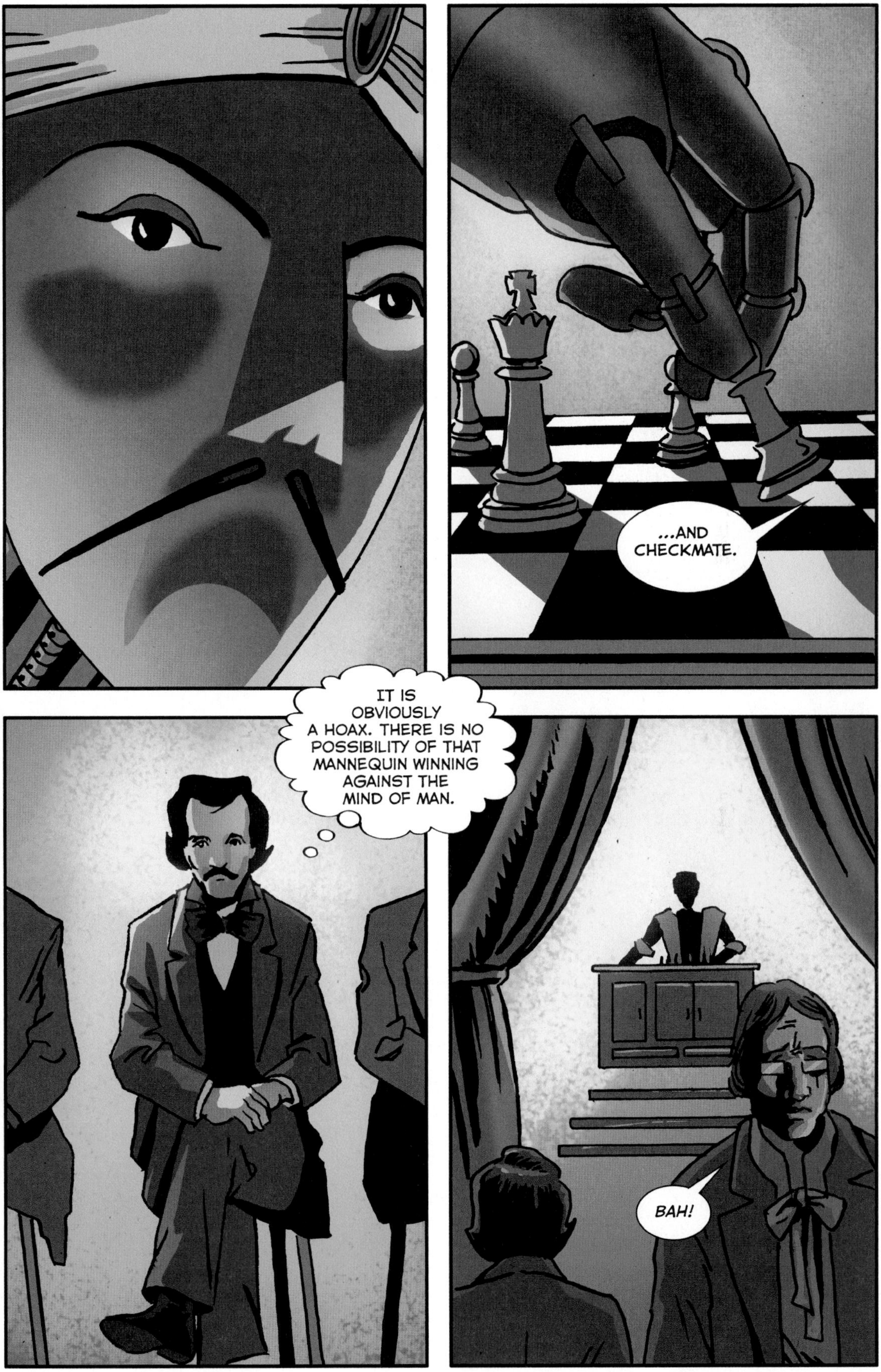
...AND CHECKMATE.
IT IS OBVIOUSLY A HOAX. THERE IS NO POSSIBILITY OF THAT MANNEQUIN WINNING AGAINST THE MIND OF MAN.
BAH!

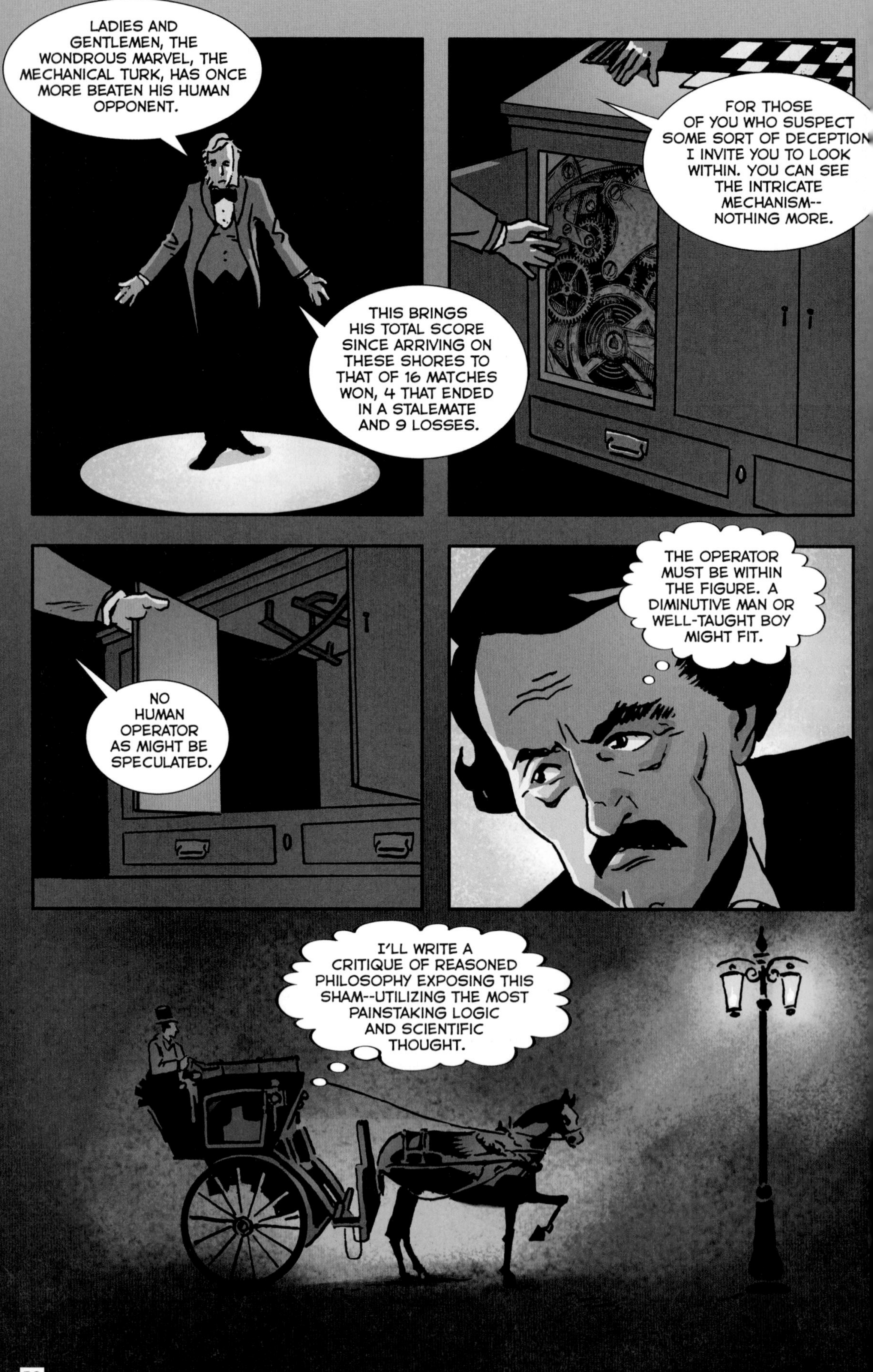
LADIES AND GENTLEMEN, THE WONDROUS MARVEL, THE MECHANICAL TURK, HAS ONCE MORE BEATEN HIS HUMAN OPPONENT.
THIS BRINGS HIS TOTAL SCORE SINCE ARRIVING ON THESE SHORES TO THAT OF 16 MATCHES WON, 4 THAT ENDED IN A STALEMATE AND 9 LOSSES.
FOR THOSE OF YOU WHO SUSPECT SOME SORT OF DECEPTION I INVITE YOU TO LOOK WITHIN. YOU CAN SEE THE INTRICATE MECHANISM-- NOTHING MORE.
NO HUMAN OPERATOR AS MIGHT BE SPECULATED.
THE OPERATOR MUST BE WITHIN THE FIGURE. A DIMINUTIVE MAN OR WELL-TAUGHT BOY MIGHT FIT.
I'LL WRITE A CRITIQUE OF REASONED PHILOSOPHY EXPOSING THIS SHAM--UTILIZING THE MOST PAINSTAKING LOGIC AND SCIENTIFIC THOUGHT.

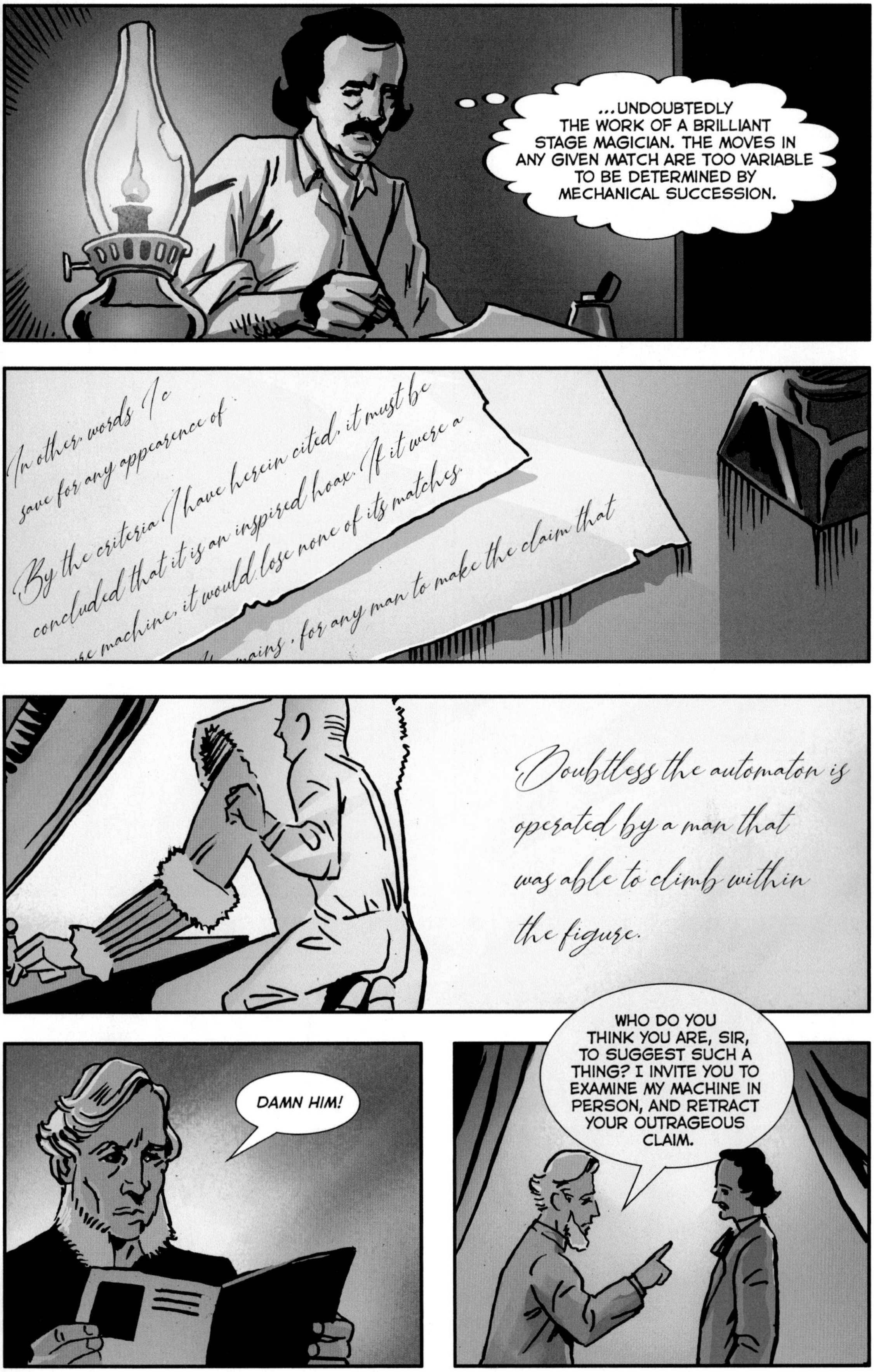
...UNDOUBTEDLY THE WORK OF A BRILLIANT STAGE MAGICIAN. THE MOVES IN ANY GIVEN MATCH ARE TOO VARIABLE TO BE DETERMINED BY MECHANICAL SUCCESSION.
In other words I c
save for any appearence of
By the criteria I have herein cited, it must be
concluded that it is an inspired hoax. If it were a
machine, it would lose none of its matches.
for any man to make the claim that
Doubtless the automaton is operated by a man that was able to climb within the figure.
DAMN HIM!
WHO DO YOU THINK YOU ARE, SIR, TO SUGGEST SUCH A THING? I INVITE YOU TO EXAMINE MY MACHINE IN PERSON, AND RETRACT YOUR OUTRAGEOUS CLAIM.

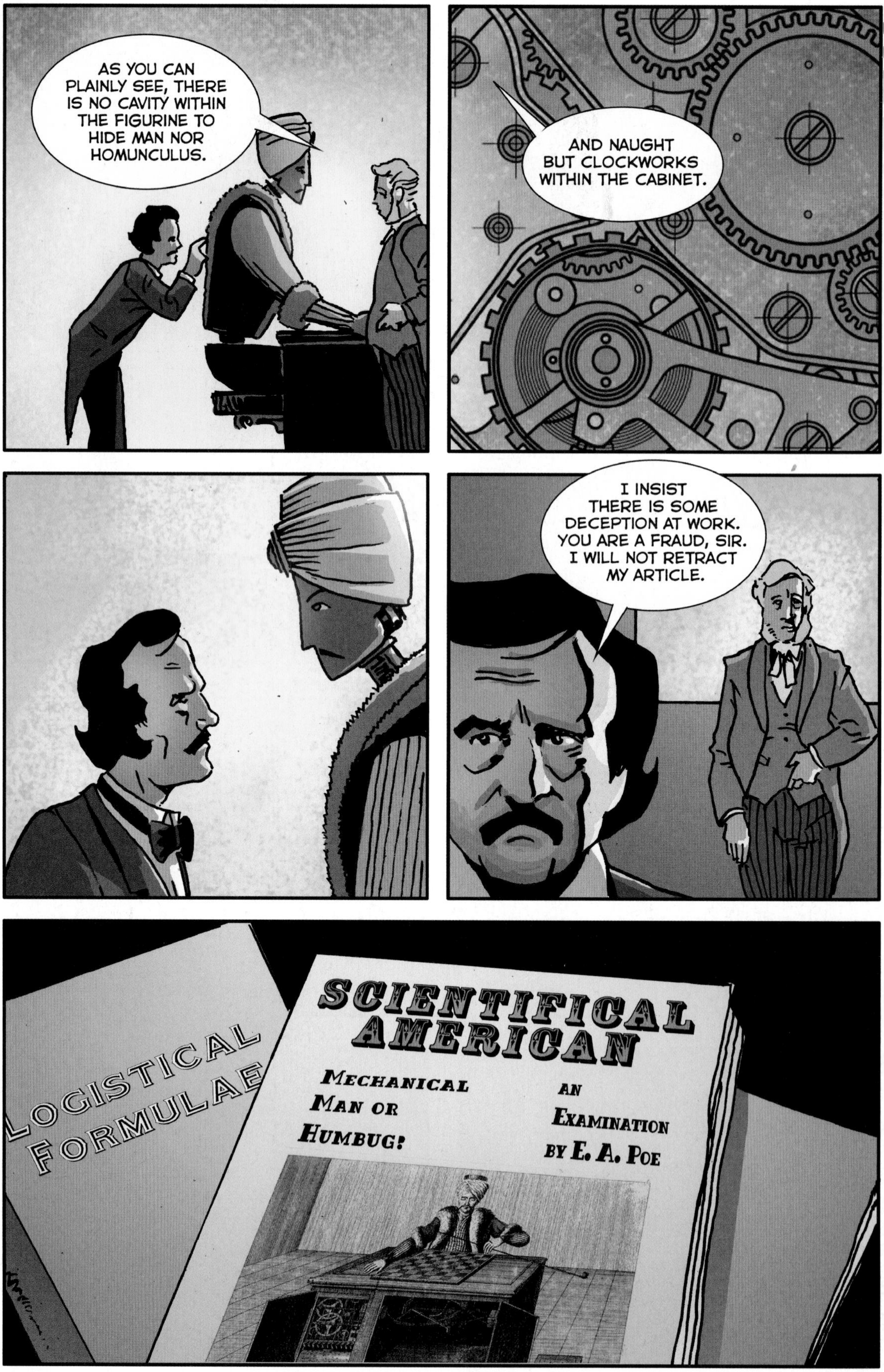
AS YOU CAN PLAINLY SEE, THERE IS NO CAVITY WITHIN THE FIGURINE TO HIDE MAN NOR HOMUNCULUS.
AND NAUGHT BUT CLOCKWORKS WITHIN THE CABINET.
I INSIST THERE IS SOME DECEPTION AT WORK. YOU ARE A FRAUD, SIR. I WILL NOT RETRACT MY ARTICLE.
LOGISTICAL FORMULAE
SCIENTIFICAL AMERICAN
MECHANICAL MAN OR HUMBUG!
AN EXAMINATION BY E. A. POE

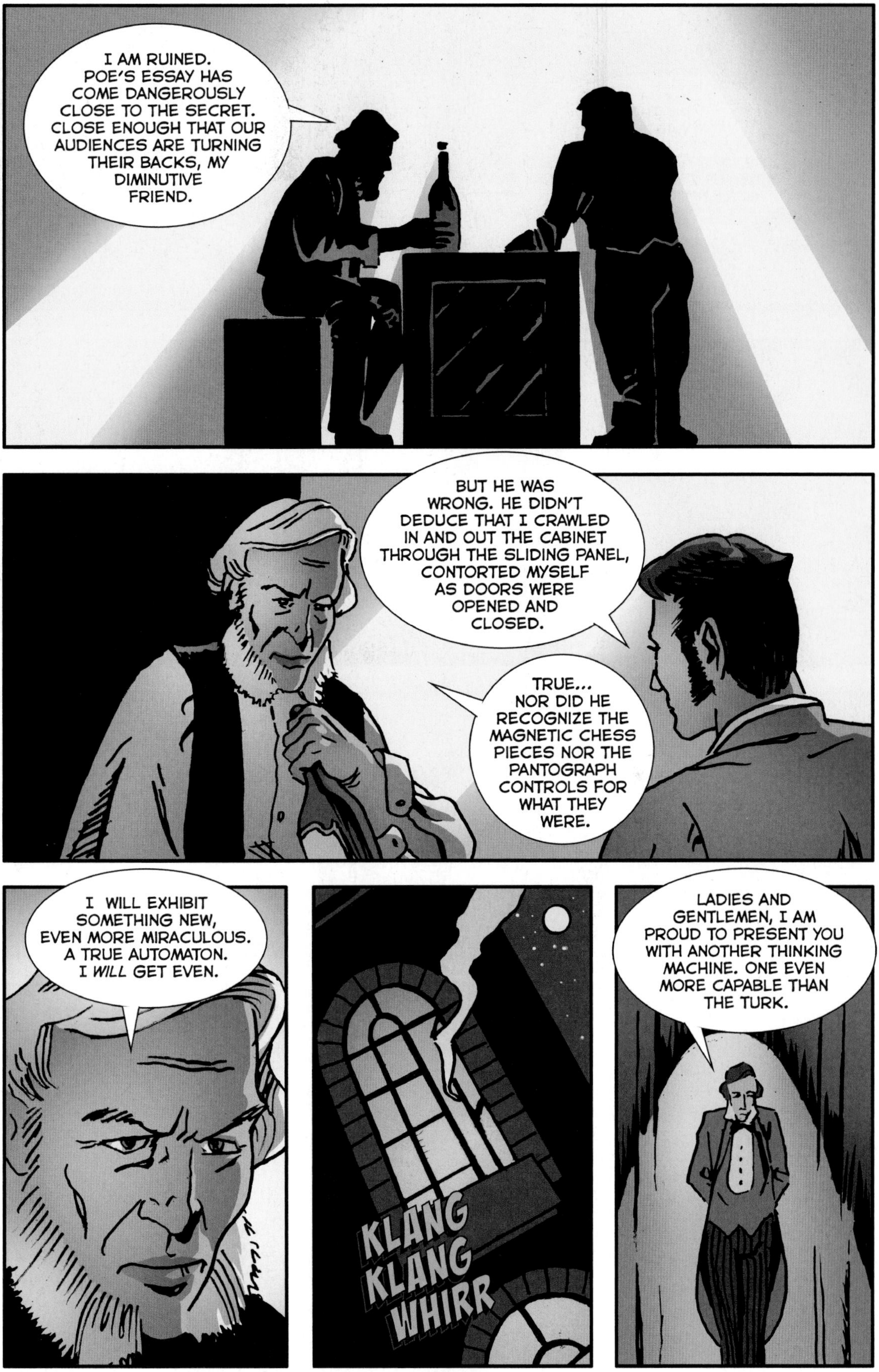
I AM RUINED. POE'S ESSAY HAS COME DANGEROUSLY CLOSE TO THE SECRET. CLOSE ENOUGH THAT OUR AUDIENCES ARE TURNING THEIR BACKS, MY DIMINUTIVE FRIEND.
BUT HE WAS WRONG. HE DIDN'T DEDUCE THAT I CRAWLED IN AND OUT THE CABINET THROUGH THE SLIDING PANEL, CONTORTED MYSELF AS DOORS WERE OPENED AND CLOSED.
TRUE... NOR DID HE RECOGNIZE THE MAGNETIC CHESS PIECES NOR THE PANTOGRAPH CONTROLS FOR WHAT THEY WERE.
I WILL EXHIBIT SOMETHING NEW, EVEN MORE MIRACULOUS. A TRUE AUTOMATON. I *WILL* GET EVEN.
KLANG
KLANG
WHIRR
LADIES AND GENTLEMEN, I AM PROUD TO PRESENT *YOU* WITH ANOTHER THINKING MACHINE. ONE EVEN MORE CAPABLE THAN THE TURK.

ONE THAT, WHEN ACTIVATED, WILL ACTUALLY WRITE-- NAY, *CREATE* VERSE. BEFORE YOUR VERY EYES. LADIES AND GENTLEMEN, I GIVE YOU...

...EDGAR, THE MECHANICAL POET!

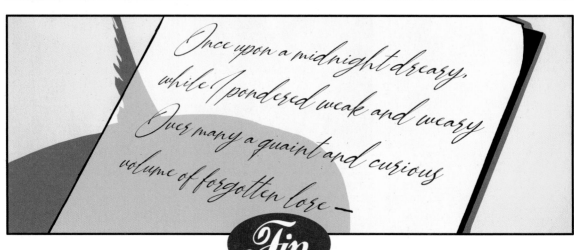

Once upon a midnight dreary, while I pondered weak and weary Over many a quaint and curious volume of forgotten lore—

Fin

ANGLE of THE ODD: A NUISANCE

IT WAS A LOATHSOMELY MUGGY AUGUST EVENING.

I HAD YET TO CONSUMMATE ANY KIND OF DINNER BEYOND A GLASS OF WINE, AND WAS SITTING ALONE IN THE LIVING ROOM, STOMACH PANGS AND EMPTY DOCUMENT TAUNTING ME IN EQUAL MEASURE.

I AM WILLING TO CONFESS THAT I FELT A LITTLE STUPID.

I HAD CHOSEN TO ADAPT ONE OF POE'S MORE RIDICULOUS WORKS...

...BUT FOUND NO SATISFACTORY APPROACH.

ANGLE OF THE ODD

THIS THING IS CONTEMPTIBLE! IT CANNOT GIVE ME WHAT I NEED.

I NEED AN ANGLE!

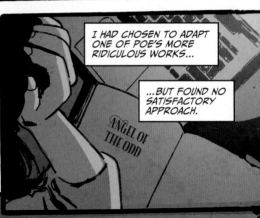

MY GOD, MAN! WHAT DRUNKARD CAN'T SEE THEIR BOUNTEOUS OPTIONS AT THIS LITERARY HOUR?

WHO ARE YOU? HOW DID YOU GET HERE?

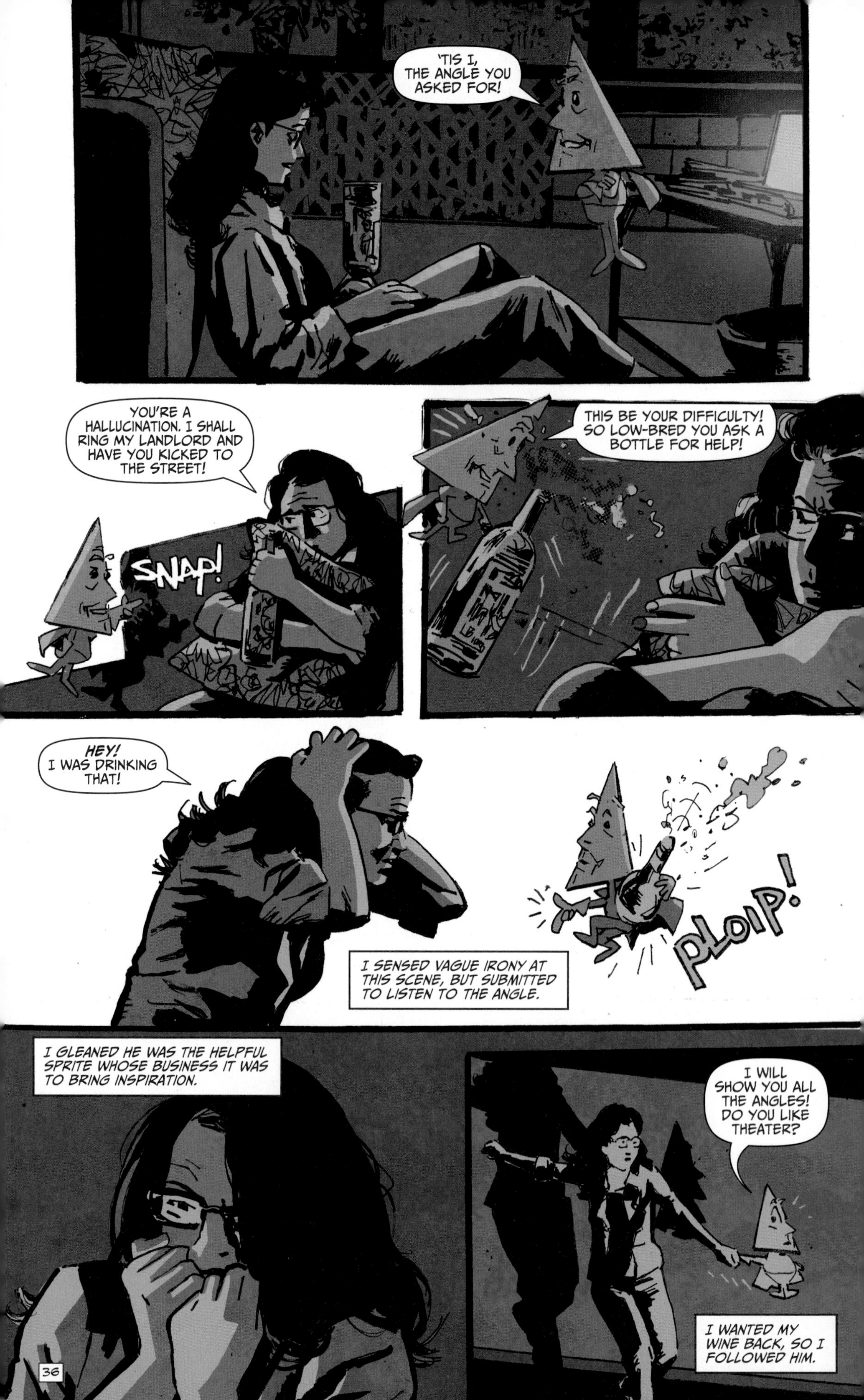
'TIS I, THE ANGLE YOU ASKED FOR!
YOU'RE A HALLUCINATION. I SHALL RING MY LANDLORD AND HAVE YOU KICKED TO THE STREET!
SNAP!
THIS BE YOUR DIFFICULTY! SO LOW-BRED YOU ASK A BOTTLE FOR HELP!
HEY! I WAS DRINKING THAT!
PLOIP!
I SENSED VAGUE IRONY AT THIS SCENE, BUT SUBMITTED TO LISTEN TO THE ANGLE.
I GLEANED HE WAS THE HELPFUL SPRITE WHOSE BUSINESS IT WAS TO BRING INSPIRATION.
I WILL SHOW YOU ALL THE ANGLES! DO YOU LIKE THEATER?
I WANTED MY WINE BACK, SO I FOLLOWED HIM.

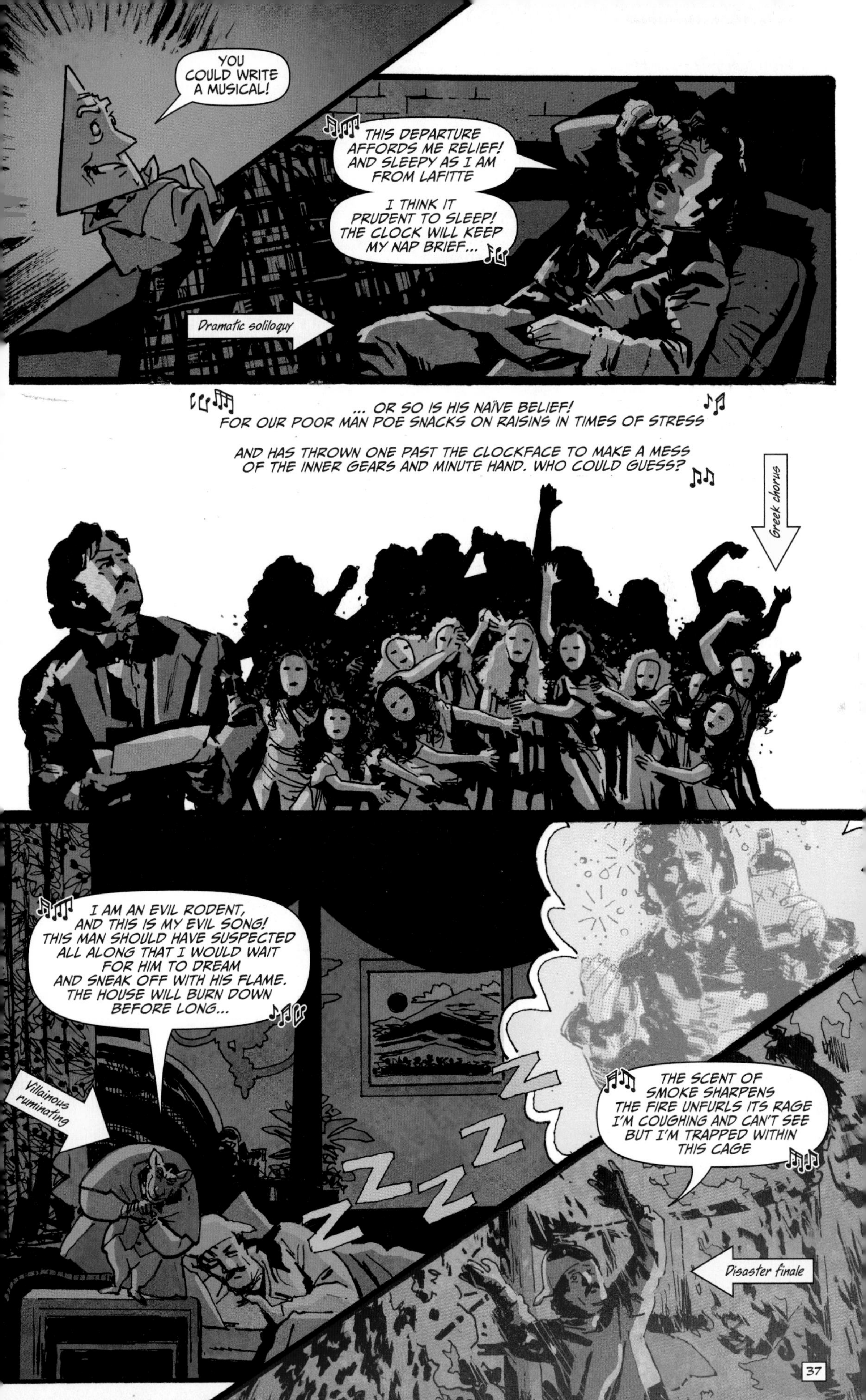
YOU COULD WRITE A MUSICAL!
THIS DEPARTURE AFFORDS ME RELIEF! AND SLEEPY AS I AM FROM LAFITTE
I THINK IT PRUDENT TO SLEEP! THE CLOCK WILL KEEP MY NAP BRIEF...
Dramatic soliloquy
... OR SO IS HIS NAÏVE BELIEF! FOR OUR POOR MAN POE SNACKS ON RAISINS IN TIMES OF STRESS
AND HAS THROWN ONE PAST THE CLOCKFACE TO MAKE A MESS OF THE INNER GEARS AND MINUTE HAND. WHO COULD GUESS?
Greek chorus
I AM AN EVIL RODENT, AND THIS IS MY EVIL SONG! THIS MAN SHOULD HAVE SUSPECTED ALL ALONG THAT I WOULD WAIT FOR HIM TO DREAM AND SNEAK OFF WITH HIS FLAME. THE HOUSE WILL BURN DOWN BEFORE LONG...
Villainous ruminating
ZZZZZ
THE SCENT OF SMOKE SHARPENS THE FIRE UNFURLS ITS RAGE I'M COUGHING AND CAN'T SEE BUT I'M TRAPPED WITHIN THIS CAGE
Disaster finale

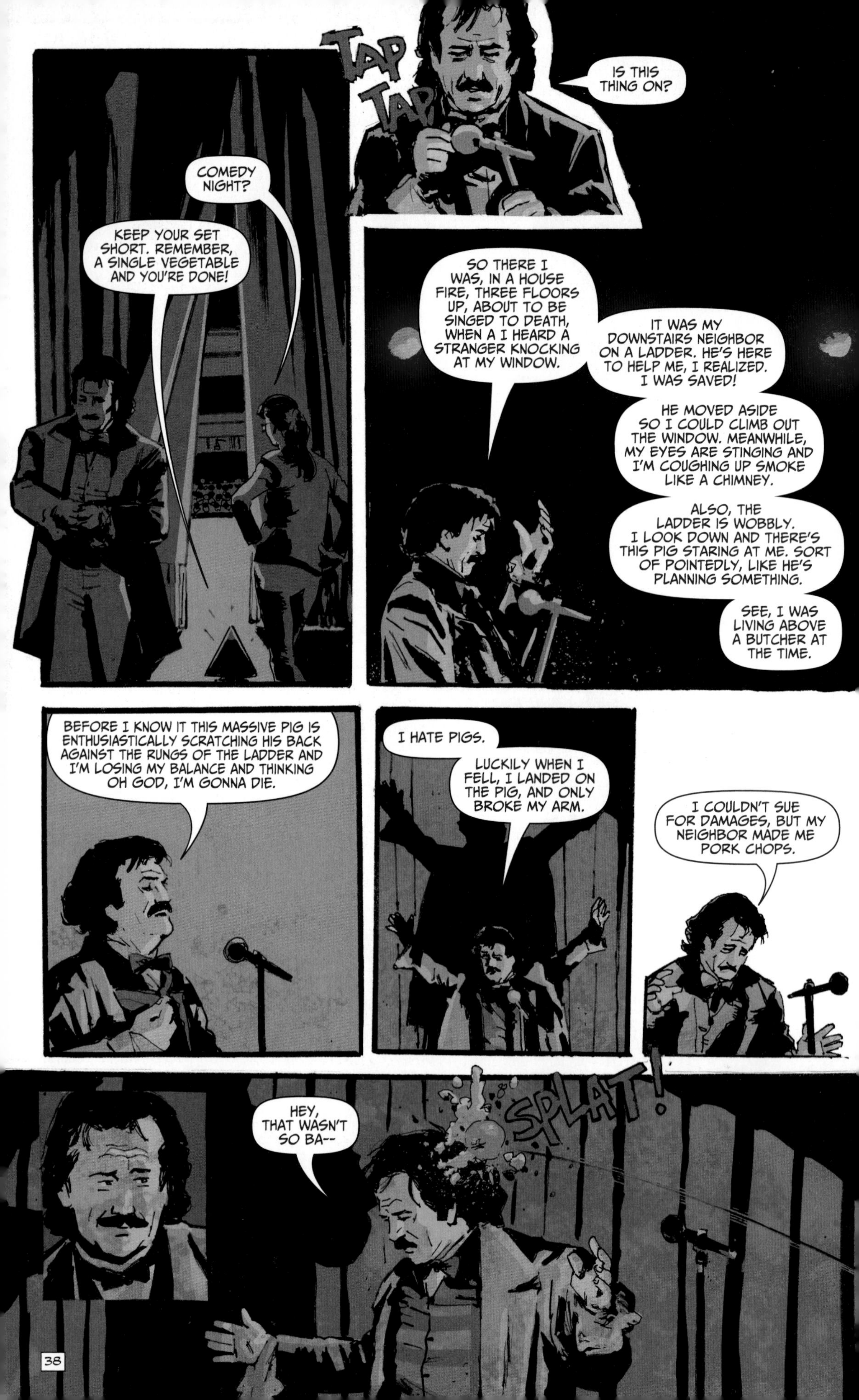
TAP
TAP
IS THIS THING ON?
COMEDY NIGHT?
KEEP YOUR SET SHORT. REMEMBER, A SINGLE VEGETABLE AND YOU'RE DONE!
SO THERE I WAS, IN A HOUSE FIRE, THREE FLOORS UP, ABOUT TO BE SINGED TO DEATH, WHEN A I HEARD A STRANGER KNOCKING AT MY WINDOW.
IT WAS MY DOWNSTAIRS NEIGHBOR ON A LADDER. HE'S HERE TO HELP ME, I REALIZED. I WAS SAVED!
HE MOVED ASIDE SO I COULD CLIMB OUT THE WINDOW. MEANWHILE, MY EYES ARE STINGING AND I'M COUGHING UP SMOKE LIKE A CHIMNEY.
ALSO, THE LADDER IS WOBBLY. I LOOK DOWN AND THERE'S THIS PIG STARING AT ME. SORT OF POINTEDLY, LIKE HE'S PLANNING SOMETHING.
SEE, I WAS LIVING ABOVE A BUTCHER AT THE TIME.
BEFORE I KNOW IT THIS MASSIVE PIG IS ENTHUSIASTICALLY SCRATCHING HIS BACK AGAINST THE RUNGS OF THE LADDER AND I'M LOSING MY BALANCE AND THINKING OH GOD, I'M GONNA DIE.
I HATE PIGS.
LUCKILY WHEN I FELL, I LANDED ON THE PIG, AND ONLY BROKE MY ARM.
I COULDN'T SUE FOR DAMAGES, BUT MY NEIGHBOR MADE ME PORK CHOPS.
HEY, THAT WASN'T SO BA--
SPLAT!

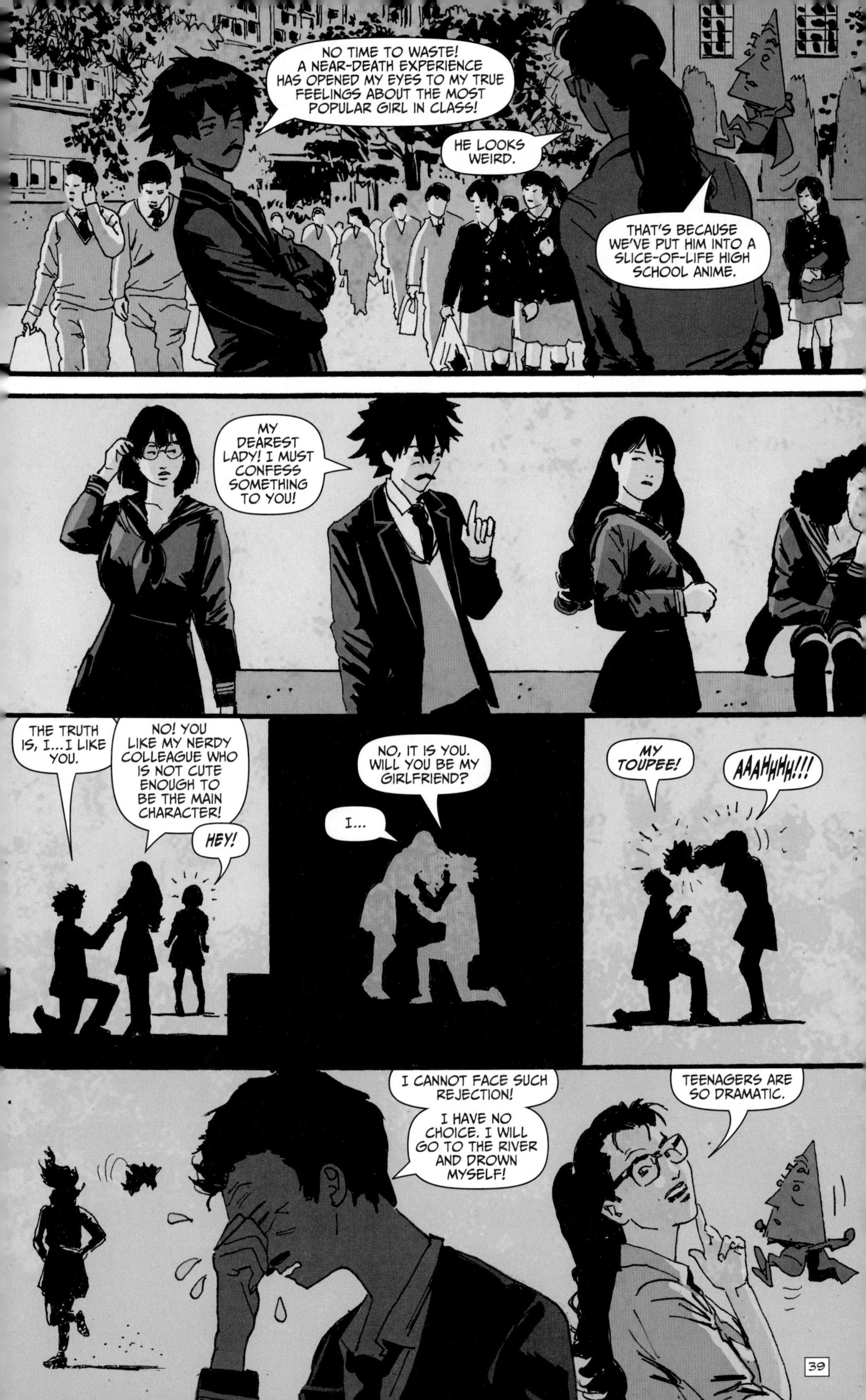
NO TIME TO WASTE! A NEAR-DEATH EXPERIENCE HAS OPENED MY EYES TO MY TRUE FEELINGS ABOUT THE MOST POPULAR GIRL IN CLASS!
HE LOOKS WEIRD.
THAT'S BECAUSE WE'VE PUT HIM INTO A SLICE-OF-LIFE HIGH SCHOOL ANIME.
MY DEAREST LADY! I MUST CONFESS SOMETHING TO YOU!
THE TRUTH IS, I...I LIKE YOU.
NO! YOU LIKE MY NERDY COLLEAGUE WHO IS NOT CUTE ENOUGH TO BE THE MAIN CHARACTER!
HEY!
NO, IT IS YOU. WILL YOU BE MY GIRLFRIEND?
I...
MY TOUPEE!
AAAHHHH!!!
I CANNOT FACE SUCH REJECTION!
I HAVE NO CHOICE. I WILL GO TO THE RIVER AND DROWN MYSELF!
TEENAGERS ARE SO DRAMATIC.

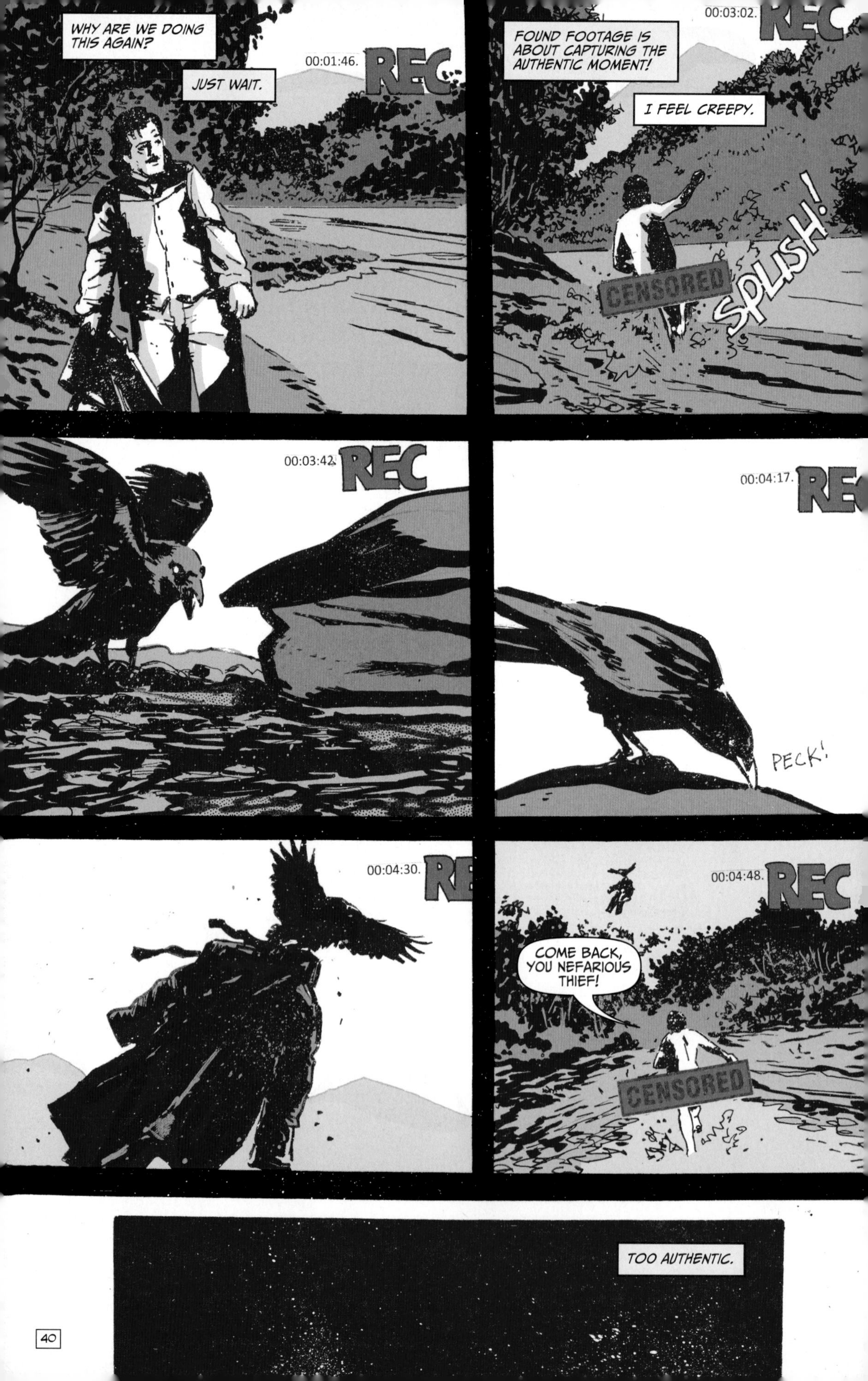
WHY ARE WE DOING THIS AGAIN?
JUST WAIT.
00:01:46.
REC
00:03:02.
REC
FOUND FOOTAGE IS ABOUT CAPTURING THE AUTHENTIC MOMENT!
I FEEL CREEPY.
CENSORED
SPLISH!
00:03:42.
REC
00:04:17.
PECK!
00:04:30.
00:04:48.
REC
COME BACK, YOU NEFARIOUS THIEF!
CENSORED
TOO AUTHENTIC.

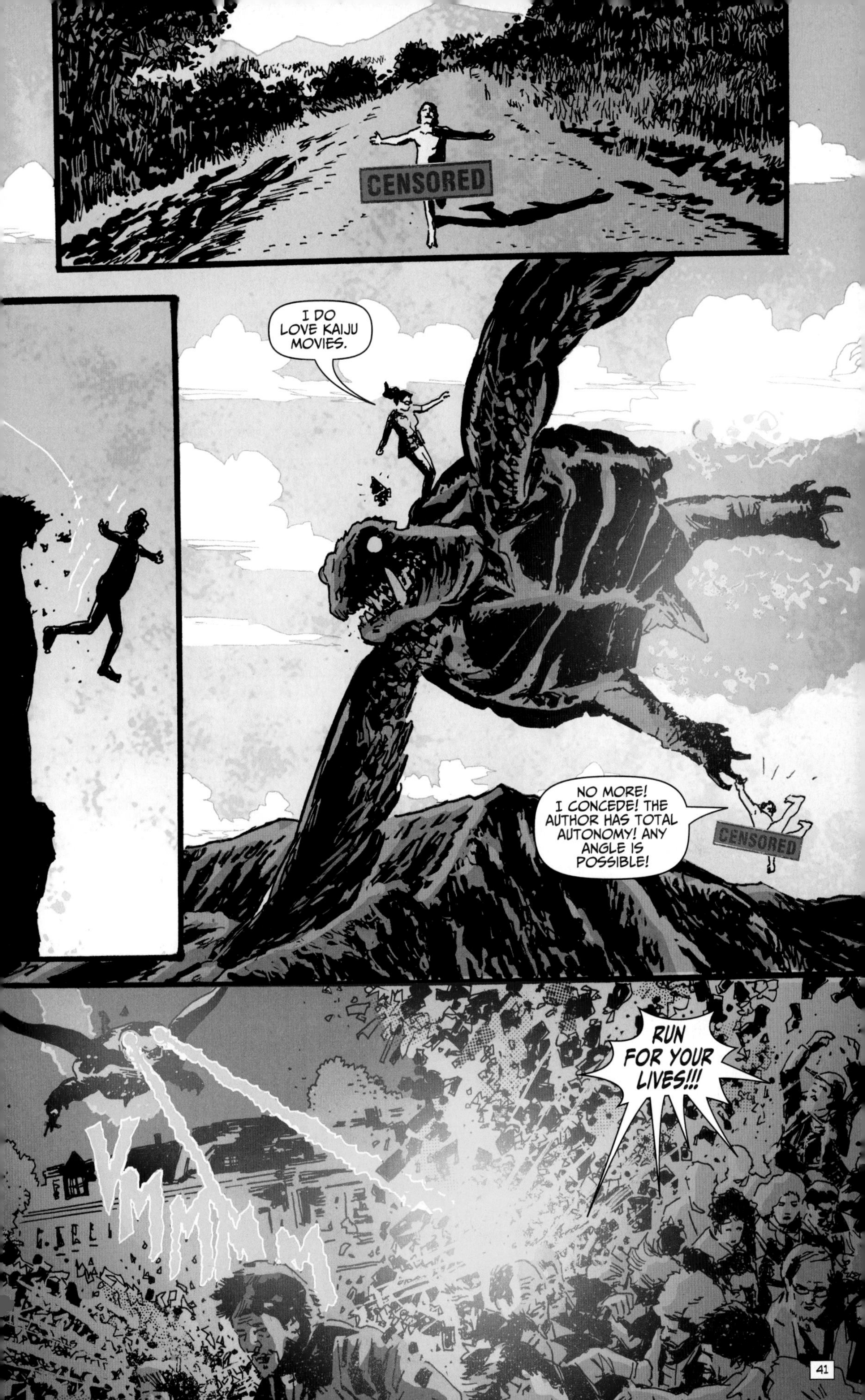
CENSORED
I DO LOVE KAIJU MOVIES.
NO MORE! I CONCEDE! THE AUTHOR HAS TOTAL AUTONOMY! ANY ANGLE IS POSSIBLE!
CENSORED
RUN FOR YOUR LIVES!!!
VMMMMM

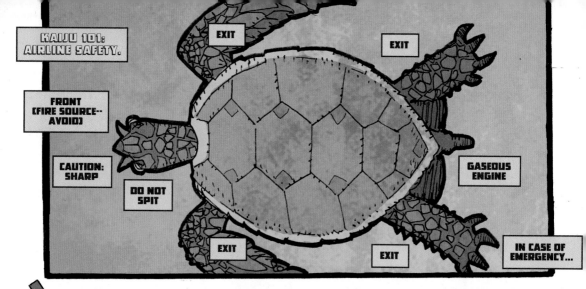

KAIJU 101:
AIRLINE SAFETY.

EXIT

EXIT

FRONT
(FIRE SOURCE--
AVOID)

CAUTION:
SHARP

DO NOT
SPIT

GASEOUS
ENGINE

EXIT

EXIT

IN CASE OF
EMERGENCY...

CENSORED

FRUMPH!

CENSORED

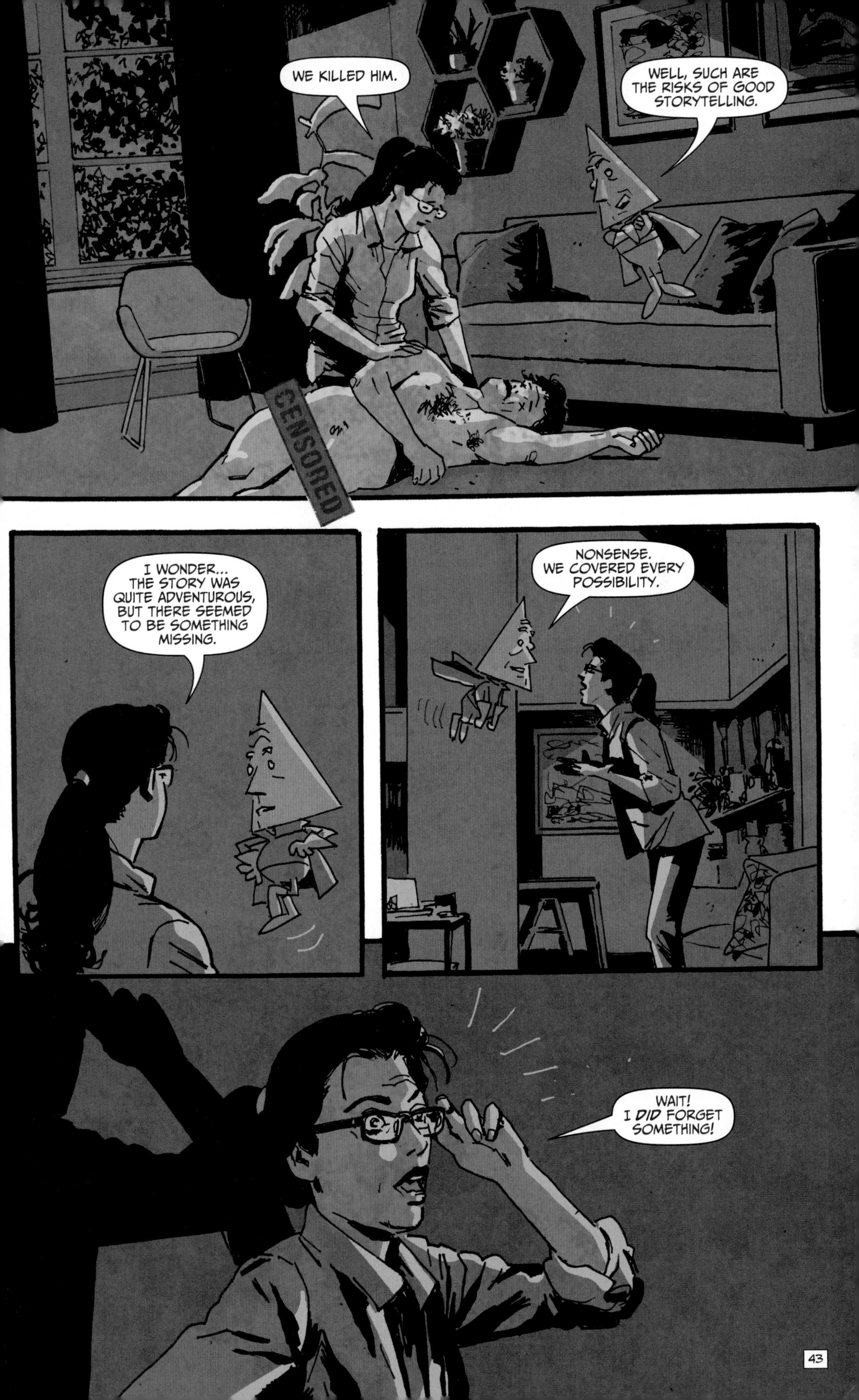
WE KILLED HIM.
WELL, SUCH ARE THE RISKS OF GOOD STORYTELLING.
CENSORED
I WONDER... THE STORY WAS QUITE ADVENTUROUS, BUT THERE SEEMED TO BE SOMETHING MISSING.
NONSENSE. WE COVERED EVERY POSSIBILITY.
WAIT! I *DID* FORGET SOMETHING!

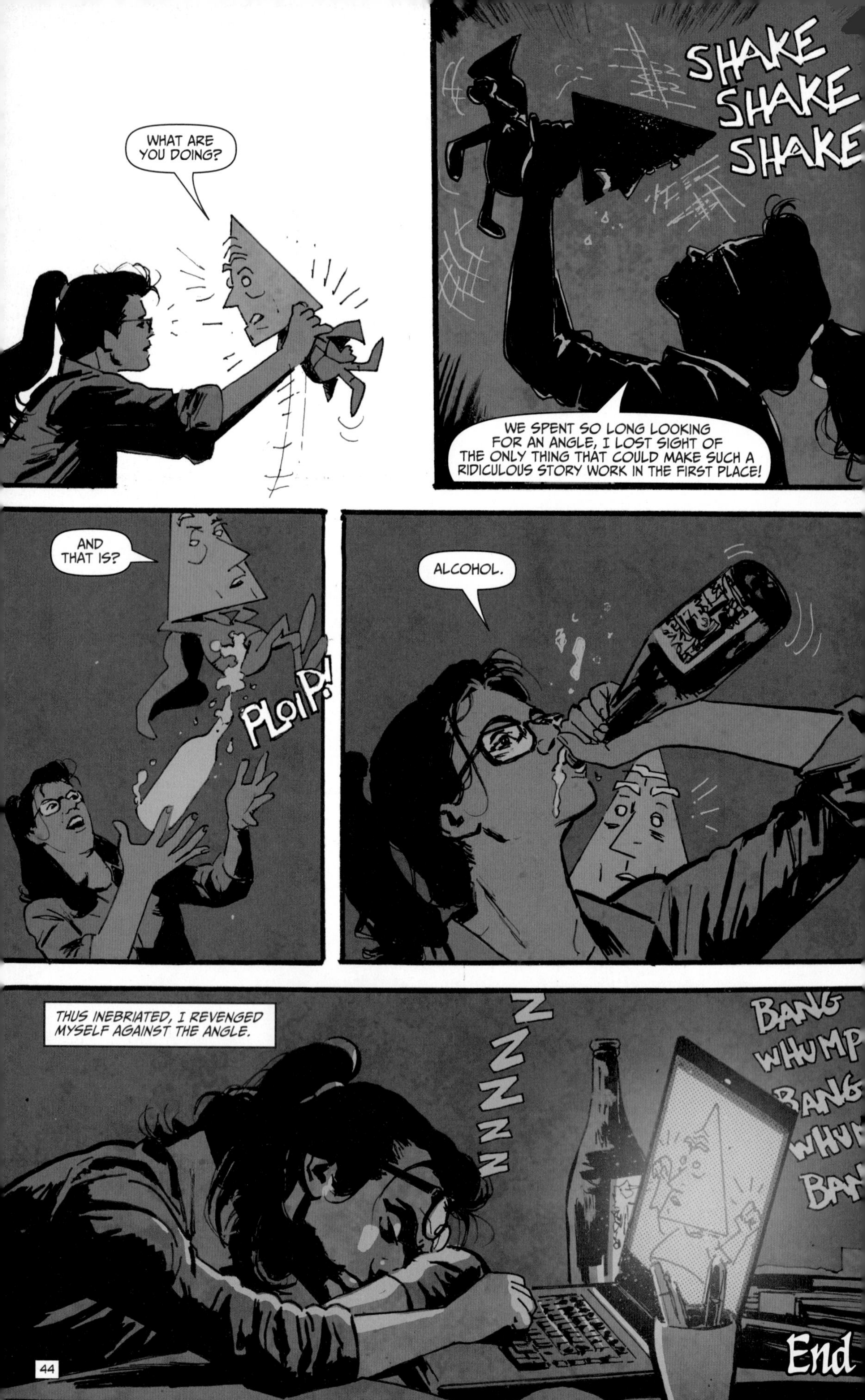
WHAT ARE YOU DOING?
SHAKE SHAKE SHAKE
WE SPENT SO LONG LOOKING FOR AN ANGLE, I LOST SIGHT OF THE ONLY THING THAT COULD MAKE SUCH A RIDICULOUS STORY WORK IN THE FIRST PLACE!
AND THAT IS?
PLOIP!
ALCOHOL.
THUS INEBRIATED, I REVENGED MYSELF AGAINST THE ANGLE.
ZZZZZ
BANG
WHUMP
BANG
End

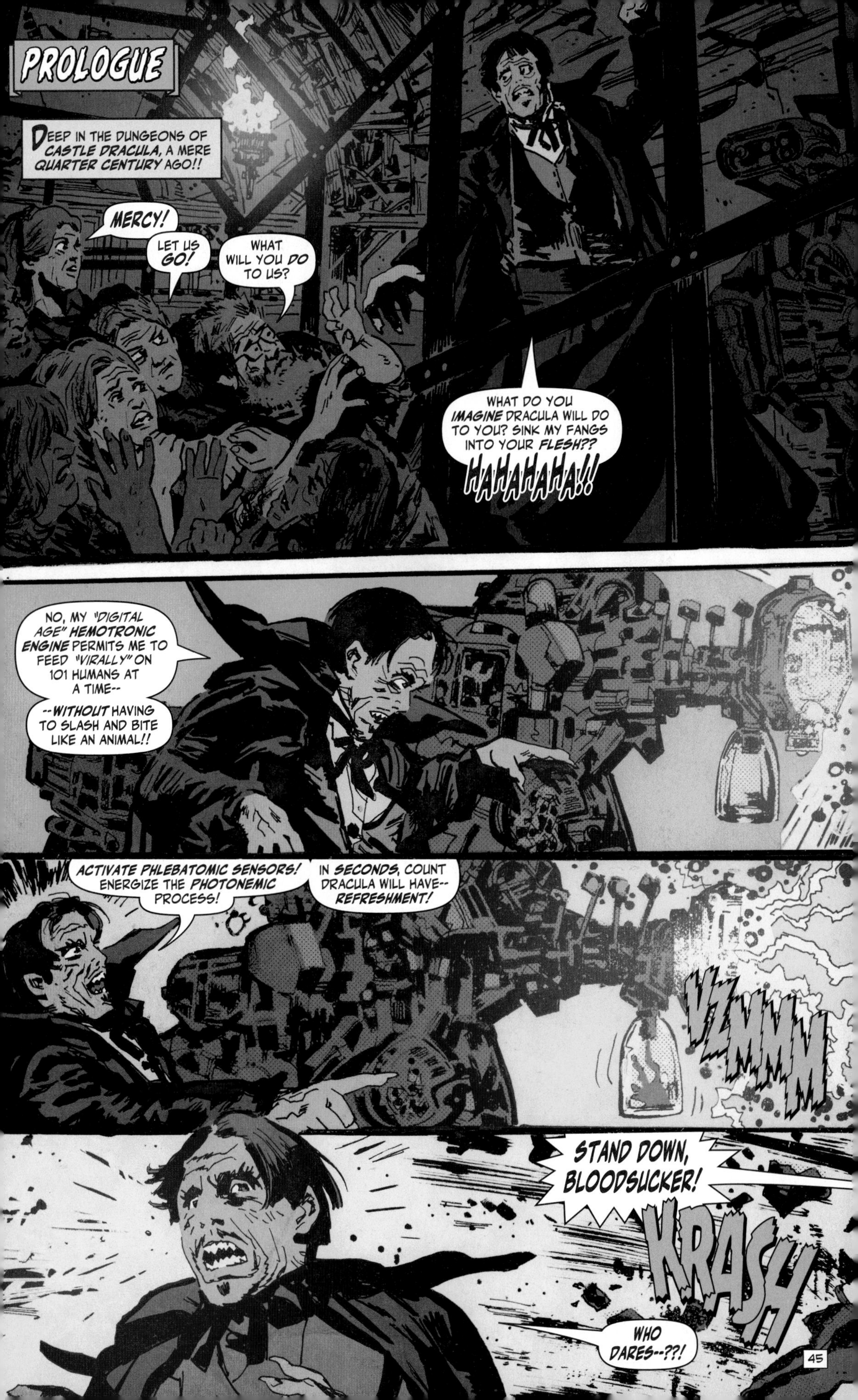
PROLOGUE
DEEP IN THE DUNGEONS OF CASTLE DRACULA, A MERE QUARTER CENTURY AGO!!
MERCY!
LET US GO!
WHAT WILL YOU DO TO US?
WHAT DO YOU IMAGINE DRACULA WILL DO TO YOU? SINK MY FANGS INTO YOUR FLESH?? HAHAHAHA!!
NO, MY "DIGITAL AGE" HEMOTRONIC ENGINE PERMITS ME TO FEED "VIRALLY" ON 101 HUMANS AT A TIME--
--WITHOUT HAVING TO SLASH AND BITE LIKE AN ANIMAL!!
ACTIVATE PHLEBATOMIC SENSORS! ENERGIZE THE PHOTONEMIC PROCESS!
IN SECONDS, COUNT DRACULA WILL HAVE-- REFRESHMENT!
VZMMM
STAND DOWN, BLOODSUCKER!
KRASH
WHO DARES--??!

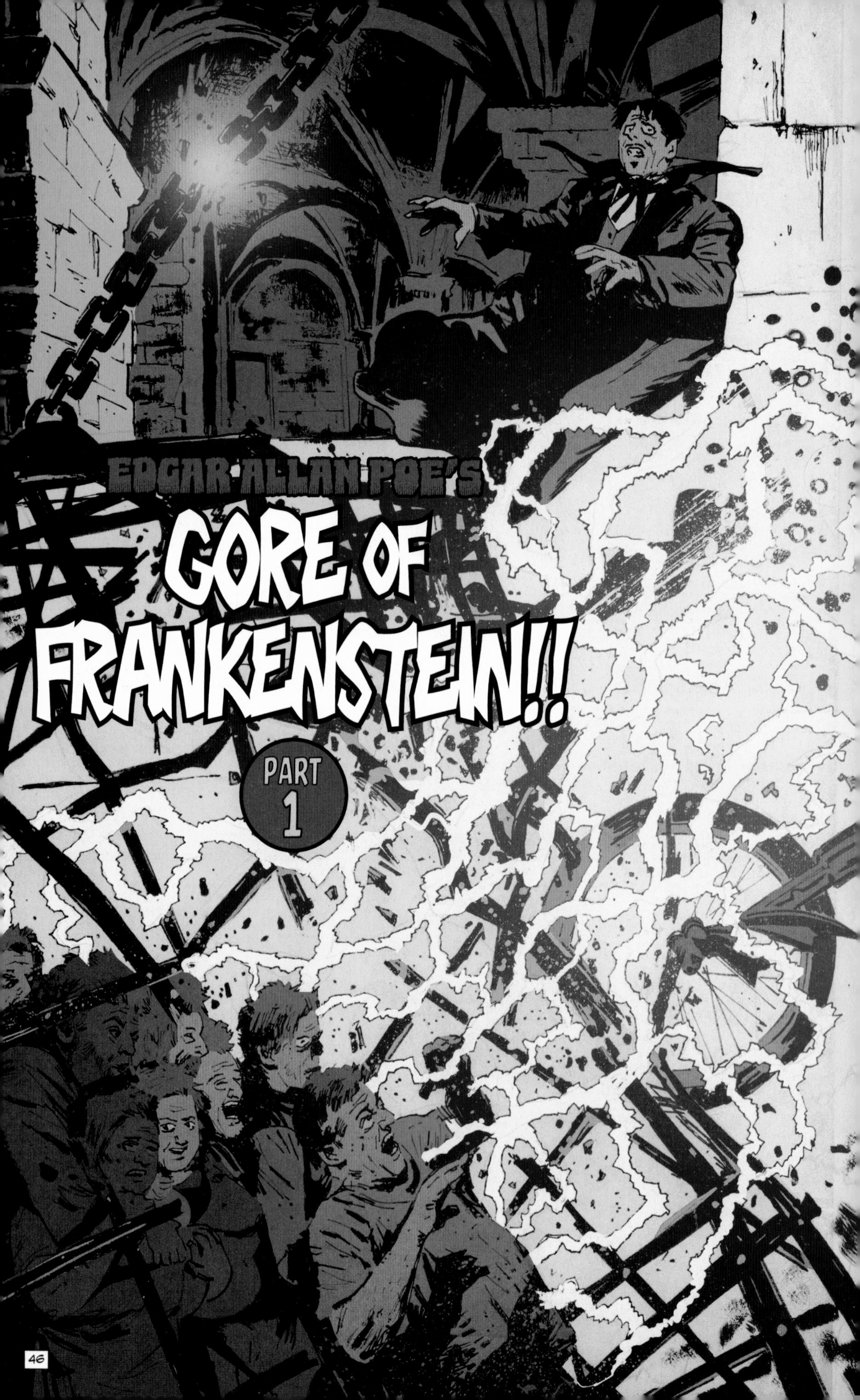
EDGAR ALLAN POE'S
GORE OF FRANKENSTEIN!!
PART 1

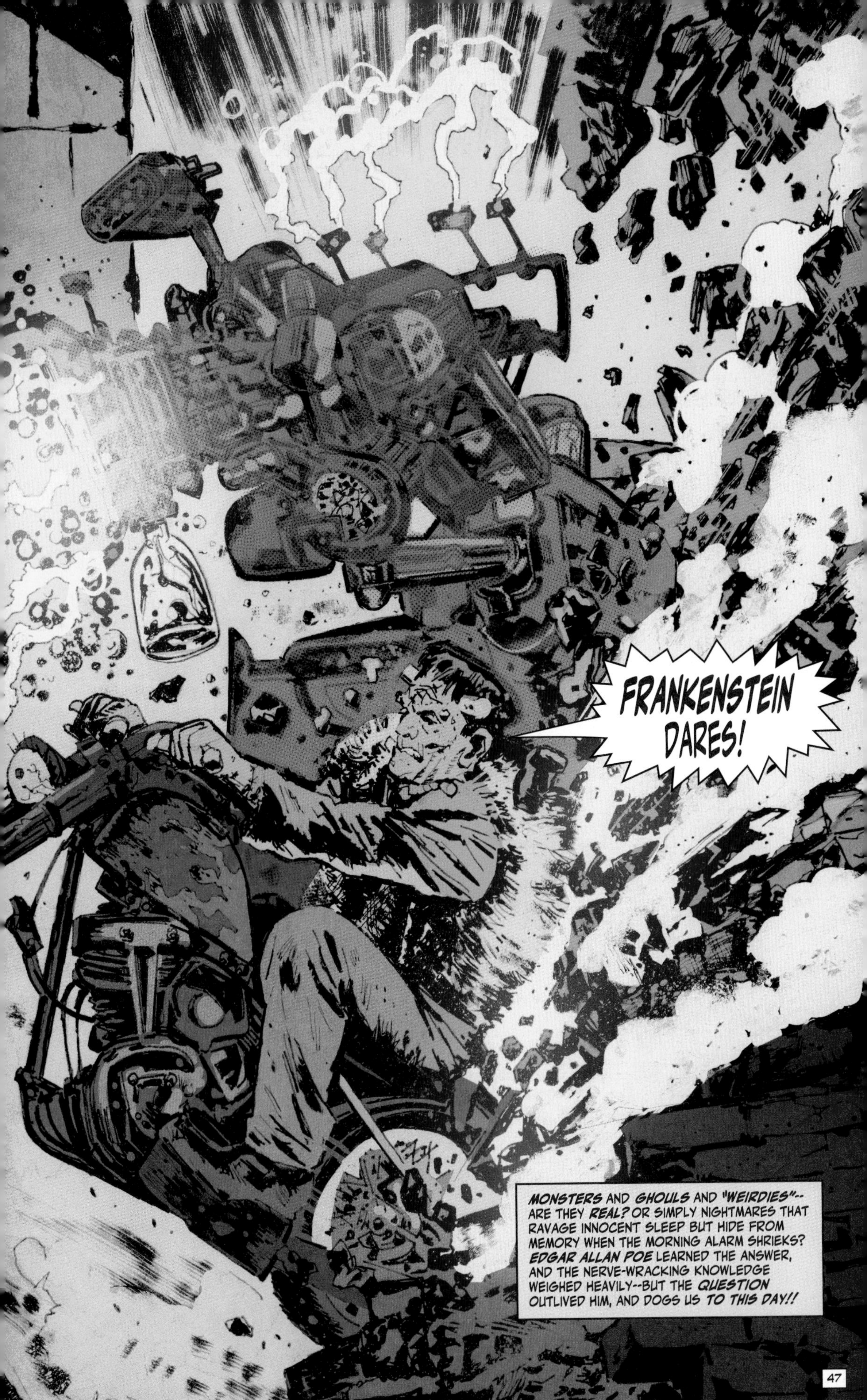
FRANKENSTEIN DARES!
MONSTERS AND GHOULS AND "WEIRDIES"--ARE THEY REAL? OR SIMPLY NIGHTMARES THAT RAVAGE INNOCENT SLEEP BUT HIDE FROM MEMORY WHEN THE MORNING ALARM SHRIEKS? EDGAR ALLAN POE LEARNED THE ANSWER, AND THE NERVE-WRACKING KNOWLEDGE WEIGHED HEAVILY--BUT THE QUESTION OUTLIVED HIM, AND DOGS US TO THIS DAY!!

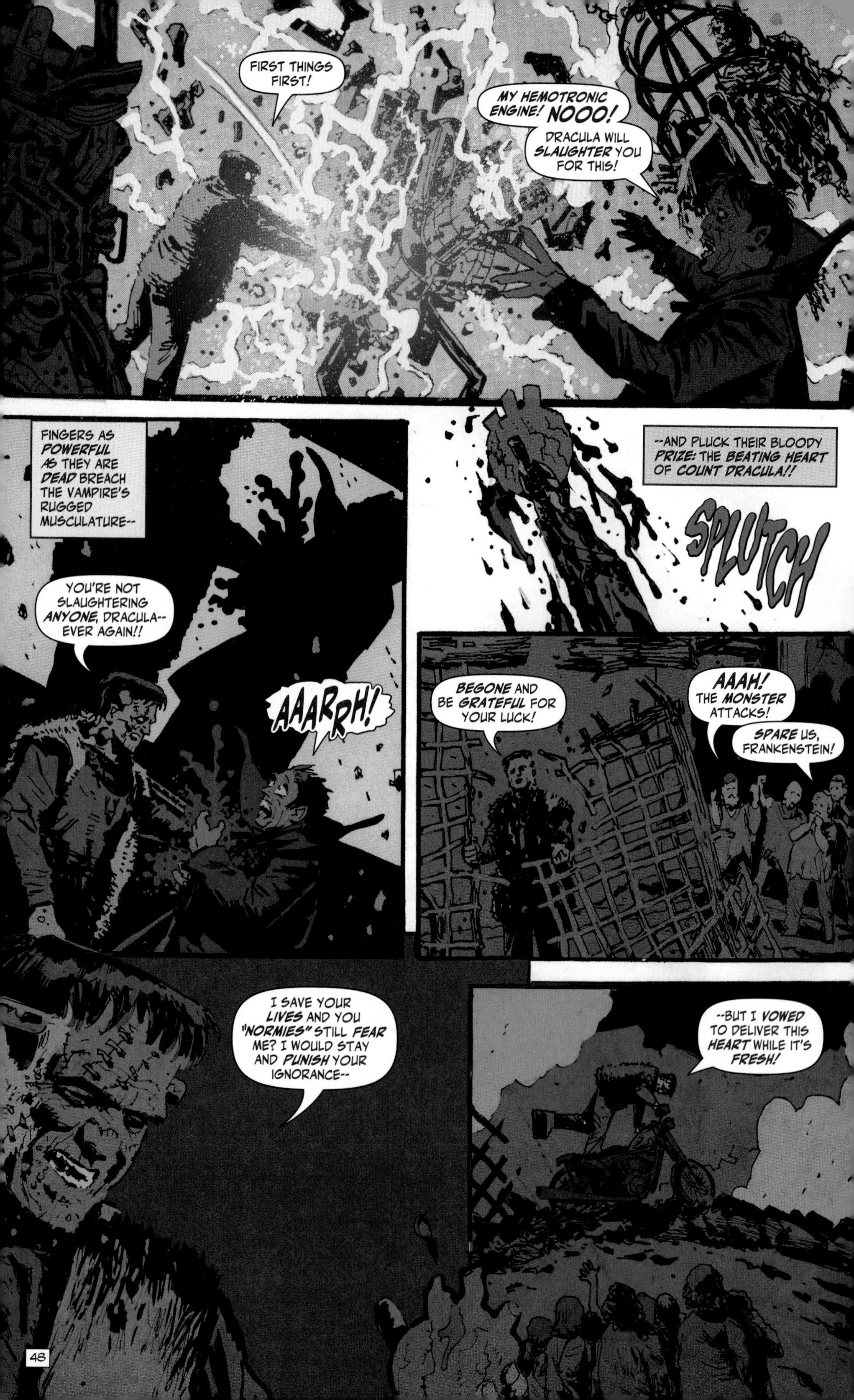
FIRST THINGS FIRST!
MY HEMOTRONIC ENGINE! NOOO!
DRACULA WILL SLAUGHTER YOU FOR THIS!
FINGERS AS POWERFUL AS THEY ARE DEAD BREACH THE VAMPIRE'S RUGGED MUSCULATURE--
YOU'RE NOT SLAUGHTERING ANYONE, DRACULA-- EVER AGAIN!!
AAARRH!
--AND PLUCK THEIR BLOODY PRIZE: THE BEATING HEART OF COUNT DRACULA!!
SPLUTCH
BEGONE AND BE GRATEFUL FOR YOUR LUCK!
AAAH! THE MONSTER ATTACKS!
SPARE US, FRANKENSTEIN!
I SAVE YOUR LIVES AND YOU "NORMIES" STILL FEAR ME? I WOULD STAY AND PUNISH YOUR IGNORANCE--
--BUT I VOWED TO DELIVER THIS HEART WHILE IT'S FRESH!

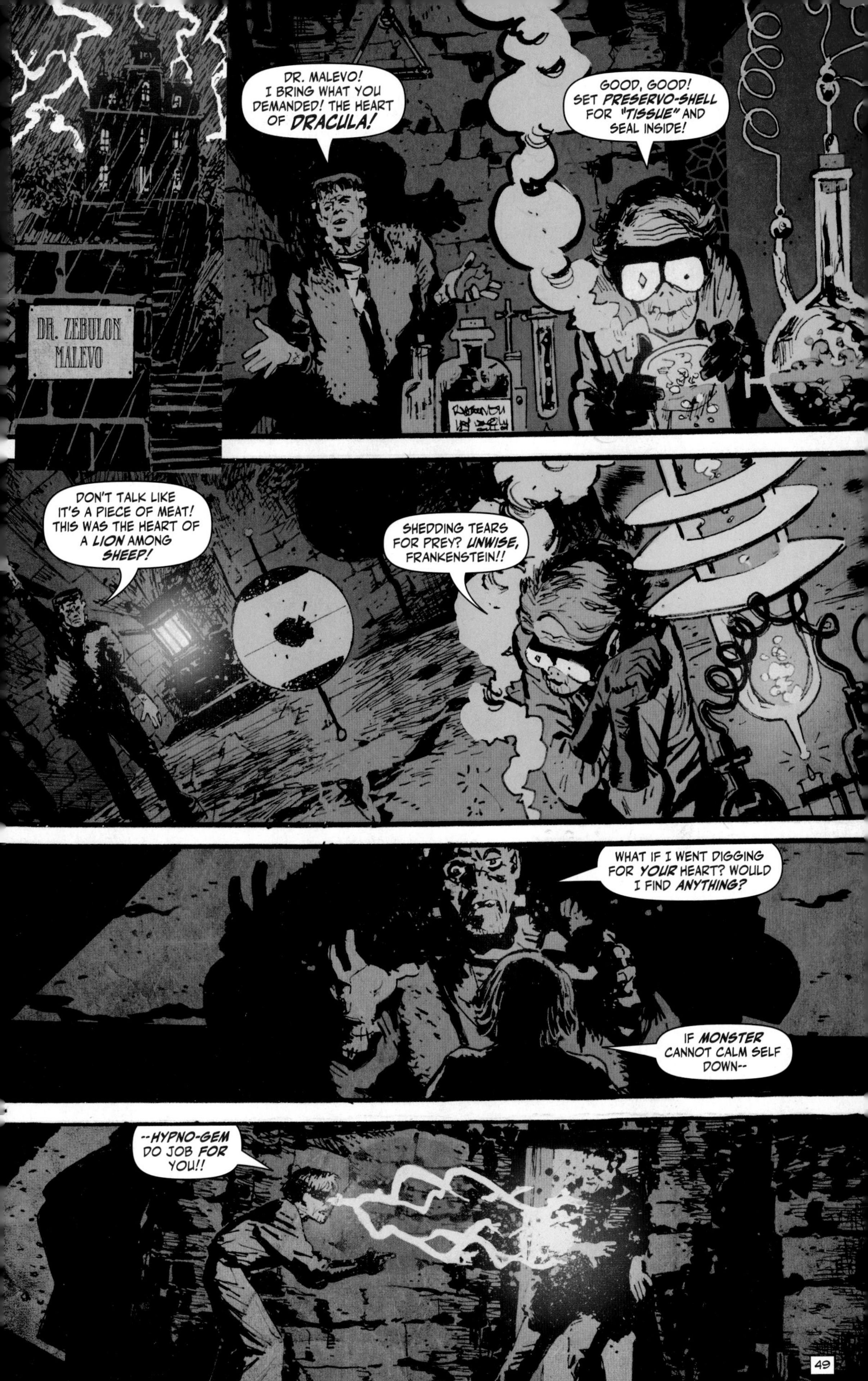
DR. ZEBULON MALEVO
DR. MALEVO! I BRING WHAT YOU DEMANDED! THE HEART OF DRACULA!
GOOD, GOOD! SET PRESERVO-SHELL FOR "TISSUE" AND SEAL INSIDE!
DON'T TALK LIKE IT'S A PIECE OF MEAT! THIS WAS THE HEART OF A LION AMONG SHEEP!
SHEDDING TEARS FOR PREY? UNWISE, FRANKENSTEIN!!
WHAT IF I WENT DIGGING FOR YOUR HEART? WOULD I FIND ANYTHING?
IF MONSTER CANNOT CALM SELF DOWN--
--HYPNO-GEM DO JOB FOR YOU!!

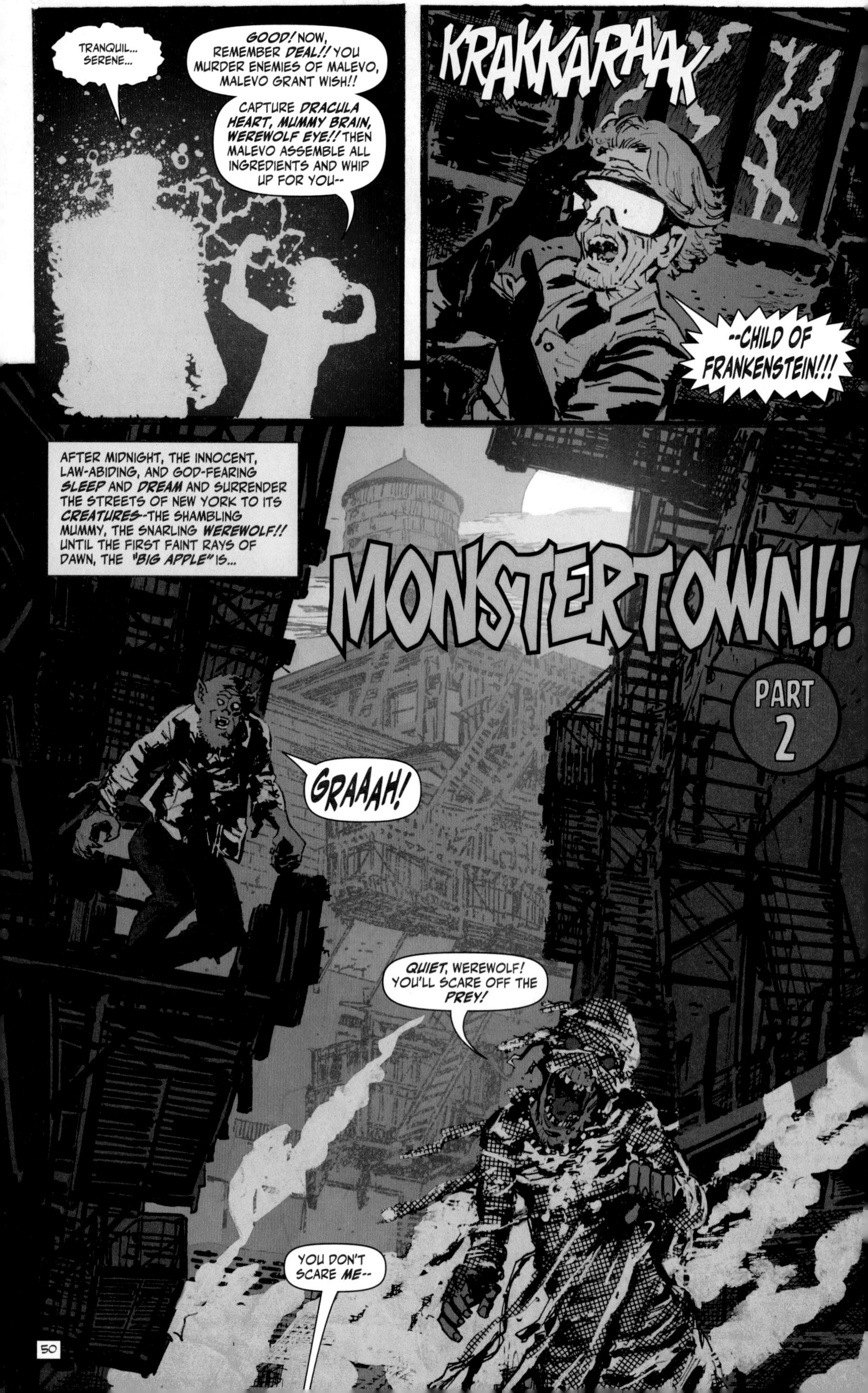
TRANQUIL... SERENE...
GOOD! NOW, REMEMBER DEAL!! YOU MURDER ENEMIES OF MALEVO, MALEVO GRANT WISH!!
CAPTURE DRACULA HEART, MUMMY BRAIN, WEREWOLF EYE!! THEN MALEVO ASSEMBLE ALL INGREDIENTS AND WHIP UP FOR YOU--
KRAKKARAAK
--CHILD OF FRANKENSTEIN!!!
AFTER MIDNIGHT, THE INNOCENT, LAW-ABIDING, AND GOD-FEARING SLEEP AND DREAM AND SURRENDER THE STREETS OF NEW YORK TO ITS CREATURES--THE SHAMBLING MUMMY, THE SNARLING WEREWOLF!! UNTIL THE FIRST FAINT RAYS OF DAWN, THE "BIG APPLE" IS...
MONSTERTOWN!!
PART 2
GRAAAH!
QUIET, WEREWOLF! YOU'LL SCARE OFF THE PREY!
YOU DON'T SCARE ME--

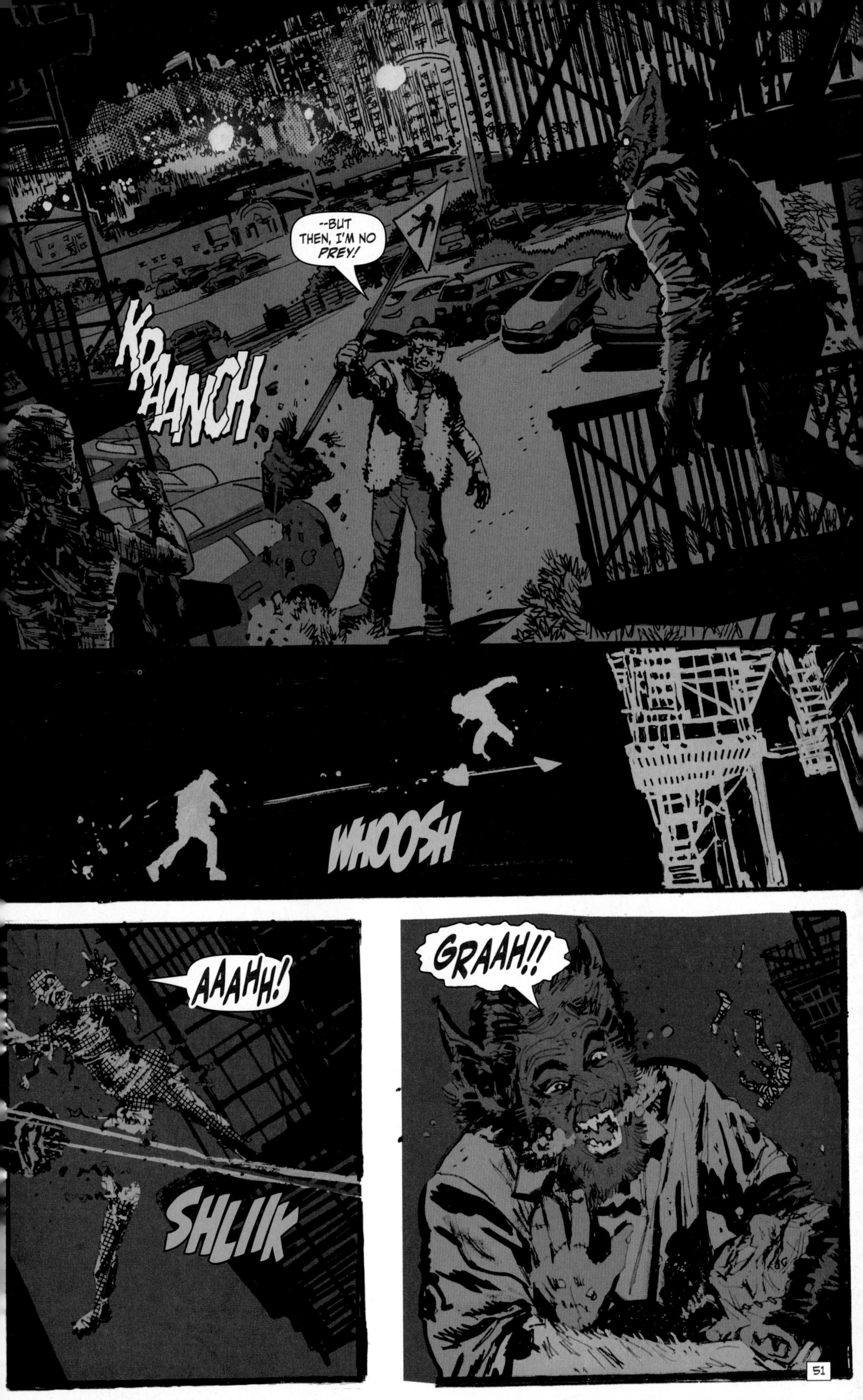
--BUT THEN, I'M NO PREY!
KRAANCH
WHOOSH
AAAHH!
SHLIIK
GRAAH!!

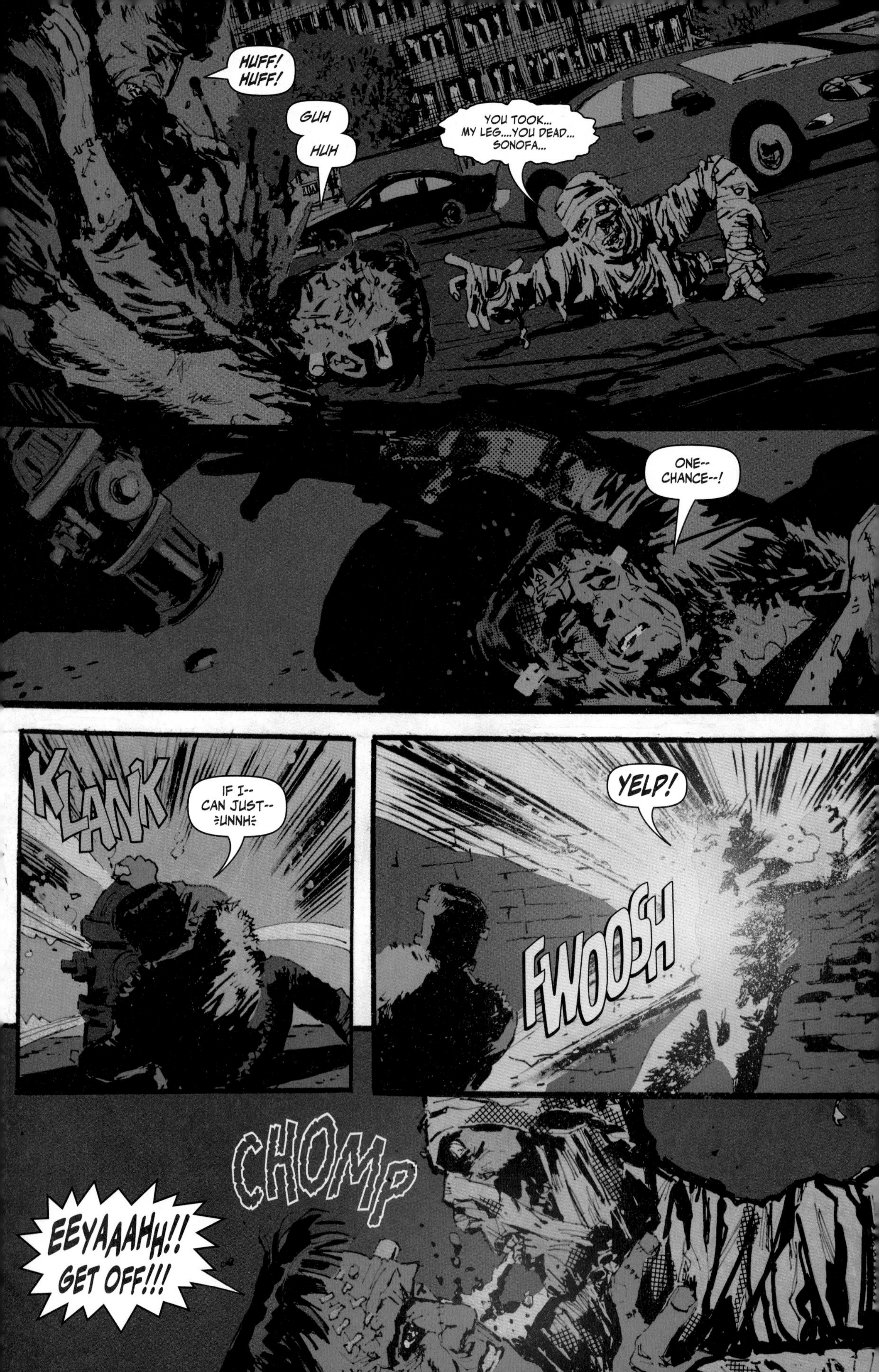
HUFF! HUFF!
GUH
HUH
YOU TOOK... MY LEG....YOU DEAD... SONOFA...
ONE-- CHANCE--!
KLANK
IF I-- CAN JUST-- =UNNH=
YELP!
FWOOSH
CHOMP
EEYAAAHH!! GET OFF!!!

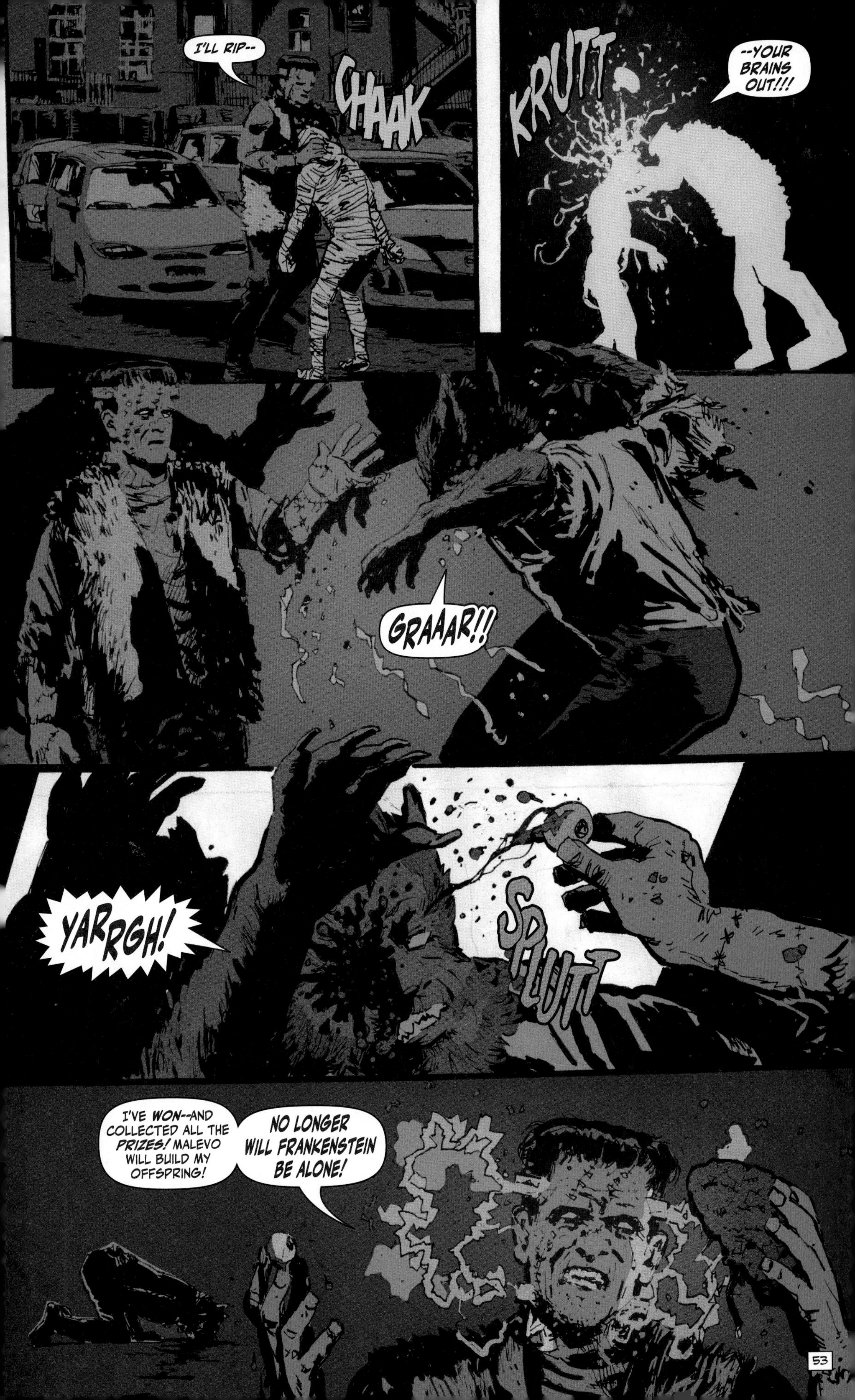
I'LL RIP--
CHAAK
KRUTT
--YOUR BRAINS OUT!!!
GRAAAR!!
YARRGH!
SPLUTT
I'VE WON--AND COLLECTED ALL THE PRIZES! MALEVO WILL BUILD MY OFFSPRING!
NO LONGER WILL FRANKENSTEIN BE ALONE!

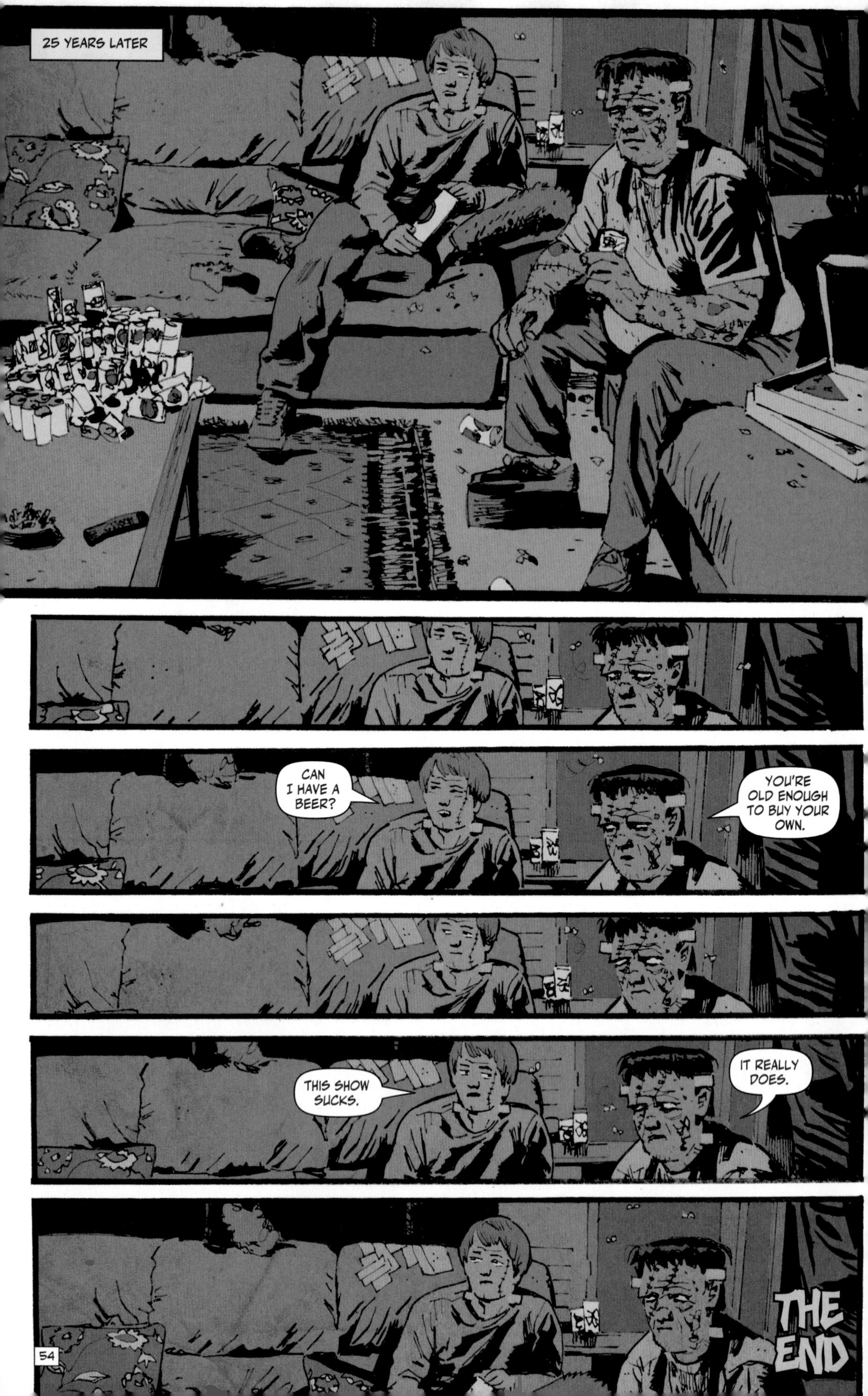
25 YEARS LATER
CAN I HAVE A BEER?
YOU'RE OLD ENOUGH TO BUY YOUR OWN.
THIS SHOW SUCKS.
IT REALLY DOES.
THE END

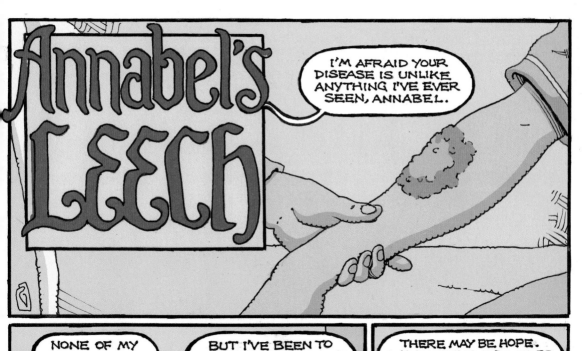

Annabel's Leech

I'M AFRAID YOUR DISEASE IS UNLIKE ANYTHING I'VE EVER SEEN, ANNABEL.

NONE OF MY METHODS HAVE WORKED.

BUT I'VE BEEN TO EVERY DOCTOR IN THE STATE! I DON'T HAVE ANY OTHER OPTIONS!

THERE MAY BE HOPE. I KNOW OF TWO DOCTORS WHO HAVE BOTH FOUND SOME SUCCESS...

THEY JUST HATE EACH OTHER.

BETWEEN THEIR INTENSE RIVALRY AND... UNIQUE METHODS, THEY'VE BEEN RELEGATED TO THE FRINGE OF THE MEDICAL COMMUNITY.

DR. KEPP
230 N. MAIN ST.

DR. RAYNARD
47 2ND AVE.

"THIS IS HOW WE MET ANNABEL."

MAYBE THEY CAN HELP. JUST DON'T TELL EITHER OF THEM YOU'RE SEEING THE OTHER.

"BUT IN THE END, SHE COULD ONLY CHOOSE ONE OF US."

DR. KEPP'S OFFICE

I KNOW THIS CAN BE INTIMIDATING, BUT LET ME EXPLAIN: MY THEORY IS THAT WE CAN TRICK YOUR BRAIN INTO HEALING YOUR BODY.

BY SHOCKING IT?!

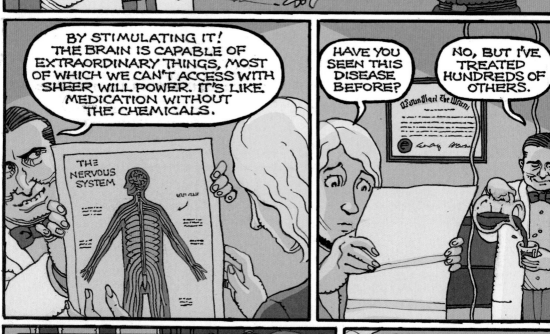

BY STIMULATING IT! THE BRAIN IS CAPABLE OF EXTRAORDINARY THINGS, MOST OF WHICH WE CAN'T ACCESS WITH SHEER WILL POWER. IT'S LIKE MEDICATION WITHOUT THE CHEMICALS.

THE NERVOUS SYSTEM

HAVE YOU SEEN THIS DISEASE BEFORE?

NO, BUT I'VE TREATED HUNDREDS OF OTHERS.

DR. RAYNARD'S OFFICE

THAT'S LYLE. HE'S ONE OF SEVERAL LEECHES I'LL TREAT YOU WITH.

TO SUCK MY BLOOD?!

AND TAKE YOUR DISEASE WITH IT! LOOK — HE'S QUITE FOND OF YOU.

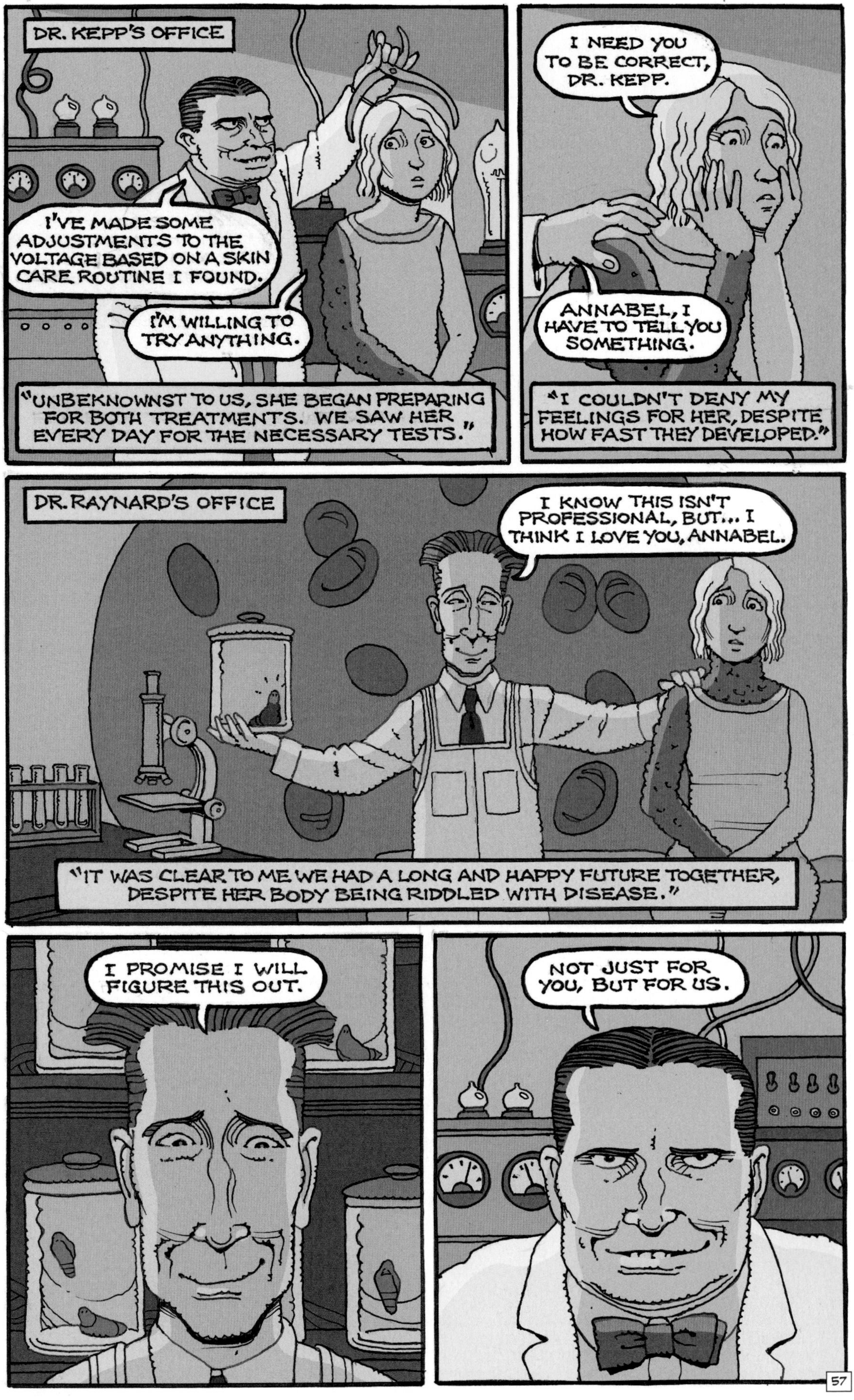
DR. KEPP'S OFFICE
I'VE MADE SOME ADJUSTMENTS TO THE VOLTAGE BASED ON A SKIN CARE ROUTINE I FOUND.
I'M WILLING TO TRY ANYTHING.
"UNBEKNOWNST TO US, SHE BEGAN PREPARING FOR BOTH TREATMENTS. WE SAW HER EVERY DAY FOR THE NECESSARY TESTS."
I NEED YOU TO BE CORRECT, DR. KEPP.
ANNABEL, I HAVE TO TELL YOU SOMETHING.
"I COULDN'T DENY MY FEELINGS FOR HER, DESPITE HOW FAST THEY DEVELOPED."
DR. RAYNARD'S OFFICE
I KNOW THIS ISN'T PROFESSIONAL, BUT... I THINK I LOVE YOU, ANNABEL.
"IT WAS CLEAR TO ME WE HAD A LONG AND HAPPY FUTURE TOGETHER, DESPITE HER BODY BEING RIDDLED WITH DISEASE."
I PROMISE I WILL FIGURE THIS OUT.
NOT JUST FOR YOU, BUT FOR US.

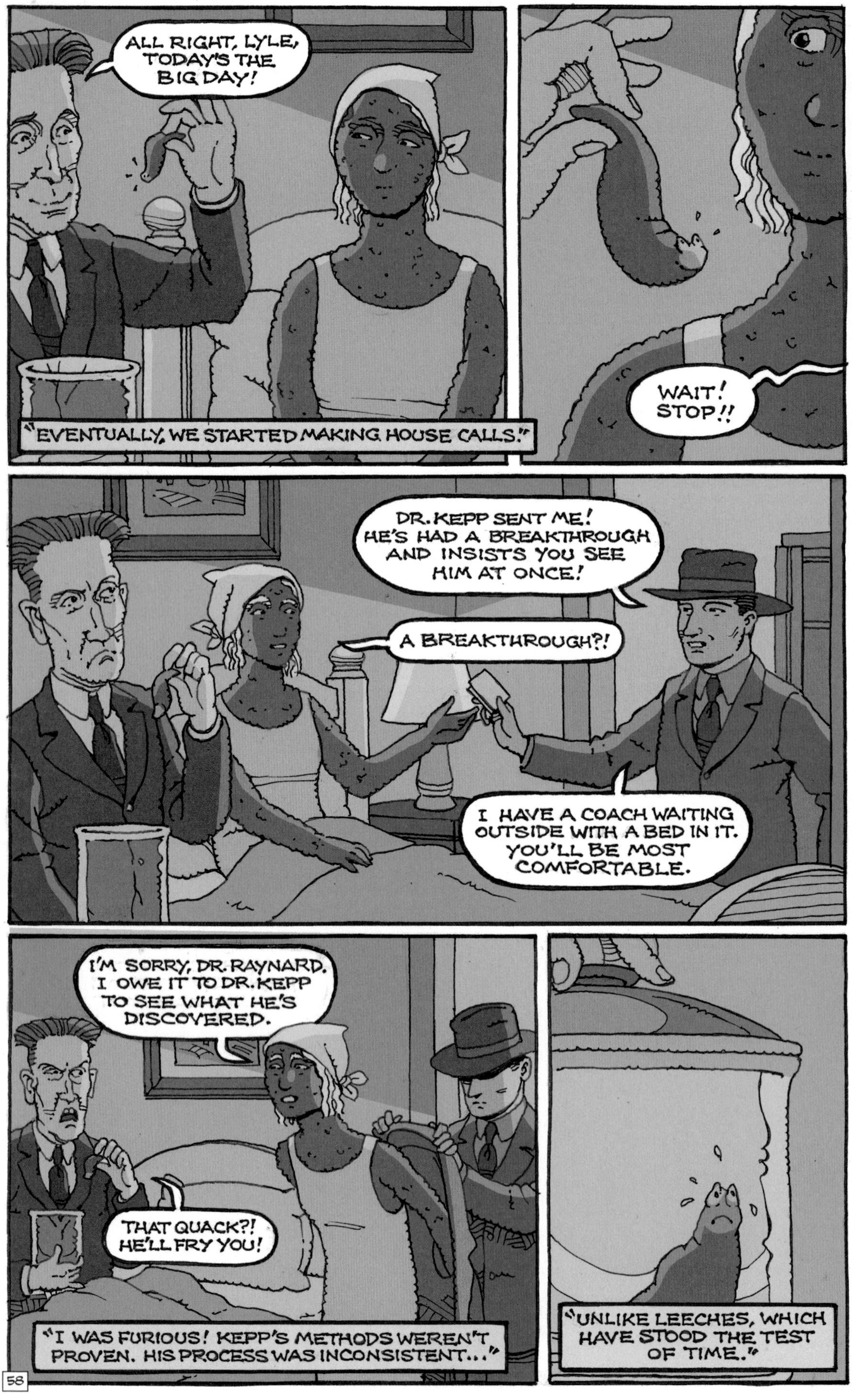
ALL RIGHT, LYLE, TODAY'S THE BIG DAY!
"EVENTUALLY, WE STARTED MAKING HOUSE CALLS."
WAIT! STOP!!
DR. KEPP SENT ME! HE'S HAD A BREAKTHROUGH AND INSISTS YOU SEE HIM AT ONCE!
A BREAKTHROUGH?!
I HAVE A COACH WAITING OUTSIDE WITH A BED IN IT. YOU'LL BE MOST COMFORTABLE.
I'M SORRY, DR. RAYNARD. I OWE IT TO DR. KEPP TO SEE WHAT HE'S DISCOVERED.
THAT QUACK?! HE'LL FRY YOU!
"I WAS FURIOUS! KEPP'S METHODS WEREN'T PROVEN. HIS PROCESS WAS INCONSISTENT..."
"UNLIKE LEECHES, WHICH HAVE STOOD THE TEST OF TIME."

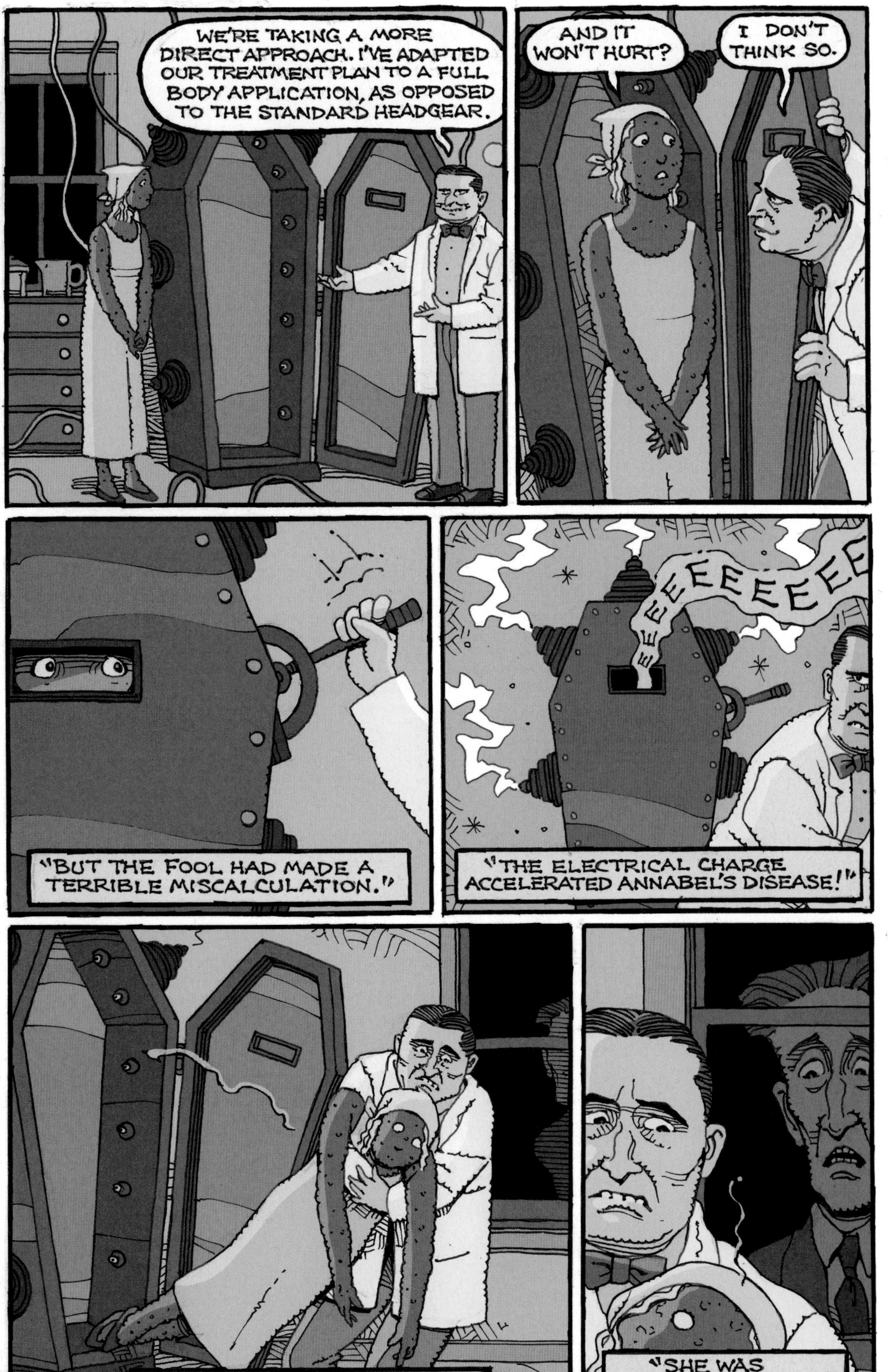
WE'RE TAKING A MORE DIRECT APPROACH. I'VE ADAPTED OUR TREATMENT PLAN TO A FULL BODY APPLICATION, AS OPPOSED TO THE STANDARD HEADGEAR.
AND IT WON'T HURT?
I DON'T THINK SO.
"BUT THE FOOL HAD MADE A TERRIBLE MISCALCULATION."
EEEEEEEEEEEE
"THE ELECTRICAL CHARGE ACCELERATED ANNABEL'S DISEASE!"
"AND WHEN HE WAS DONE..."
"SHE WAS UNRECOGNIZABLE!"

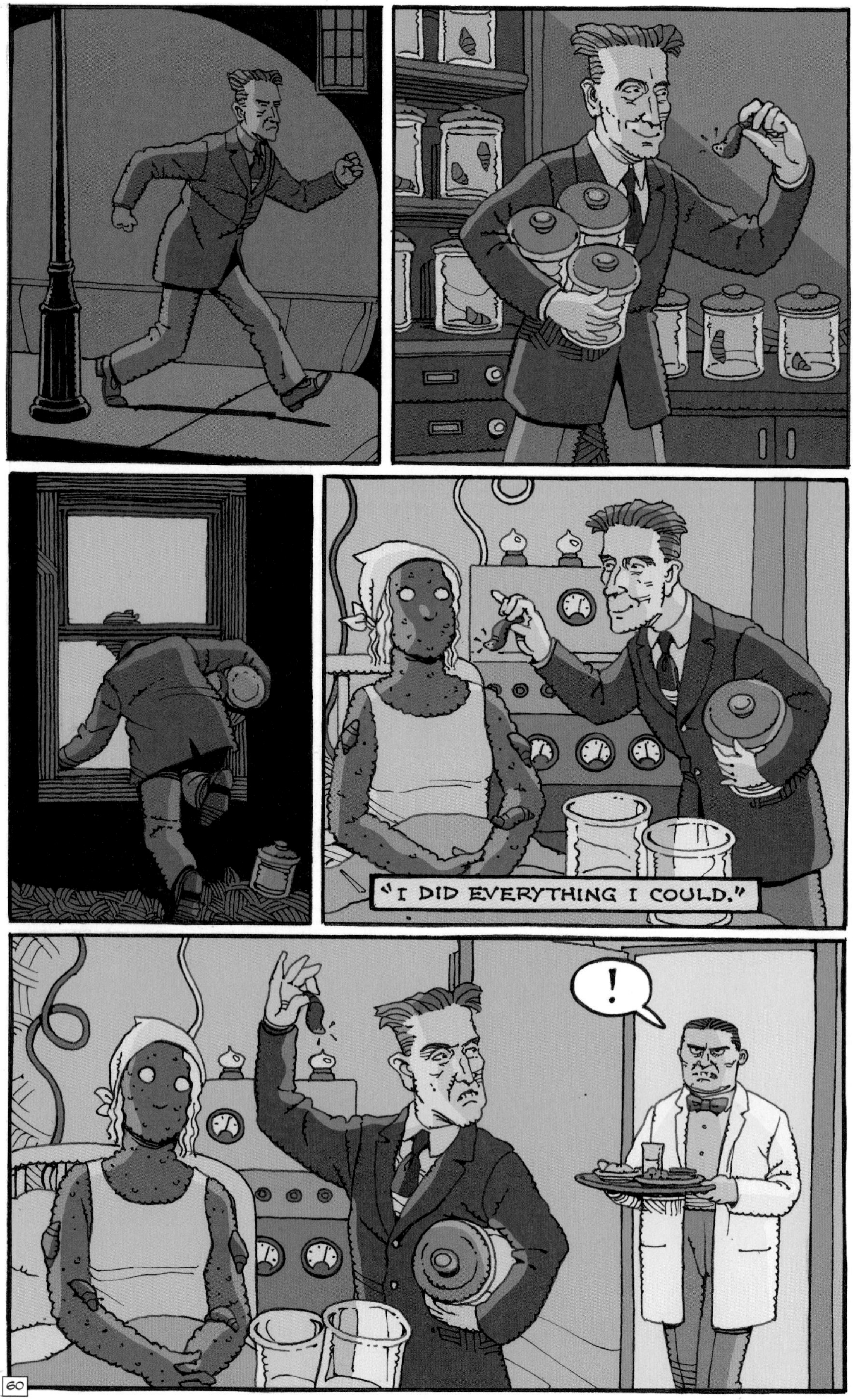
"I DID EVERYTHING I COULD."
!

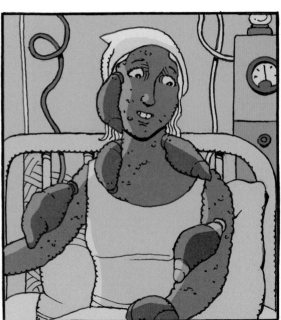

"I COULD TELL KEPP HAD THE UPPER HAND WHEN IT CAME TO GRAPPLING."

HEY, LOOK! IT'S WORKING!

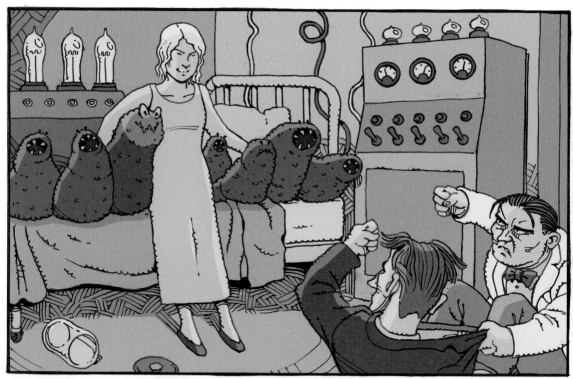

"KEPP WAS THE FIRST TO GO — ON PRINCIPLE."

"RAYNARD WAS NEXT. WE HATED THOSE AWFUL JARS."

"BUT HEY, HE INTRODUCED ME TO ANNABEL. I MUST SAY..."

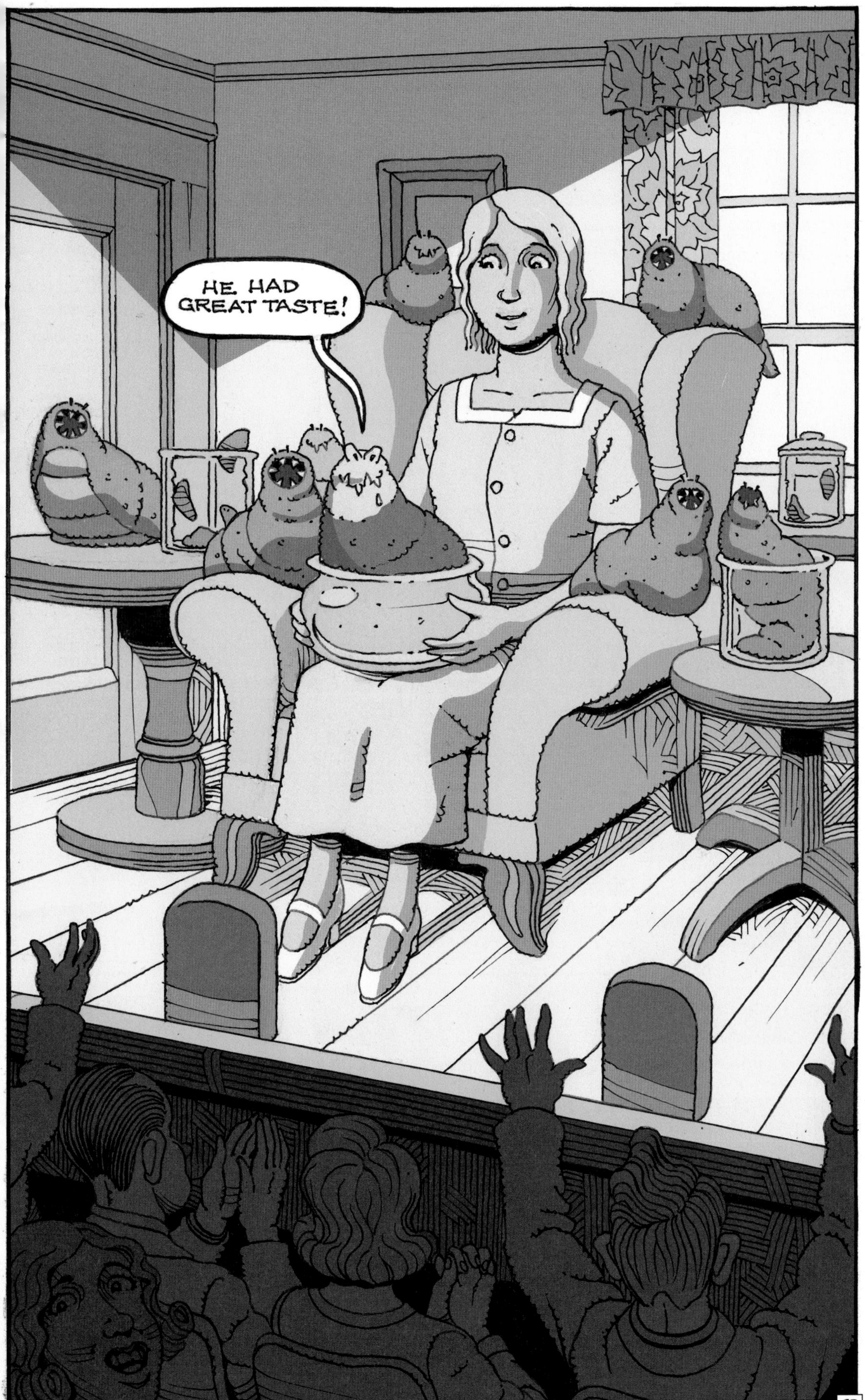
HE HAD GREAT TASTE!

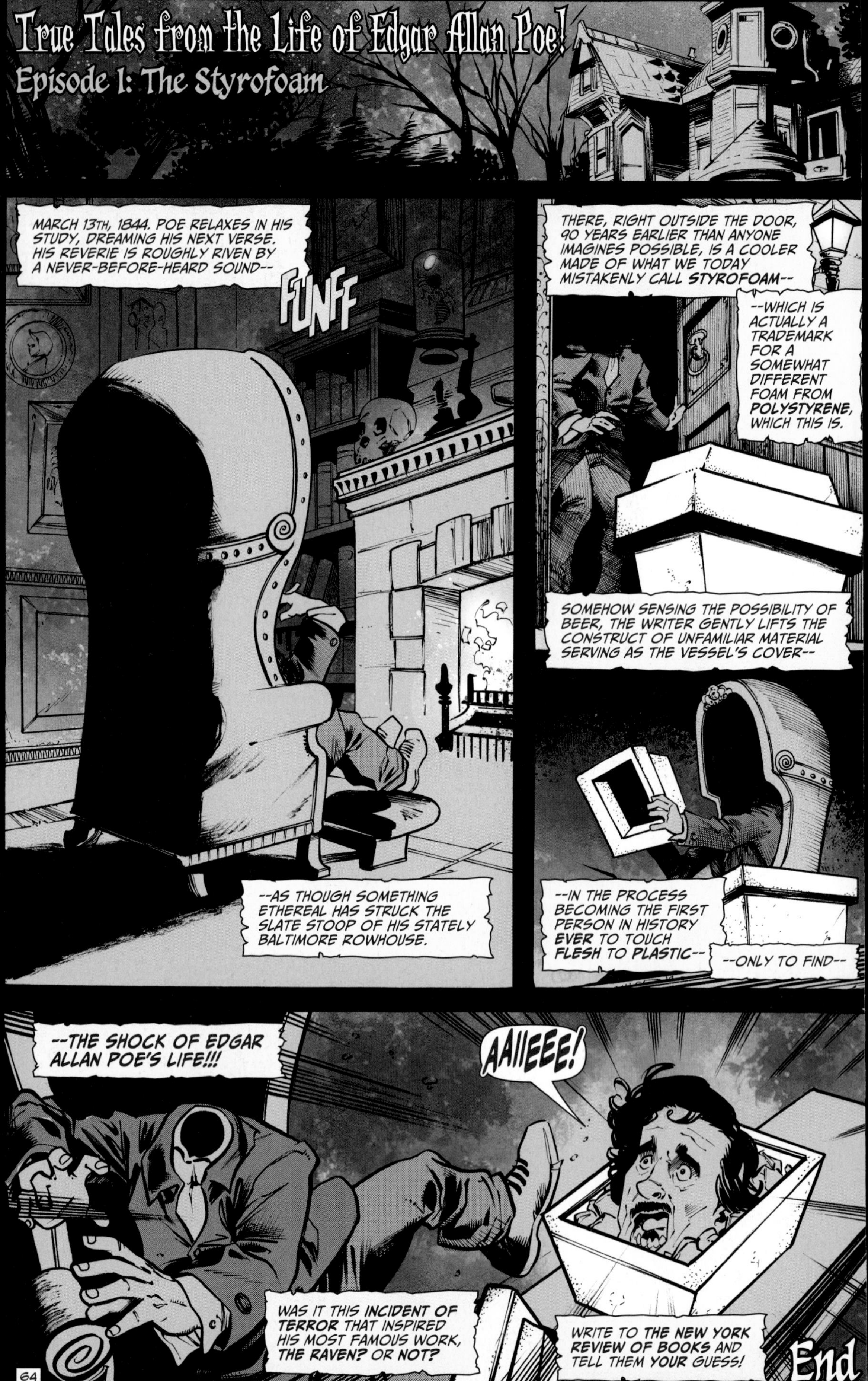
True Tales from the Life of Edgar Allan Poe!
Episode 1: The Styrofoam
MARCH 13TH, 1844. POE RELAXES IN HIS STUDY, DREAMING HIS NEXT VERSE. HIS REVERIE IS ROUGHLY RIVEN BY A NEVER-BEFORE-HEARD SOUND--
FUNFF
--AS THOUGH SOMETHING ETHEREAL HAS STRUCK THE SLATE STOOP OF HIS STATELY BALTIMORE ROWHOUSE.
THERE, RIGHT OUTSIDE THE DOOR, 90 YEARS EARLIER THAN ANYONE IMAGINES POSSIBLE, IS A COOLER MADE OF WHAT WE TODAY MISTAKENLY CALL STYROFOAM--
--WHICH IS ACTUALLY A TRADEMARK FOR A SOMEWHAT DIFFERENT FOAM FROM POLYSTYRENE, WHICH THIS IS.
SOMEHOW SENSING THE POSSIBILITY OF BEER, THE WRITER GENTLY LIFTS THE CONSTRUCT OF UNFAMILIAR MATERIAL SERVING AS THE VESSEL'S COVER--
--IN THE PROCESS BECOMING THE FIRST PERSON IN HISTORY EVER TO TOUCH FLESH TO PLASTIC--
--ONLY TO FIND--
--THE SHOCK OF EDGAR ALLAN POE'S LIFE!!!
AAIIEEE!
WAS IT THIS INCIDENT OF TERROR THAT INSPIRED HIS MOST FAMOUS WORK, THE RAVEN? OR NOT?
WRITE TO THE NEW YORK REVIEW OF BOOKS AND TELL THEM YOUR GUESS!
End

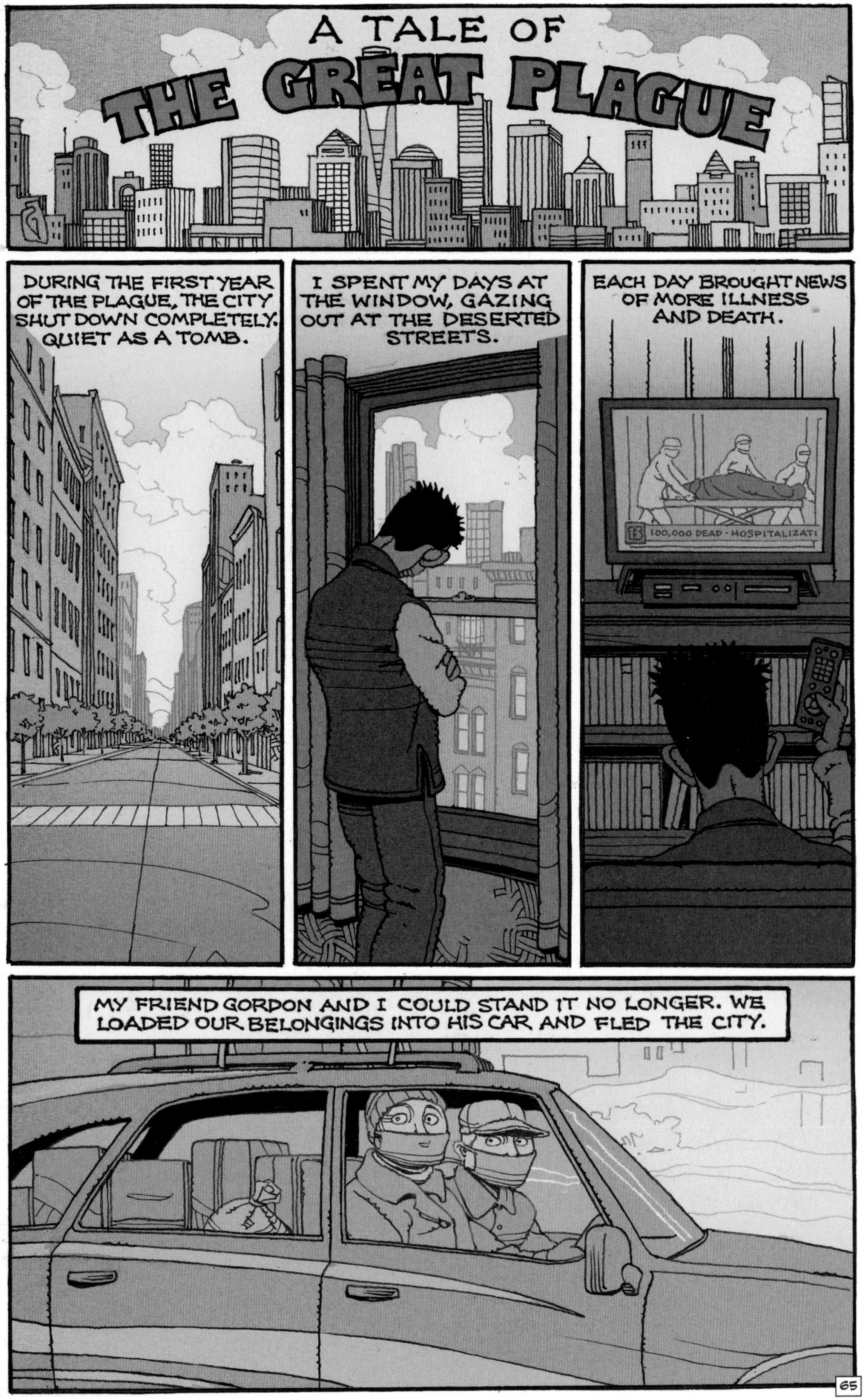
A TALE OF
THE GREAT PLAGUE
DURING THE FIRST YEAR OF THE PLAGUE, THE CITY SHUT DOWN COMPLETELY. QUIET AS A TOMB.
I SPENT MY DAYS AT THE WINDOW, GAZING OUT AT THE DESERTED STREETS.
EACH DAY BROUGHT NEWS OF MORE ILLNESS AND DEATH.
13
100,000 DEAD - HOSPITALIZATI
MY FRIEND GORDON AND I COULD STAND IT NO LONGER. WE LOADED OUR BELONGINGS INTO HIS CAR AND FLED THE CITY.

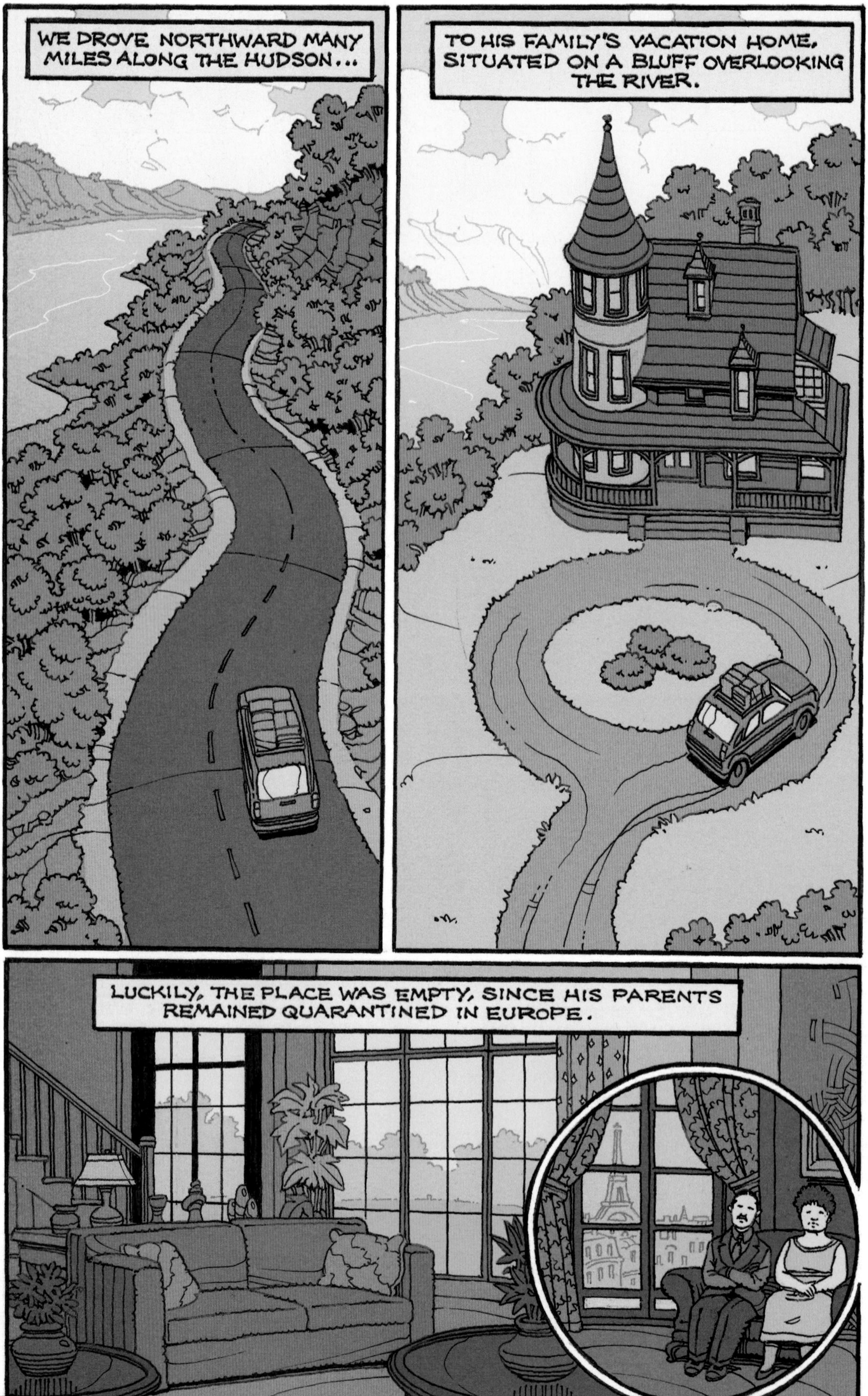
WE DROVE NORTHWARD MANY MILES ALONG THE HUDSON...
TO HIS FAMILY'S VACATION HOME, SITUATED ON A BLUFF OVERLOOKING THE RIVER.
LUCKILY, THE PLACE WAS EMPTY, SINCE HIS PARENTS REMAINED QUARANTINED IN EUROPE.

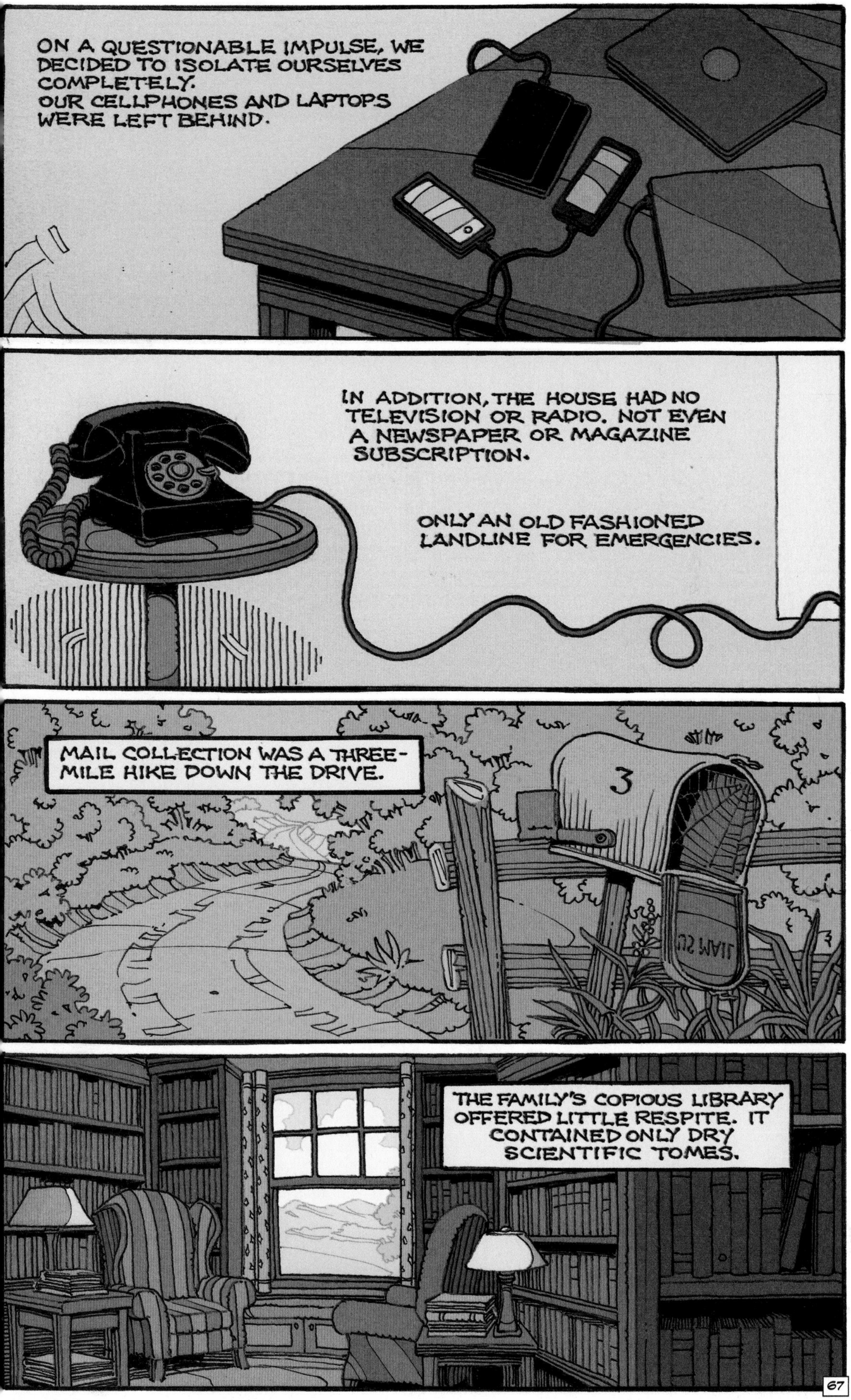

ON A QUESTIONABLE IMPULSE, WE DECIDED TO ISOLATE OURSELVES COMPLETELY.
OUR CELLPHONES AND LAPTOPS WERE LEFT BEHIND.
IN ADDITION, THE HOUSE HAD NO TELEVISION OR RADIO. NOT EVEN A NEWSPAPER OR MAGAZINE SUBSCRIPTION.
ONLY AN OLD FASHIONED LANDLINE FOR EMERGENCIES.
MAIL COLLECTION WAS A THREE-MILE HIKE DOWN THE DRIVE.
3
US MAIL
THE FAMILY'S COPIOUS LIBRARY OFFERED LITTLE RESPITE. IT CONTAINED ONLY DRY SCIENTIFIC TOMES.

WHEN NECESSARY, WE TOOK TURNS VISITING THE LOCAL MARKET, ALL PRECAUTIONS TAKEN, OF COURSE.

SURELY, GIVEN THE CIRCUMSTANCES, WE WERE ABOUT AS SAFE AS ANYONE COULD BE.

AND YET I WORRIED. YOU SEE, I'M SOMEWHAT OF A NERVOUS TYPE, APT TO LET MY IMAGINATION RUN TO ITS DARKEST CORNERS.

TO ME, THE VERY AIR FROM THE SOUTH SEEMED REDOLENT OF DEATH.

SUCH THOUGHTS INVADED MY CONSCIOUSNESS, UNBIDDEN, AS I RECLINED IN THE LIBRARY ONE AFTERNOON.

THEN, AS I INDOLENTLY REGARDED THE HILLS ALONG THE RIVER, MY EYES WERE MET WITH A HORRIFYING SIGHT.

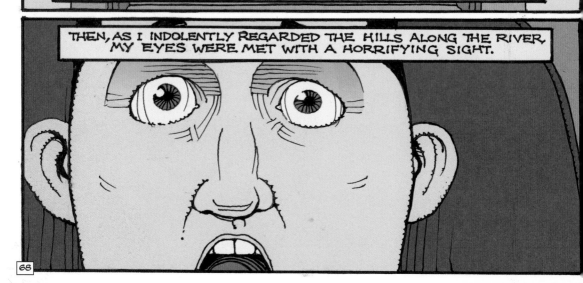

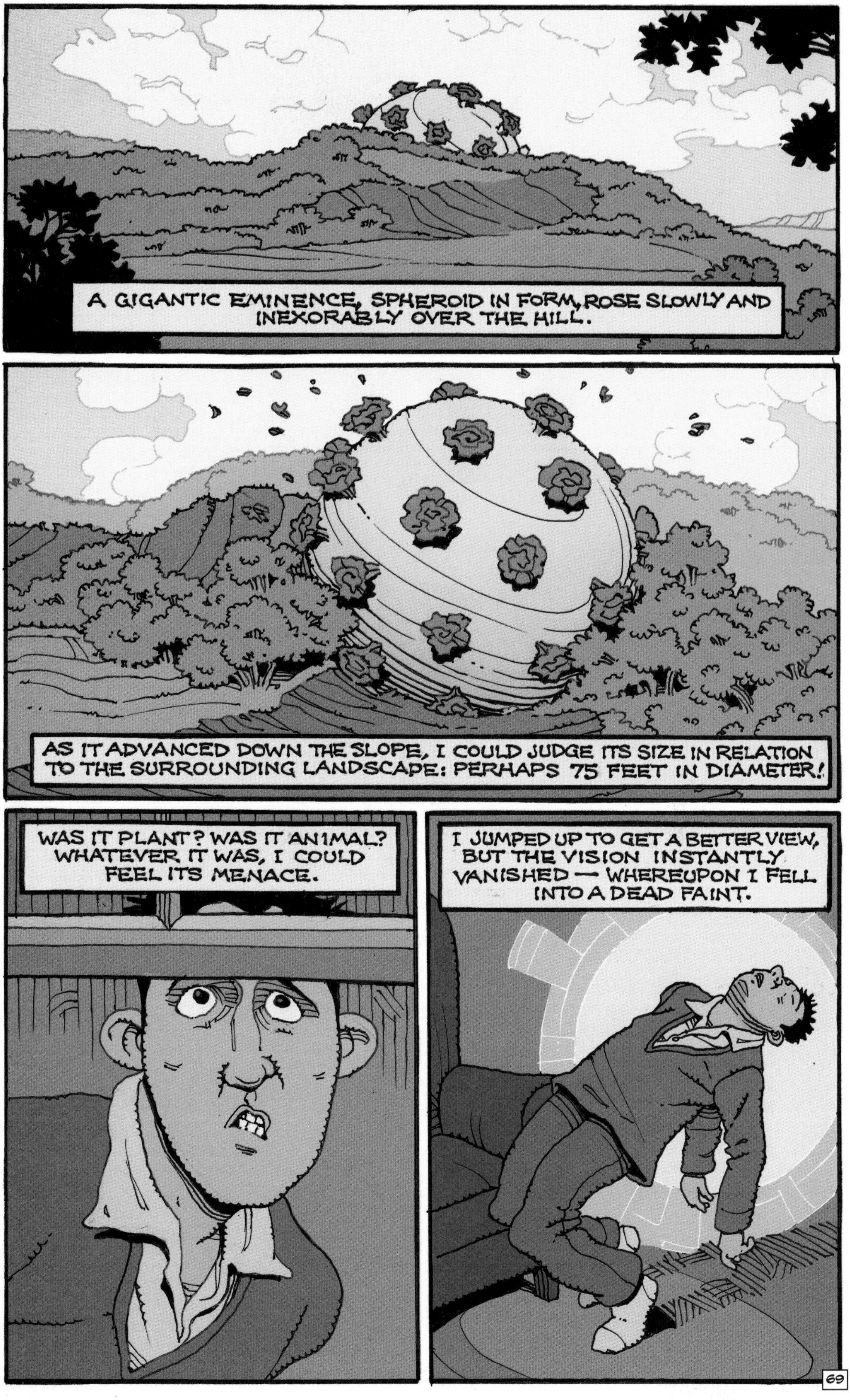
A GIGANTIC EMINENCE, SPHEROID IN FORM, ROSE SLOWLY AND INEXORABLY OVER THE HILL.
AS IT ADVANCED DOWN THE SLOPE, I COULD JUDGE ITS SIZE IN RELATION TO THE SURROUNDING LANDSCAPE: PERHAPS 75 FEET IN DIAMETER!
WAS IT PLANT? WAS IT ANIMAL? WHATEVER IT WAS, I COULD FEEL ITS MENACE.
I JUMPED UP TO GET A BETTER VIEW, BUT THE VISION INSTANTLY VANISHED — WHEREUPON I FELL INTO A DEAD FAINT.

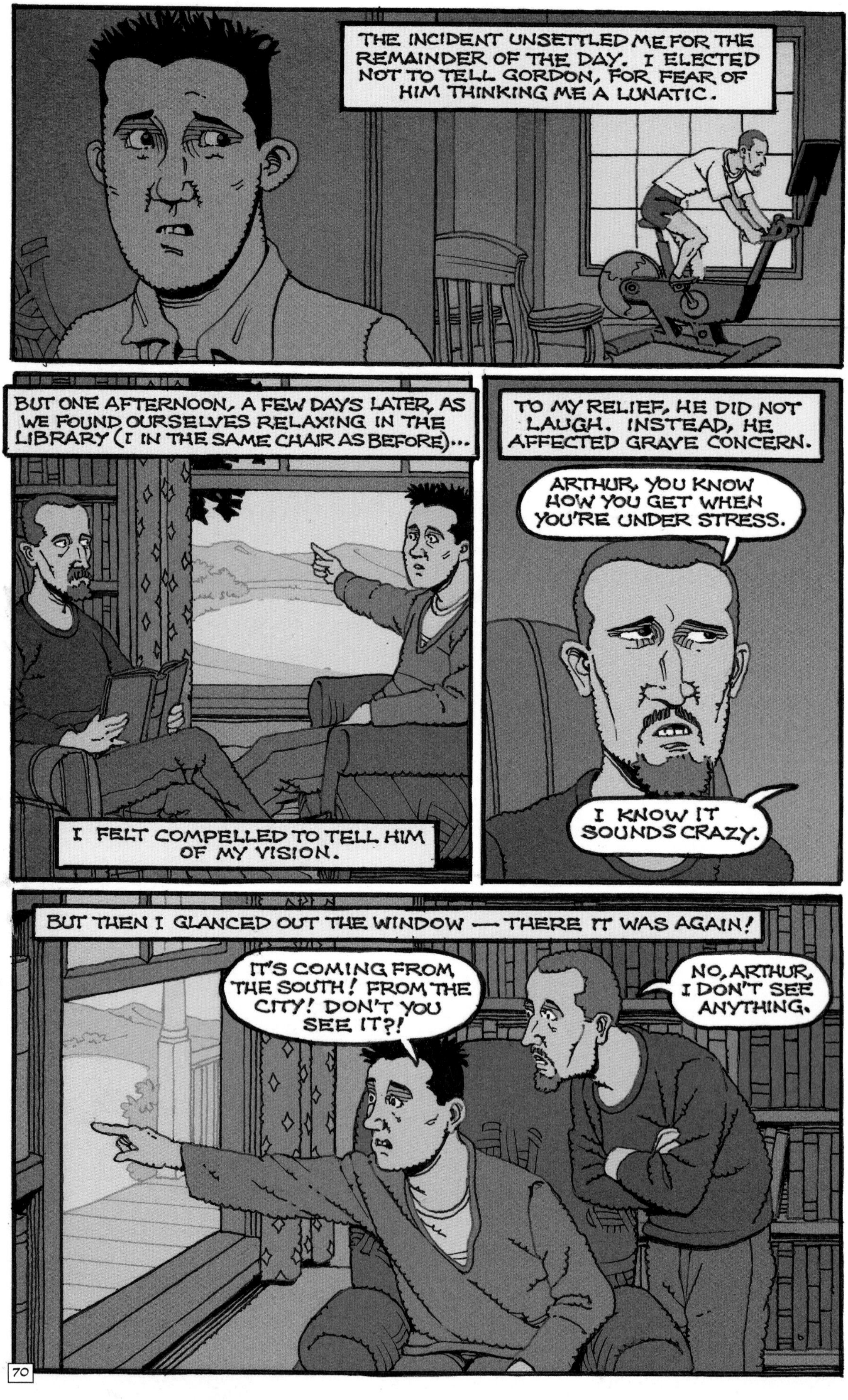
THE INCIDENT UNSETTLED ME FOR THE REMAINDER OF THE DAY. I ELECTED NOT TO TELL GORDON, FOR FEAR OF HIM THINKING ME A LUNATIC.
BUT ONE AFTERNOON, A FEW DAYS LATER, AS WE FOUND OURSELVES RELAXING IN THE LIBRARY (I IN THE SAME CHAIR AS BEFORE)...
I FELT COMPELLED TO TELL HIM OF MY VISION.
TO MY RELIEF, HE DID NOT LAUGH. INSTEAD, HE AFFECTED GRAVE CONCERN.
ARTHUR, YOU KNOW HOW YOU GET WHEN YOU'RE UNDER STRESS.
I KNOW IT SOUNDS CRAZY.
BUT THEN I GLANCED OUT THE WINDOW — THERE IT WAS AGAIN!
IT'S COMING FROM THE SOUTH! FROM THE CITY! DON'T YOU SEE IT?!
NO, ARTHUR, I DON'T SEE ANYTHING.

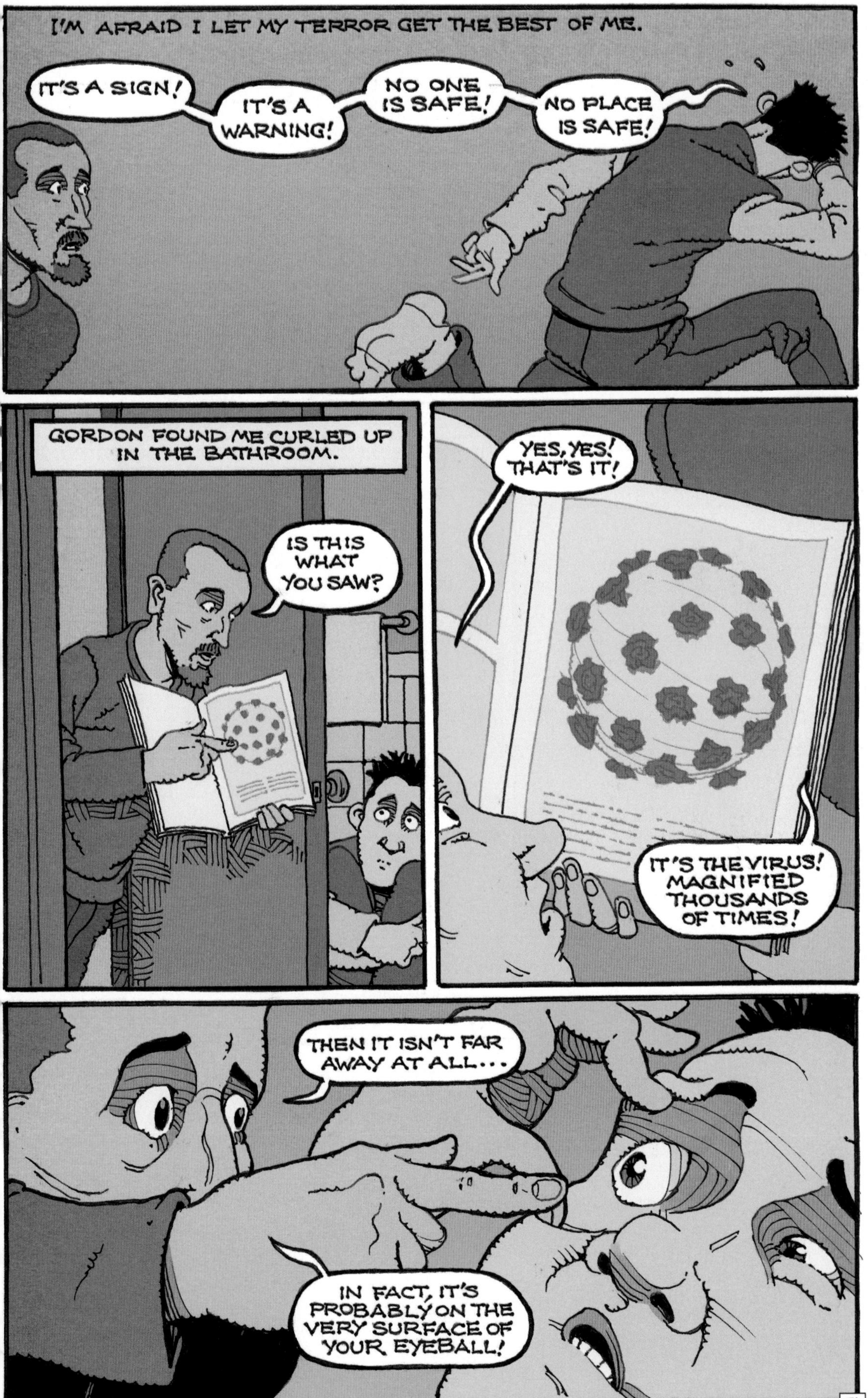
I'M AFRAID I LET MY TERROR GET THE BEST OF ME.
IT'S A SIGN!
IT'S A WARNING!
NO ONE IS SAFE!
NO PLACE IS SAFE!
GORDON FOUND ME CURLED UP IN THE BATHROOM.
IS THIS WHAT YOU SAW?
YES, YES! THAT'S IT!
IT'S THE VIRUS! MAGNIFIED THOUSANDS OF TIMES!
THEN IT ISN'T FAR AWAY AT ALL...
IN FACT, IT'S PROBABLY ON THE VERY SURFACE OF YOUR EYEBALL!

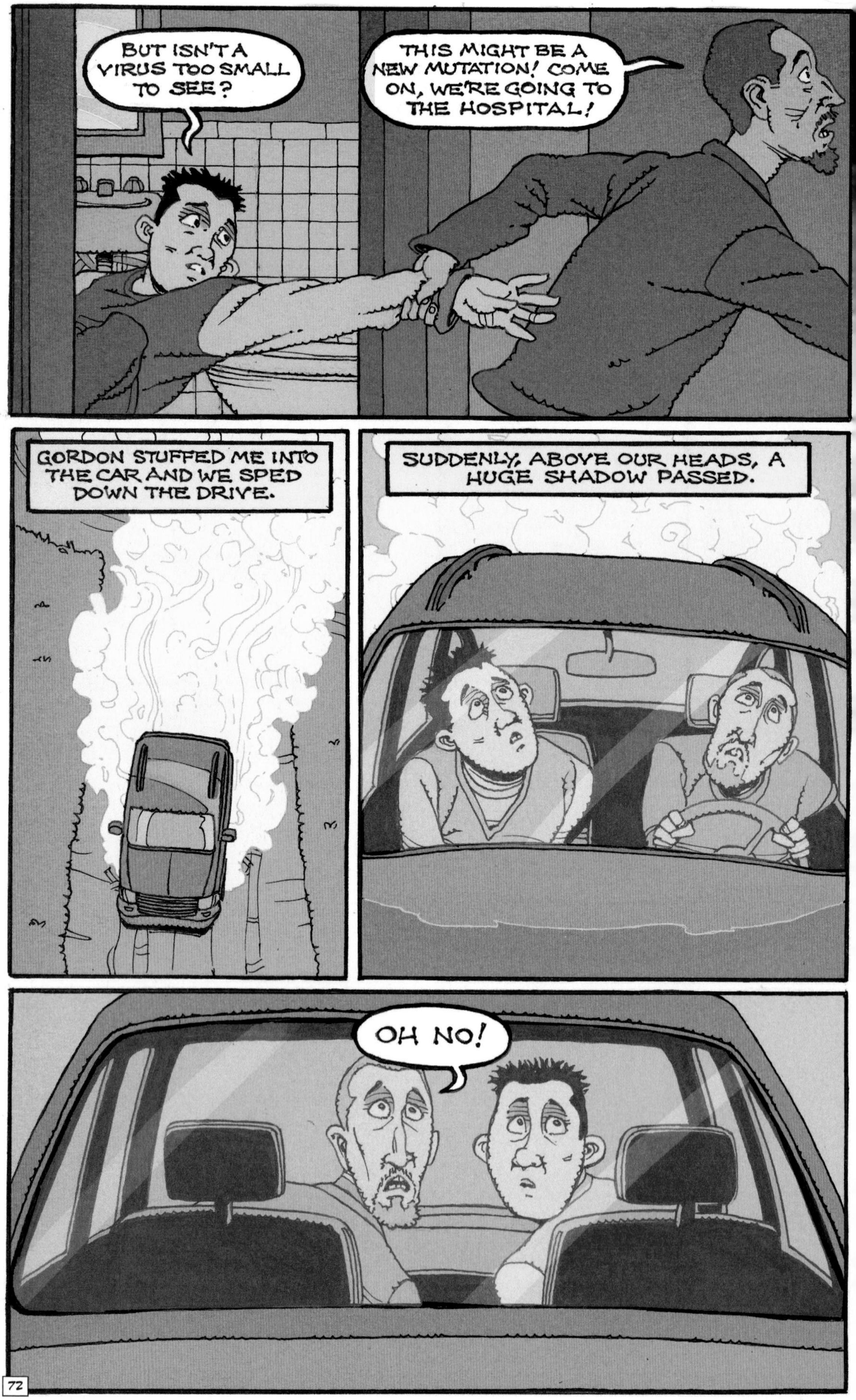
BUT ISN'T A VIRUS TOO SMALL TO SEE?
THIS MIGHT BE A NEW MUTATION! COME ON, WE'RE GOING TO THE HOSPITAL!
GORDON STUFFED ME INTO THE CAR AND WE SPED DOWN THE DRIVE.
SUDDENLY, ABOVE OUR HEADS, A HUGE SHADOW PASSED.
OH NO!

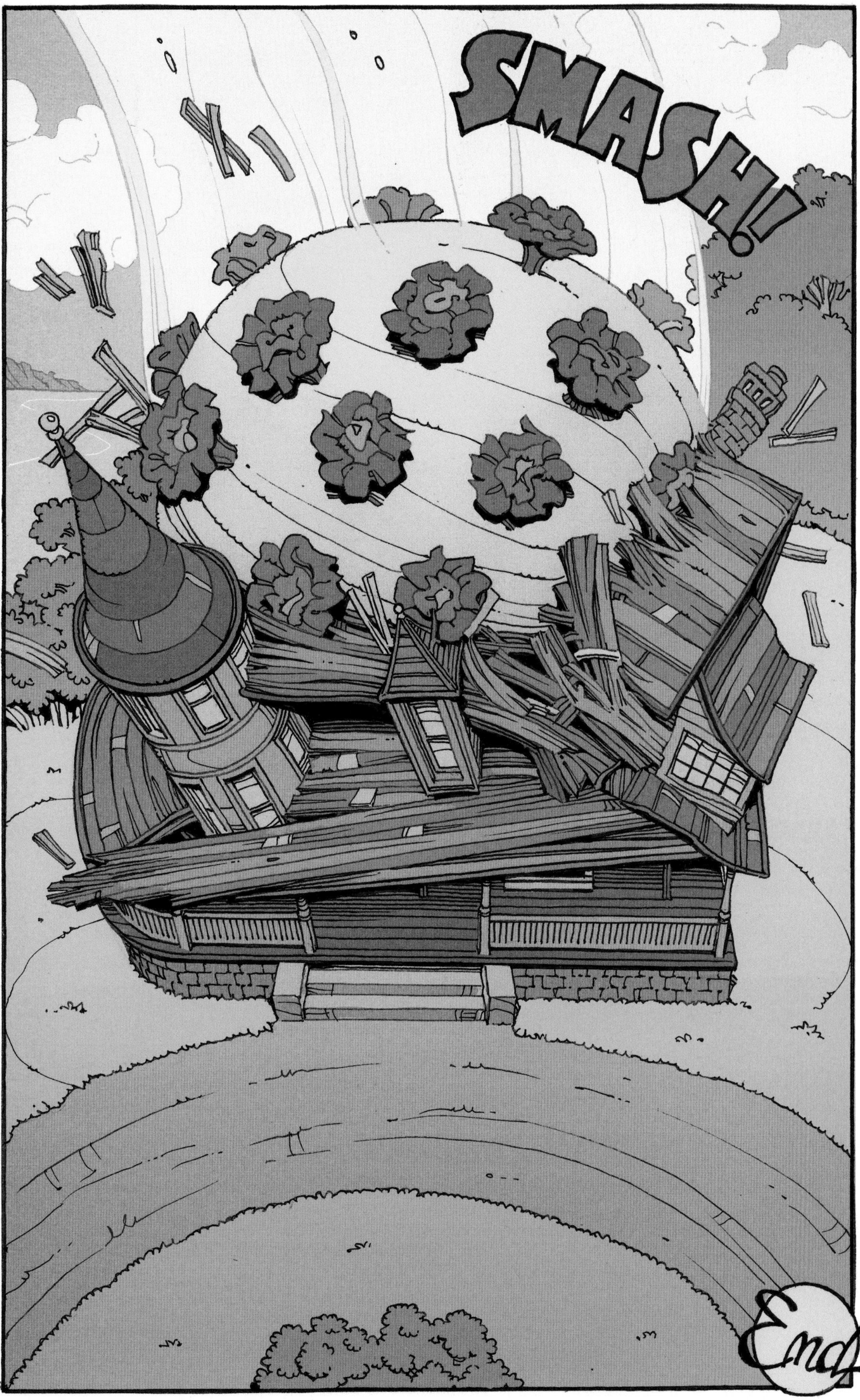
SMASH!
End

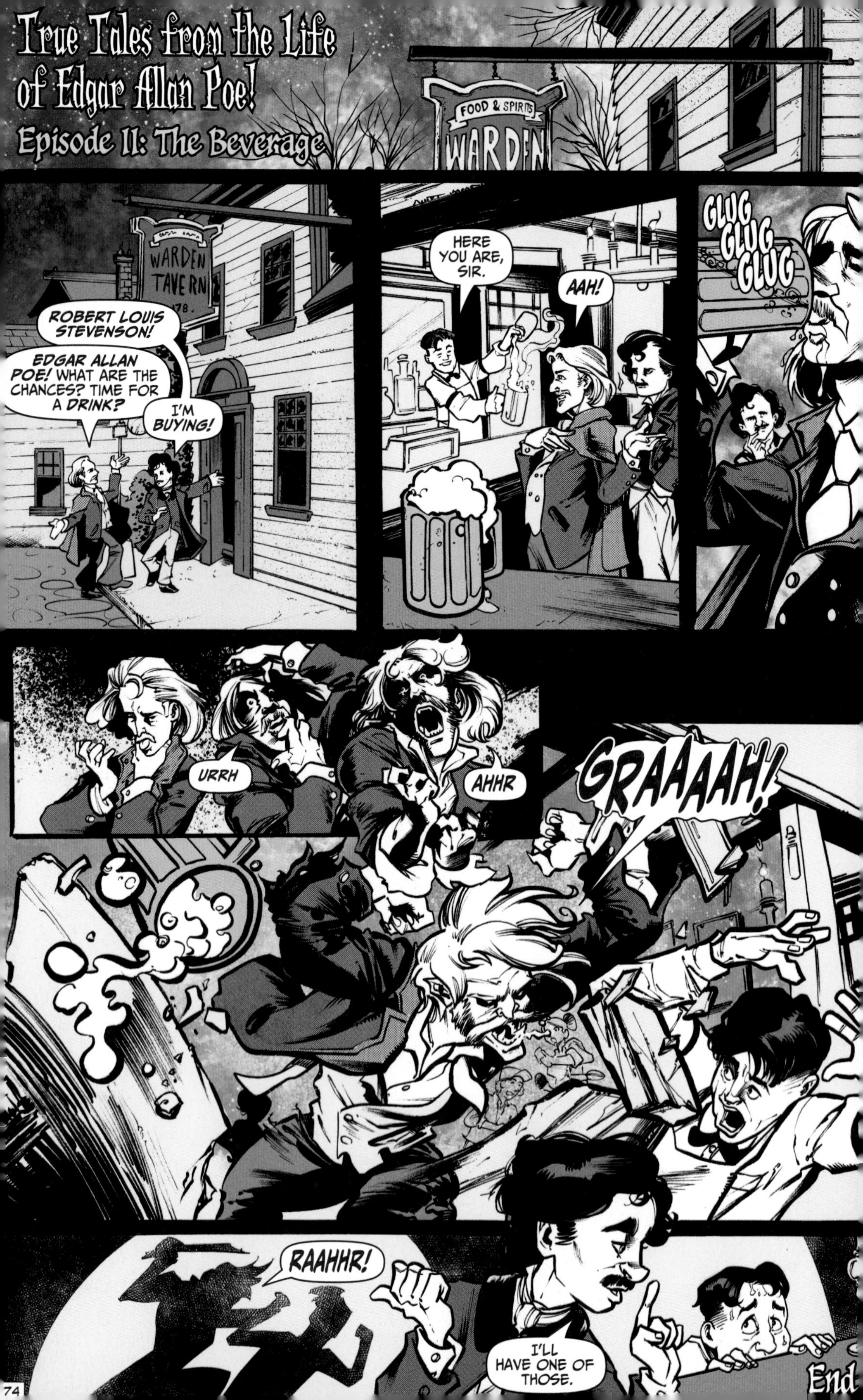

True Tales from the Life of Edgar Allan Poe!
Episode 11: The Beverage
FOOD & SPIRITS
WARDEN
WARDEN TAVERN
ROBERT LOUIS STEVENSON!
EDGAR ALLAN POE! WHAT ARE THE CHANCES? TIME FOR A DRINK?
I'M BUYING!
HERE YOU ARE, SIR.
AAH!
GLUG GLUG GLUG
URRH
AHHR
GRAAAAH!
RAAHHR!
I'LL HAVE ONE OF THOSE.
End

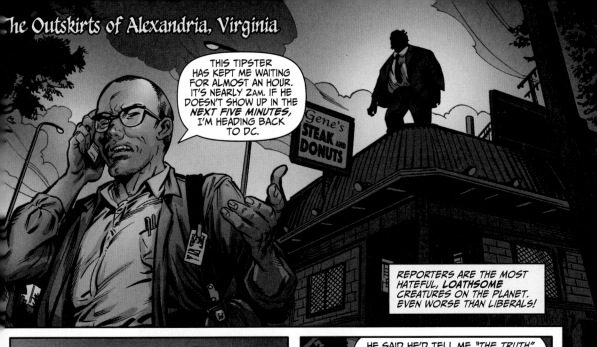

The Outskirts of Alexandria, Virginia
THIS TIPSTER HAS KEPT ME WAITING FOR ALMOST AN HOUR. IT'S NEARLY 2AM. IF HE DOESN'T SHOW UP IN THE NEXT FIVE MINUTES, I'M HEADING BACK TO DC.
Gene's STEAK AND DONUTS
REPORTERS ARE THE MOST HATEFUL, LOATHSOME CREATURES ON THE PLANET. EVEN WORSE THAN LIBERALS!
MY FIANCÉE AND I HAVE BEEN FIGHTING. I HATE WHEN WE FIGHT. SO I LURED GRIFF TO THIS DESERTED SPOT. IT ALWAYS CHEERS ME UP TO MURDER A REPORTER.
HE SAID HE'D TELL ME "THE TRUTH" ABOUT SEN. McCONNELL. I FEEL LIKE A SUCKER FOR DRIVING ALL THE WAY OUT HERE...
BUT I'D NEVER FORGIVE MYSELF IF I MISSED A CHANCE TO TAKE DOWN MOSCOW MITCH. IF IT WASN'T FOR TEDDY CRUISE, McCONNELL WOULD BE THE BIGGEST ASSHOLE IN CONGRESS.
WHAT THE FRICK. HE JUST CALLED ME AN ASSHOLE.
HEY! JERK! I'M NOT THE BIGGEST ASSHOLE. YOU'RE THE BIGGEST ASSHOLE!
SENATOR CRUISE?! TEDDY CRUISE? WHAT THE HELL. WHERE ARE YOUR PANTS?
I TOOK THEM OFF SO THEY WOULDN'T GET RIPPED. AND I'D RATHER BE ADDRESSED AS...

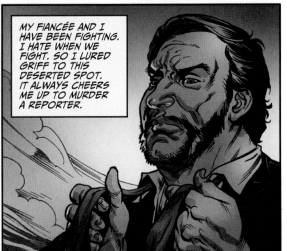

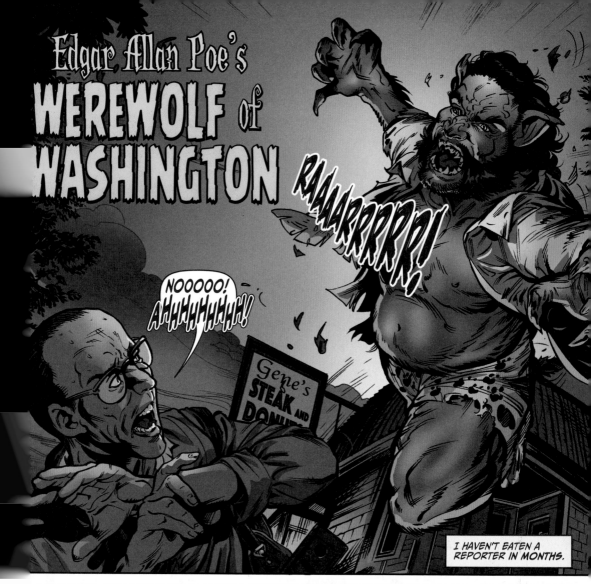

Edgar Allan Poe's
WEREWOLF of WASHINGTON

RAAAARRRRR!

NOOOOO! AHHHHHHHH!

Gene's STEAK AND DONUTS

I HAVEN'T EATEN A REPORTER IN MONTHS.

IT'S EASY TO FORGET HOW DELICIOUS THEY ARE WHEN THEY'RE PEPPERING YOU WITH ASININE QUESTIONS.

HINT OF CARAMEL. REALLY EXCELLENT.

SLURRRRP

MUNNNCH

THAT CHEERED ME UP A LITTLE, BUT I WISH I HADN'T LOST MY TEMPER. I RUINED A GOOD DRESS SHIRT. AND I'M NOT AN ASSHOLE.

I MEAN, ANYONE WHO THINKS THAT IS JUST JEALOUS OF THE FACT THAT I'M SO DAMN GOOD AT BEING A US SENATOR.

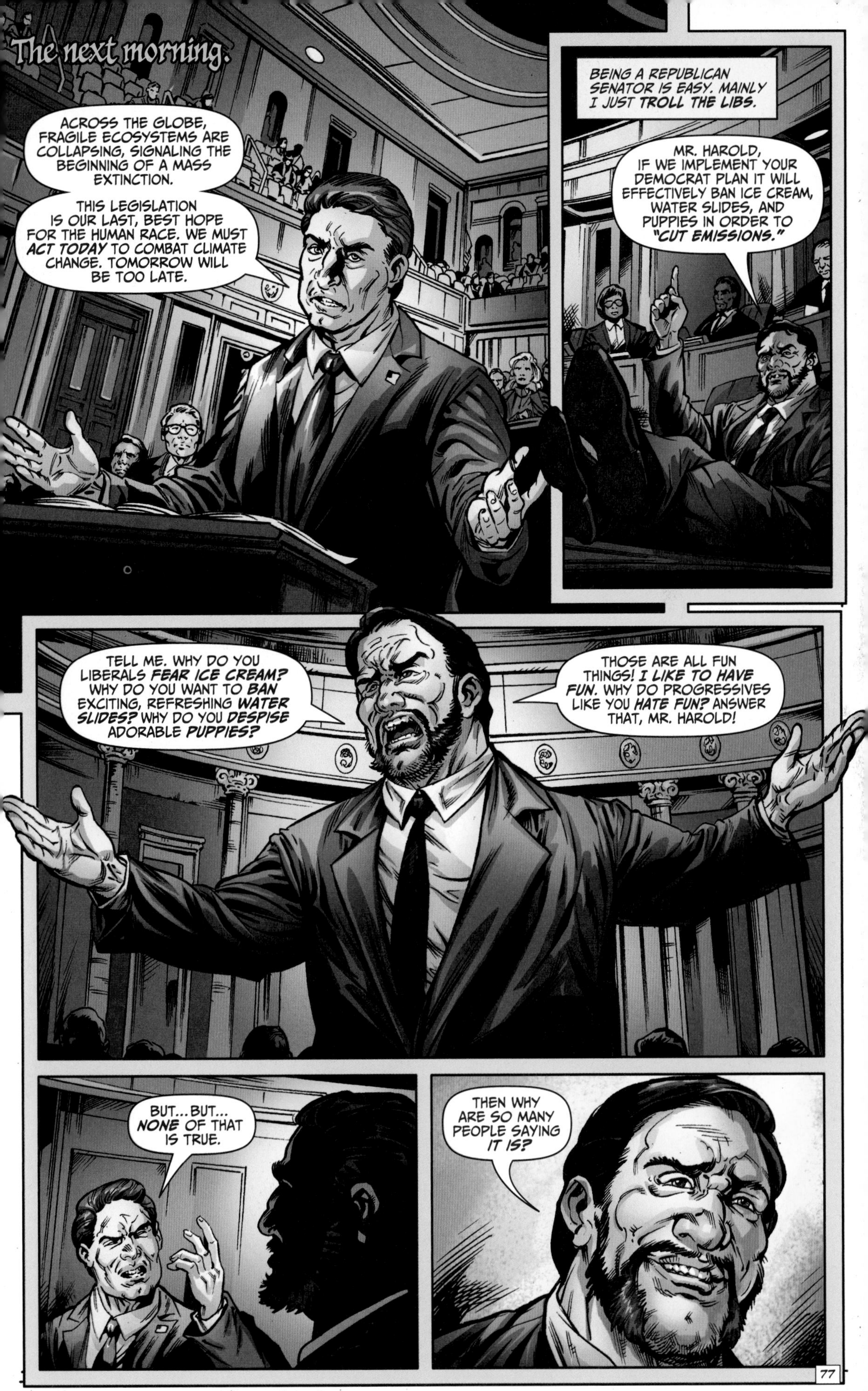
The next morning.
ACROSS THE GLOBE, FRAGILE ECOSYSTEMS ARE COLLAPSING, SIGNALING THE BEGINNING OF A MASS EXTINCTION.
THIS LEGISLATION IS OUR LAST, BEST HOPE FOR THE HUMAN RACE. WE MUST ACT TODAY TO COMBAT CLIMATE CHANGE. TOMORROW WILL BE TOO LATE.
BEING A REPUBLICAN SENATOR IS EASY. MAINLY I JUST TROLL THE LIBS.
MR. HAROLD, IF WE IMPLEMENT YOUR DEMOCRAT PLAN IT WILL EFFECTIVELY BAN ICE CREAM, WATER SLIDES, AND PUPPIES IN ORDER TO "CUT EMISSIONS."
TELL ME. WHY DO YOU LIBERALS FEAR ICE CREAM? WHY DO YOU WANT TO BAN EXCITING, REFRESHING WATER SLIDES? WHY DO YOU DESPISE ADORABLE PUPPIES?
THOSE ARE ALL FUN THINGS! I LIKE TO HAVE FUN. WHY DO PROGRESSIVES LIKE YOU HATE FUN? ANSWER THAT, MR. HAROLD!
BUT... BUT... NONE OF THAT IS TRUE.
THEN WHY ARE SO MANY PEOPLE SAYING IT IS?

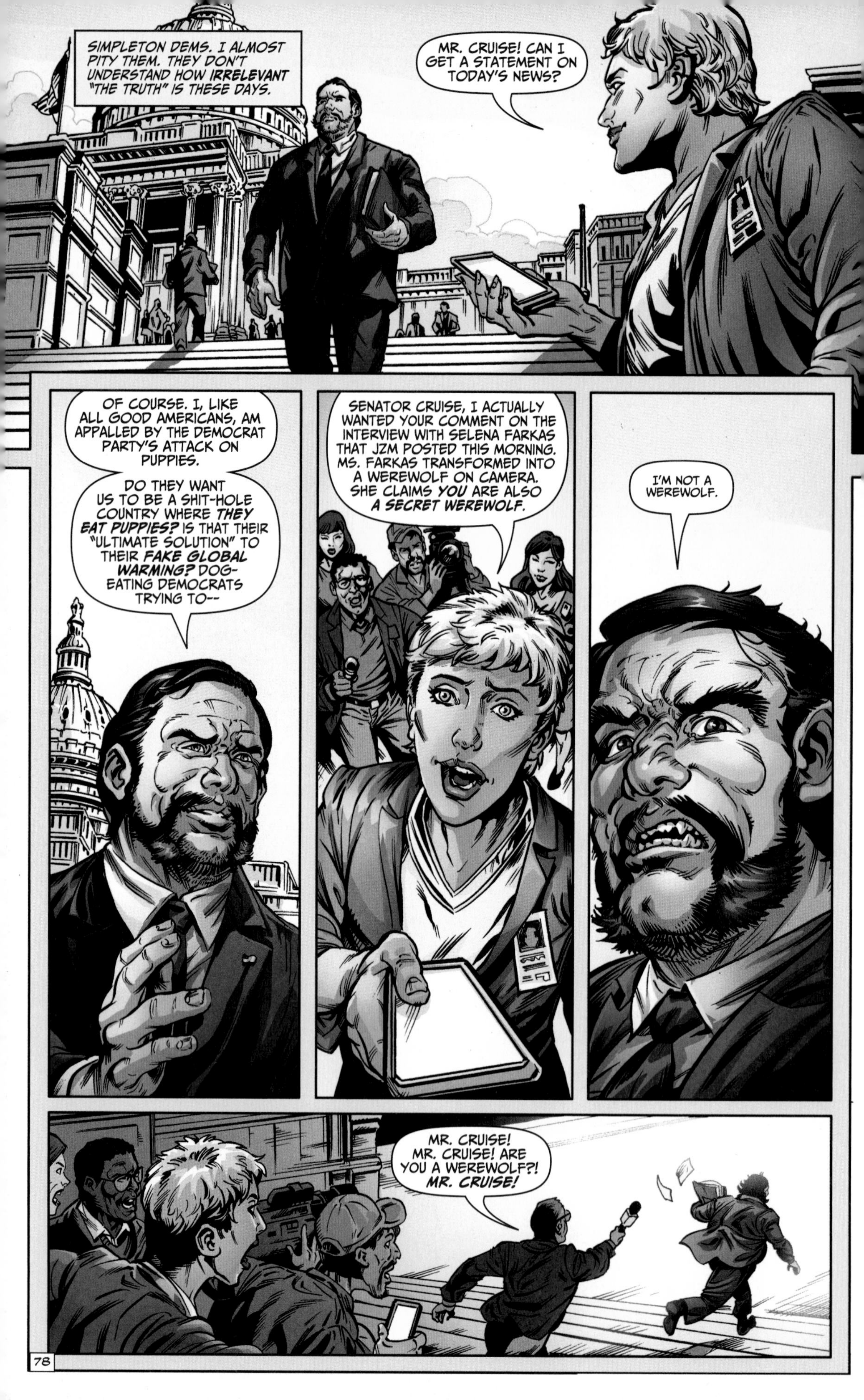
SIMPLETON DEMS. I ALMOST PITY THEM. THEY DON'T UNDERSTAND HOW IRRELEVANT "THE TRUTH" IS THESE DAYS.
MR. CRUISE! CAN I GET A STATEMENT ON TODAY'S NEWS?
OF COURSE. I, LIKE ALL GOOD AMERICANS, AM APPALLED BY THE DEMOCRAT PARTY'S ATTACK ON PUPPIES.
DO THEY WANT US TO BE A SHIT-HOLE COUNTRY WHERE THEY EAT PUPPIES? IS THAT THEIR "ULTIMATE SOLUTION" TO THEIR FAKE GLOBAL WARMING? DOG-EATING DEMOCRATS TRYING TO--
SENATOR CRUISE, I ACTUALLY WANTED YOUR COMMENT ON THE INTERVIEW WITH SELENA FARKAS THAT JZM POSTED THIS MORNING. MS. FARKAS TRANSFORMED INTO A WEREWOLF ON CAMERA. SHE CLAIMS YOU ARE ALSO A SECRET WEREWOLF.
I'M NOT A WEREWOLF.
MR. CRUISE! MR. CRUISE! ARE YOU A WEREWOLF?! MR. CRUISE!

JUST BECAUSE PEOPLE ARE **SCARED** IT DOESN'T EXCUSE **BIGOTRY.** DISCRIMINATION IS **ALWAYS** WRONG.

SELENA HAD THIS IDEA THAT WE SHOULD STOP HIDING OUR TRUE NATURES. LET PEOPLE SEE US IN ALL OUR **WEREWOLF** GLORY.

OHMYGOD! WHAT ARE YOU--

I TOLD HER SHE WAS **CRAZY.**

I SHOULD'VE **KNOWN** BETTER. SHE HAS A **TEMPER.**

YOU'RE...A WEREWOLF.

YES. AND MY FIANCÉ, SEN. CRUISE... HE'S A **WEREWOLF** TOO.

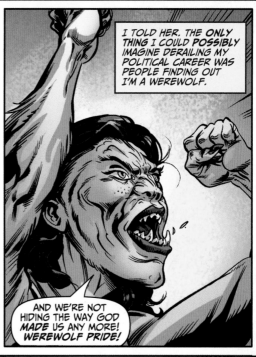

I TOLD HER. THE **ONLY** THING I COULD **POSSIBLY** IMAGINE DERAILING MY POLITICAL CAREER WAS PEOPLE FINDING OUT I'M A WEREWOLF.

AND WE'RE NOT HIDING THE WAY GOD **MADE** US ANY MORE! **WEREWOLF PRIDE!**

AND SELENA WON'T EVEN RETURN MY CALLS. I'M LOSING MY JOB AND MY FIANCÉE.

WHAT A **DISASTER.**

OR **IS** IT?

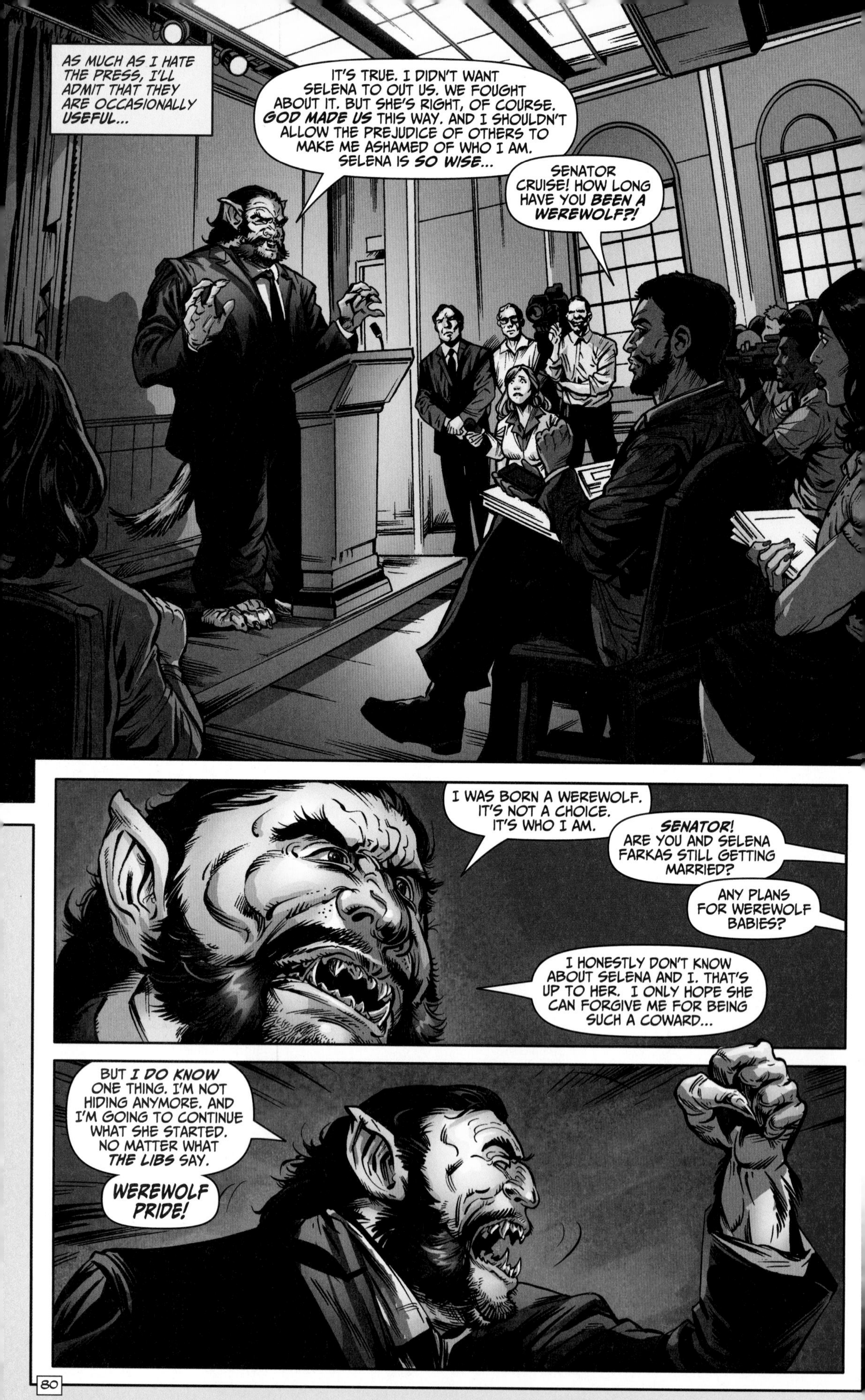
AS MUCH AS I HATE THE PRESS, I'LL ADMIT THAT THEY ARE OCCASIONALLY USEFUL...
IT'S TRUE. I DIDN'T WANT SELENA TO OUT US. WE FOUGHT ABOUT IT. BUT SHE'S RIGHT, OF COURSE. GOD MADE US THIS WAY. AND I SHOULDN'T ALLOW THE PREJUDICE OF OTHERS TO MAKE ME ASHAMED OF WHO I AM. SELENA IS SO WISE...
SENATOR CRUISE! HOW LONG HAVE YOU BEEN A WEREWOLF?!
I WAS BORN A WEREWOLF. IT'S NOT A CHOICE. IT'S WHO I AM.
SENATOR! ARE YOU AND SELENA FARKAS STILL GETTING MARRIED?
ANY PLANS FOR WEREWOLF BABIES?
I HONESTLY DON'T KNOW ABOUT SELENA AND I. THAT'S UP TO HER. I ONLY HOPE SHE CAN FORGIVE ME FOR BEING SUCH A COWARD...
BUT I DO KNOW ONE THING. I'M NOT HIDING ANYMORE. AND I'M GOING TO CONTINUE WHAT SHE STARTED. NO MATTER WHAT THE LIBS SAY.
WEREWOLF PRIDE!

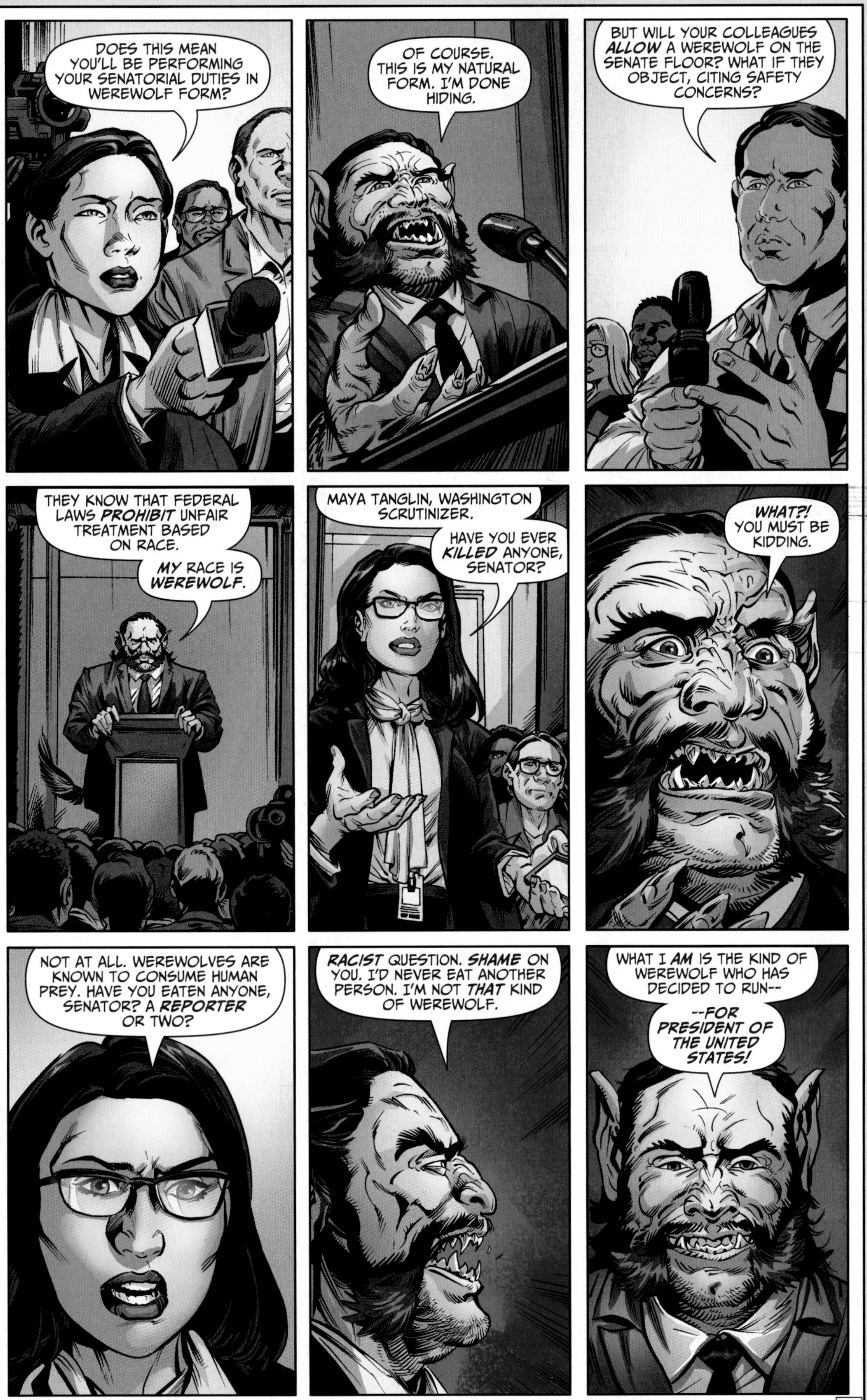
DOES THIS MEAN YOU'LL BE PERFORMING YOUR SENATORIAL DUTIES IN WEREWOLF FORM?
OF COURSE. THIS IS MY NATURAL FORM. I'M DONE HIDING.
BUT WILL YOUR COLLEAGUES ALLOW A WEREWOLF ON THE SENATE FLOOR? WHAT IF THEY OBJECT, CITING SAFETY CONCERNS?
THEY KNOW THAT FEDERAL LAWS PROHIBIT UNFAIR TREATMENT BASED ON RACE.
MY RACE IS WEREWOLF.
MAYA TANGLIN, WASHINGTON SCRUTINIZER.
HAVE YOU EVER KILLED ANYONE, SENATOR?
WHAT?! YOU MUST BE KIDDING.
NOT AT ALL. WEREWOLVES ARE KNOWN TO CONSUME HUMAN PREY. HAVE YOU EATEN ANYONE, SENATOR? A REPORTER OR TWO?
RACIST QUESTION. SHAME ON YOU. I'D NEVER EAT ANOTHER PERSON. I'M NOT THAT KIND OF WEREWOLF.
WHAT I AM IS THE KIND OF WEREWOLF WHO HAS DECIDED TO RUN--
--FOR PRESIDENT OF THE UNITED STATES!

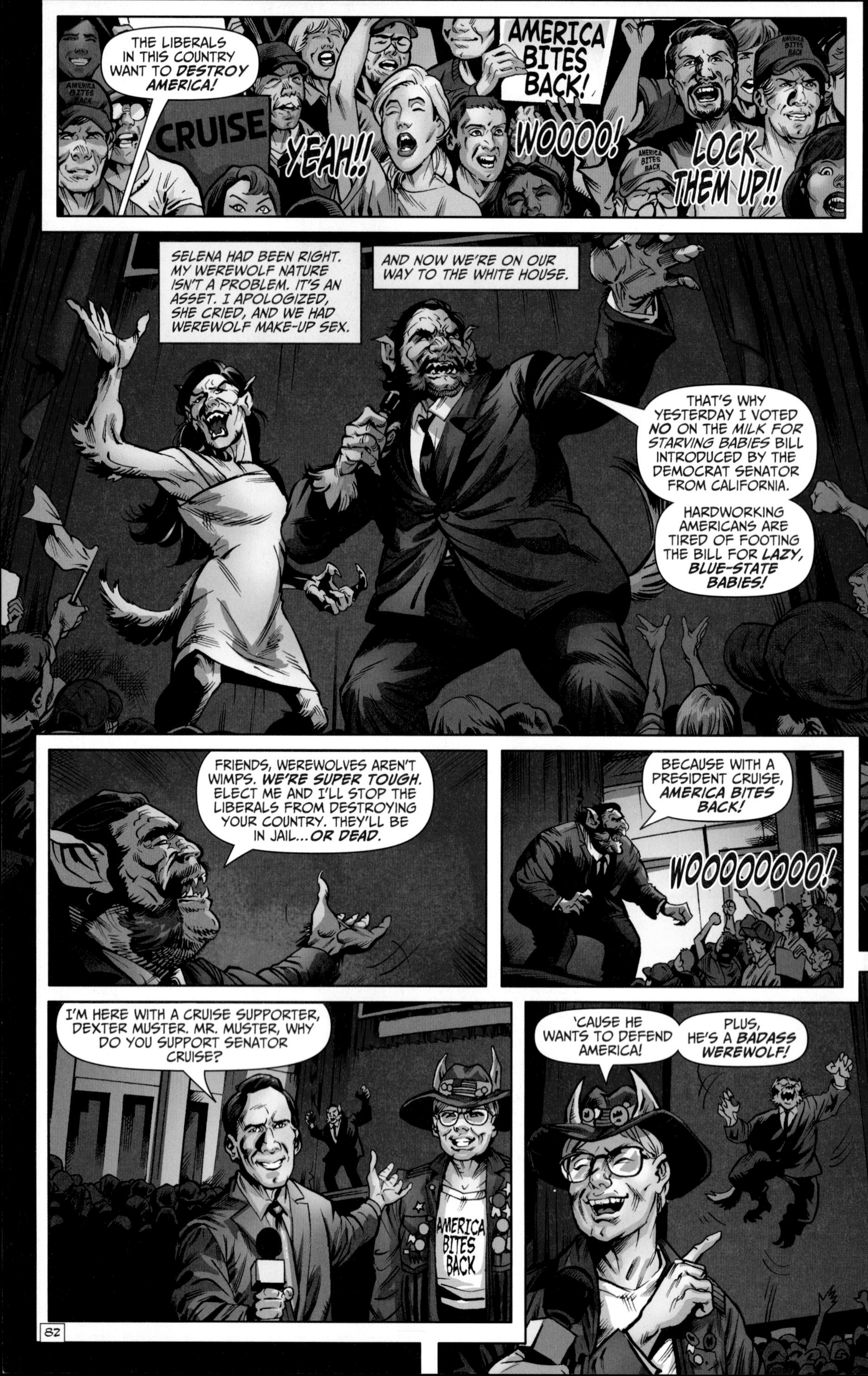

THE LIBERALS IN THIS COUNTRY WANT TO DESTROY AMERICA!
AMERICA BITES BACK!
CRUISE
AMERICA BITES BACK
YEAH!!
WOOOO!
LOCK THEM UP!!
SELENA HAD BEEN RIGHT. MY WEREWOLF NATURE ISN'T A PROBLEM. IT'S AN ASSET. I APOLOGIZED, SHE CRIED, AND WE HAD WEREWOLF MAKE-UP SEX.
AND NOW WE'RE ON OUR WAY TO THE WHITE HOUSE.
THAT'S WHY YESTERDAY I VOTED NO ON THE MILK FOR STARVING BABIES BILL INTRODUCED BY THE DEMOCRAT SENATOR FROM CALIFORNIA.
HARDWORKING AMERICANS ARE TIRED OF FOOTING THE BILL FOR LAZY, BLUE-STATE BABIES!
FRIENDS, WEREWOLVES AREN'T WIMPS. WE'RE SUPER TOUGH. ELECT ME AND I'LL STOP THE LIBERALS FROM DESTROYING YOUR COUNTRY. THEY'LL BE IN JAIL...OR DEAD.
BECAUSE WITH A PRESIDENT CRUISE, AMERICA BITES BACK!
WOOOOOOOO!
I'M HERE WITH A CRUISE SUPPORTER, DEXTER MUSTER. MR. MUSTER, WHY DO YOU SUPPORT SENATOR CRUISE?
AMERICA BITES BACK
'CAUSE HE WANTS TO DEFEND AMERICA!
PLUS, HE'S A BADASS WEREWOLF!

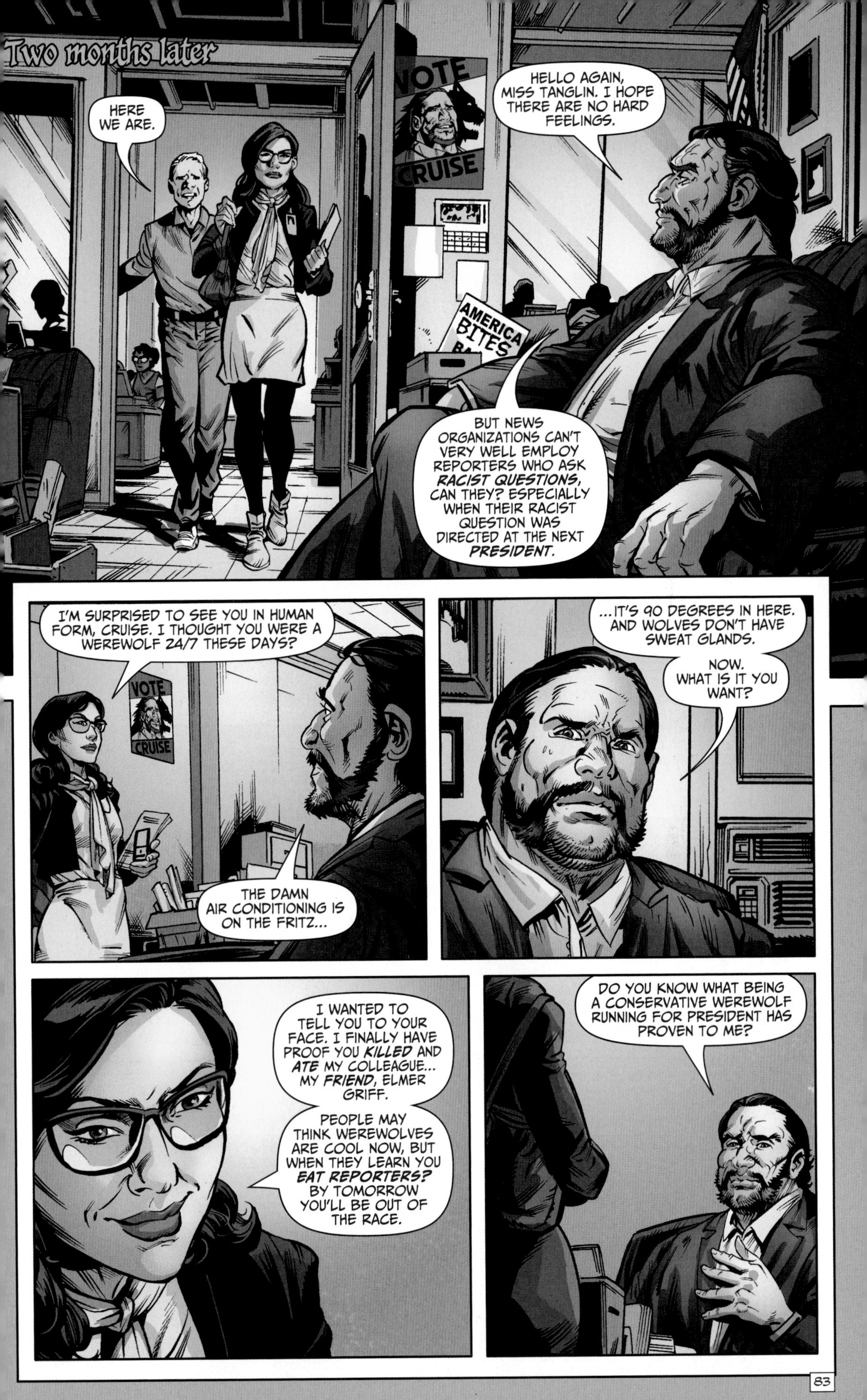
Two months later
HERE WE ARE.
VOTE CRUISE
HELLO AGAIN, MISS TANGLIN. I HOPE THERE ARE NO HARD FEELINGS.
AMERICA BITES
BUT NEWS ORGANIZATIONS CAN'T VERY WELL EMPLOY REPORTERS WHO ASK RACIST QUESTIONS, CAN THEY? ESPECIALLY WHEN THEIR RACIST QUESTION WAS DIRECTED AT THE NEXT PRESIDENT.
I'M SURPRISED TO SEE YOU IN HUMAN FORM, CRUISE. I THOUGHT YOU WERE A WEREWOLF 24/7 THESE DAYS?
VOTE CRUISE
THE DAMN AIR CONDITIONING IS ON THE FRITZ...
...IT'S 90 DEGREES IN HERE. AND WOLVES DON'T HAVE SWEAT GLANDS.
NOW. WHAT IS IT YOU WANT?
I WANTED TO TELL YOU TO YOUR FACE. I FINALLY HAVE PROOF YOU KILLED AND ATE MY COLLEAGUE... MY FRIEND, ELMER GRIFF.
PEOPLE MAY THINK WEREWOLVES ARE COOL NOW, BUT WHEN THEY LEARN YOU EAT REPORTERS? BY TOMORROW YOU'LL BE OUT OF THE RACE.
DO YOU KNOW WHAT BEING A CONSERVATIVE WEREWOLF RUNNING FOR PRESIDENT HAS PROVEN TO ME?

THEY DON'T CARE. I CAN LIE. I CAN PROMOTE INSURRECTION. I CAN KILL AND EAT. AS LONG AS I'M DOING THOSE THINGS TO PEOPLE MY SUPPORTERS HATE.

AMERICA BITES BACK!

PEOPLE LIKE *YOU*!!!

NOOOOOOO!

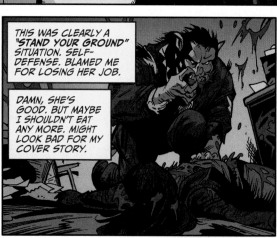

THIS WAS CLEARLY A "STAND YOUR GROUND" SITUATION. SELF-DEFENSE. BLAMED ME FOR LOSING HER JOB.

DAMN, SHE'S GOOD. BUT MAYBE I SHOULDN'T EAT ANY MORE. MIGHT LOOK BAD FOR MY COVER STORY.

AND IF IT COMES OUT THAT I KILLED HER FRIEND, THAT WAS A "STAND YOUR GROUND" SITUATION TOO. THESE REPORTERS ARE GETTING VIOLENT LATELY!

WE'LL ROUND THEM UP ONCE I'M INAUGURATED. FOR PUBLIC SAFETY. AND SNACKS.

JUST ONE MORE BITE. MAYBE TWO. I SHOULDN'T WORRY. IT'S EASY TO CONVINCE PEOPLE OF ANYTHING...

...WHEN THEY WANT TO BELIEVE THE LIE.

End

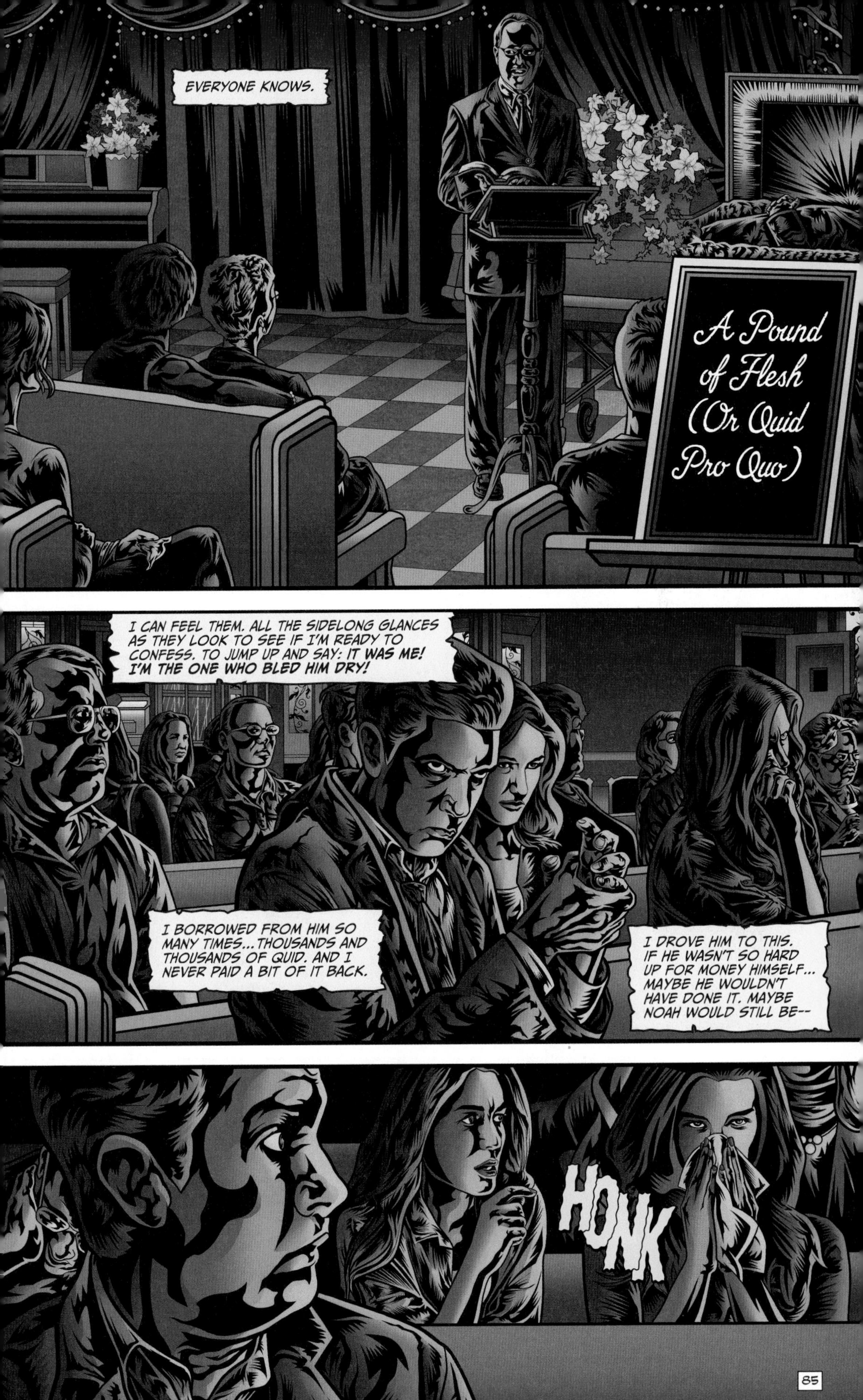
EVERYONE KNOWS.
A Pound of Flesh (Or Quid Pro Quo)
I CAN FEEL THEM. ALL THE SIDELONG GLANCES AS THEY LOOK TO SEE IF I'M READY TO CONFESS. TO JUMP UP AND SAY: IT WAS ME! I'M THE ONE WHO BLED HIM DRY!
I BORROWED FROM HIM SO MANY TIMES...THOUSANDS AND THOUSANDS OF QUID. AND I NEVER PAID A BIT OF IT BACK.
I DROVE HIM TO THIS. IF HE WASN'T SO HARD UP FOR MONEY HIMSELF... MAYBE HE WOULDN'T HAVE DONE IT. MAYBE NOAH WOULD STILL BE--
HONK

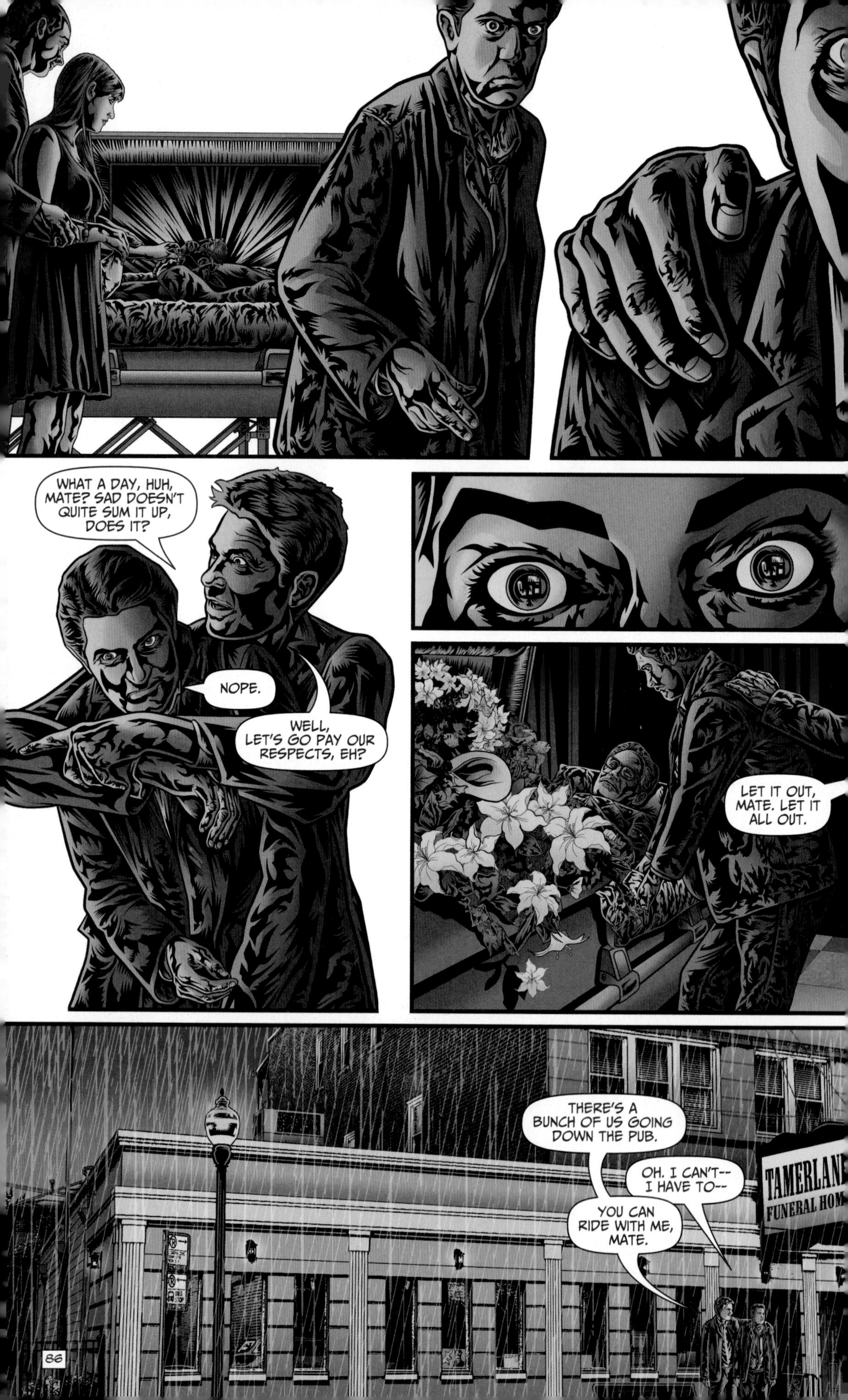
WHAT A DAY, HUH, MATE? SAD DOESN'T QUITE SUM IT UP, DOES IT?
NOPE.
WELL, LET'S GO PAY OUR RESPECTS, EH?
LET IT OUT, MATE. LET IT ALL OUT.
THERE'S A BUNCH OF US GOING DOWN THE PUB.
OH. I CAN'T-- I HAVE TO--
YOU CAN RIDE WITH ME, MATE.
TAMERLANE
FUNERAL HOM

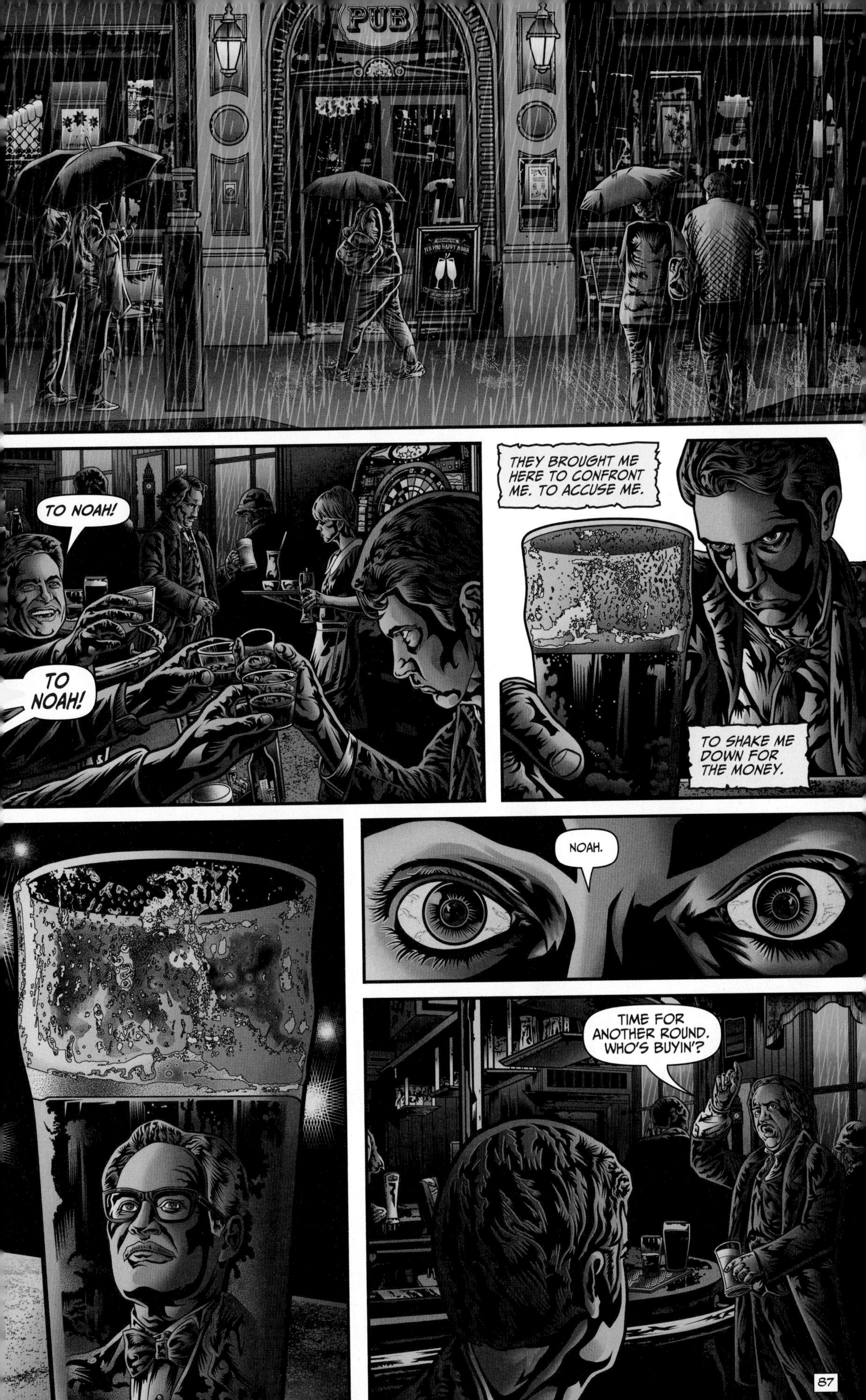
PUB
TO NOAH!
TO NOAH!
THEY BROUGHT ME HERE TO CONFRONT ME. TO ACCUSE ME.
TO SHAKE ME DOWN FOR THE MONEY.
NOAH.
TIME FOR ANOTHER ROUND. WHO'S BUYIN'?

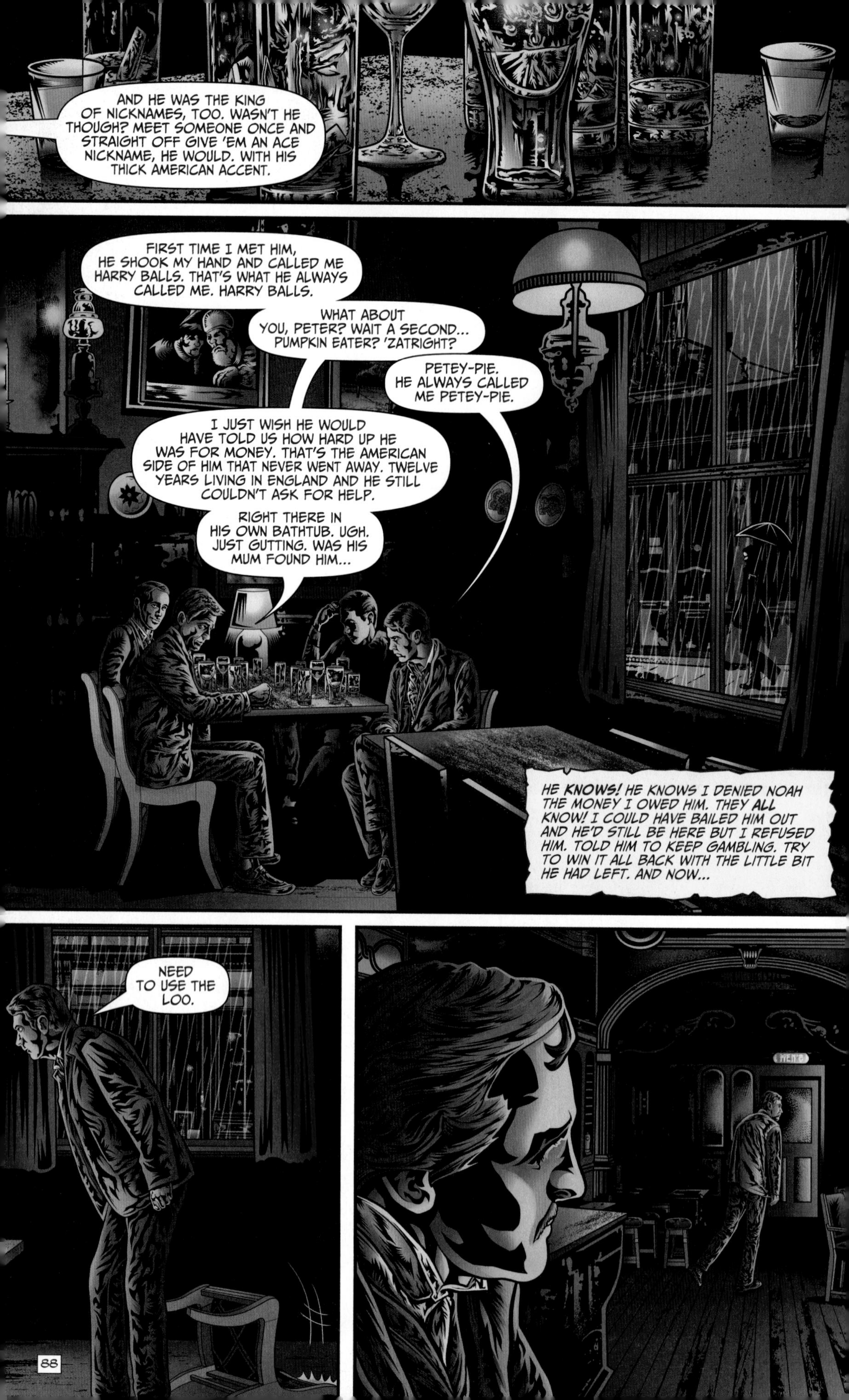
AND HE WAS THE KING OF NICKNAMES, TOO. WASN'T HE THOUGH? MEET SOMEONE ONCE AND STRAIGHT OFF GIVE 'EM AN ACE NICKNAME, HE WOULD. WITH HIS THICK AMERICAN ACCENT.
FIRST TIME I MET HIM, HE SHOOK MY HAND AND CALLED ME HARRY BALLS. THAT'S WHAT HE ALWAYS CALLED ME. HARRY BALLS.
WHAT ABOUT YOU, PETER? WAIT A SECOND... PUMPKIN EATER? 'ZATRIGHT?
PETEY-PIE. HE ALWAYS CALLED ME PETEY-PIE.
I JUST WISH HE WOULD HAVE TOLD US HOW HARD UP HE WAS FOR MONEY. THAT'S THE AMERICAN SIDE OF HIM THAT NEVER WENT AWAY. TWELVE YEARS LIVING IN ENGLAND AND HE STILL COULDN'T ASK FOR HELP.
RIGHT THERE IN HIS OWN BATHTUB. UGH. JUST GUTTING. WAS HIS MUM FOUND HIM...
HE **KNOWS!** HE KNOWS I DENIED NOAH THE MONEY I OWED HIM. THEY **ALL** KNOW! I COULD HAVE BAILED HIM OUT AND HE'D STILL BE HERE BUT I REFUSED HIM. TOLD HIM TO KEEP GAMBLING. TRY TO WIN IT ALL BACK WITH THE LITTLE BIT HE HAD LEFT. AND NOW...
NEED TO USE THE LOO.
MEN'S

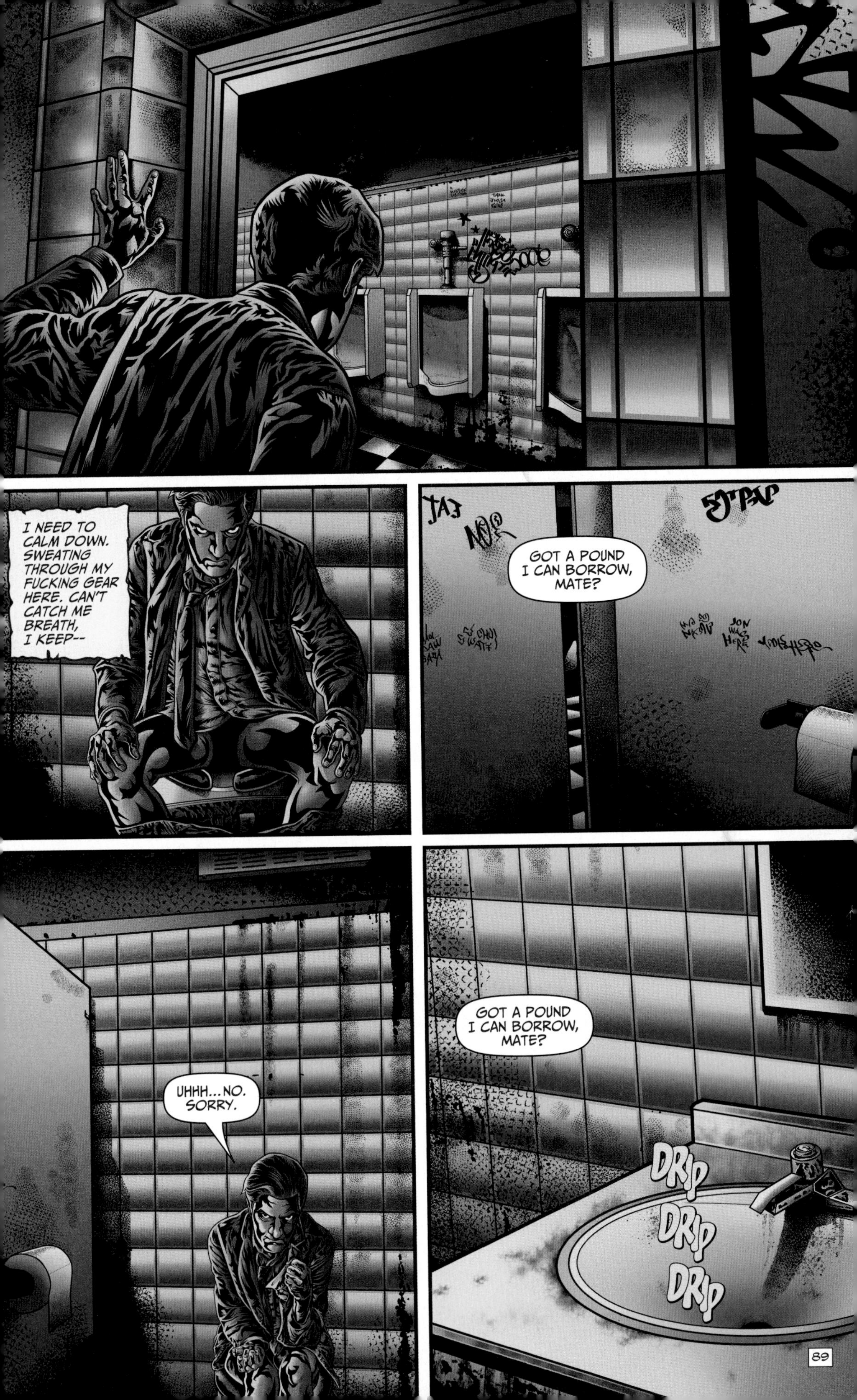
I NEED TO CALM DOWN. SWEATING THROUGH MY FUCKING GEAR HERE. CAN'T CATCH ME BREATH, I KEEP--
GOT A POUND I CAN BORROW, MATE?
JON WAS HERE
UHHH...NO. SORRY.
GOT A POUND I CAN BORROW, MATE?
DRIP
DRIP
DRIP

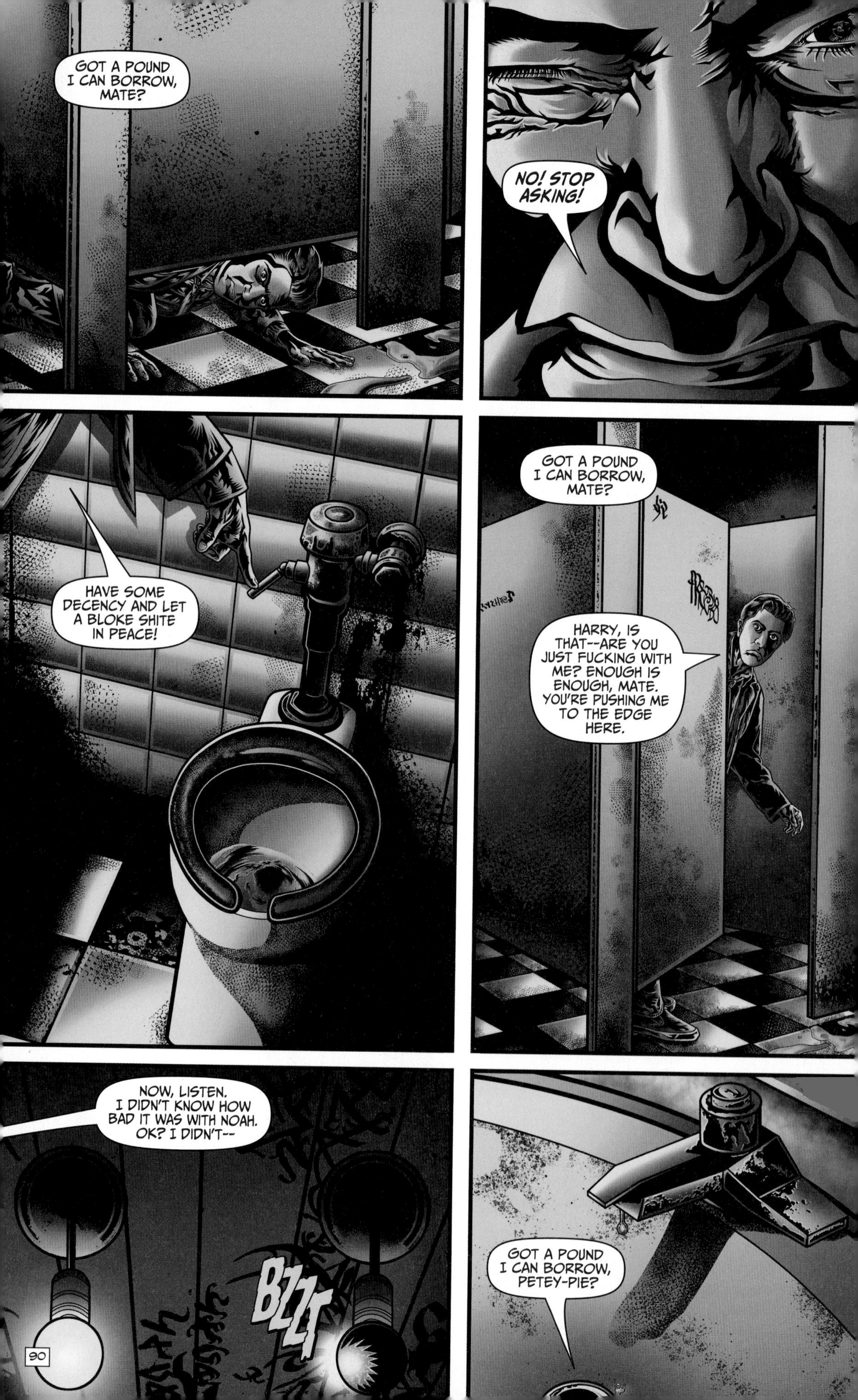
GOT A POUND I CAN BORROW, MATE?
NO! STOP ASKING!
HAVE SOME DECENCY AND LET A BLOKE SHITE IN PEACE!
GOT A POUND I CAN BORROW, MATE?
HARRY, IS THAT--ARE YOU JUST FUCKING WITH ME? ENOUGH IS ENOUGH, MATE. YOU'RE PUSHING ME TO THE EDGE HERE.
NOW, LISTEN. I DIDN'T KNOW HOW BAD IT WAS WITH NOAH. OK? I DIDN'T--
BZZT
GOT A POUND I CAN BORROW, PETEY-PIE?

IT CAN'T BE. NO, IT'S NOT... YOU'VE HAD TOO MUCH TO DRINK. YOU'RE LETTING YOUR MIND SLIP HERE.

COME ON, PETEY-PIE... CAN'T YOU LEND ME A POUND? YOU OWE ME, PAL.

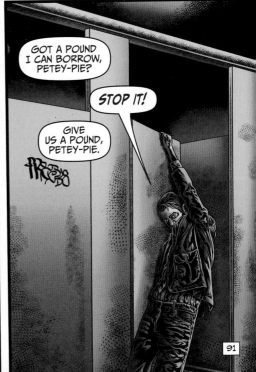

GOT A POUND I CAN BORROW, PETEY-PIE?

STOP IT!

GIVE US A POUND, PETEY-PIE.

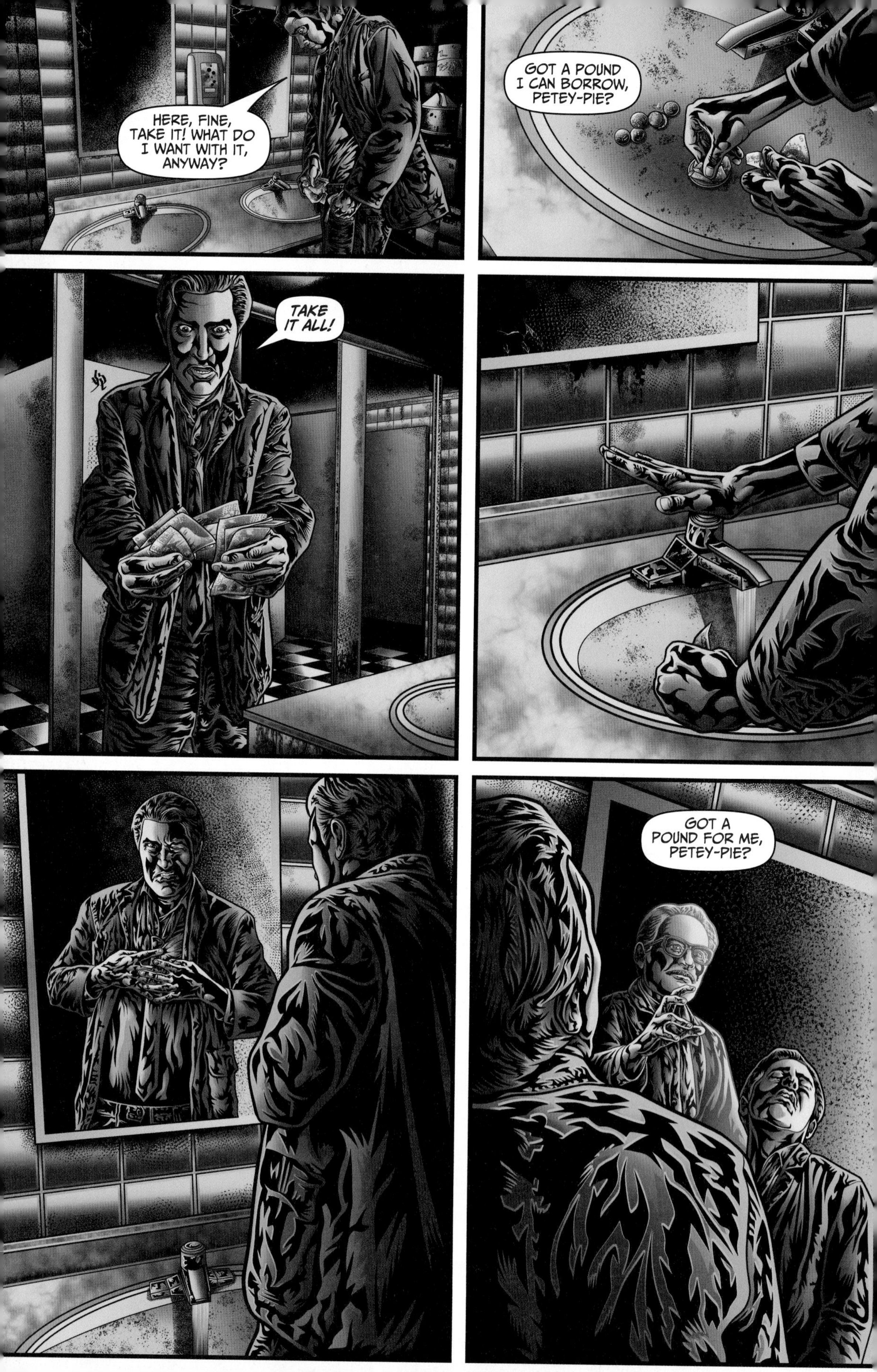
HERE, FINE, TAKE IT! WHAT DO I WANT WITH IT, ANYWAY?
GOT A POUND I CAN BORROW, PETEY-PIE?
TAKE IT ALL!
GOT A POUND FOR ME, PETEY-PIE?

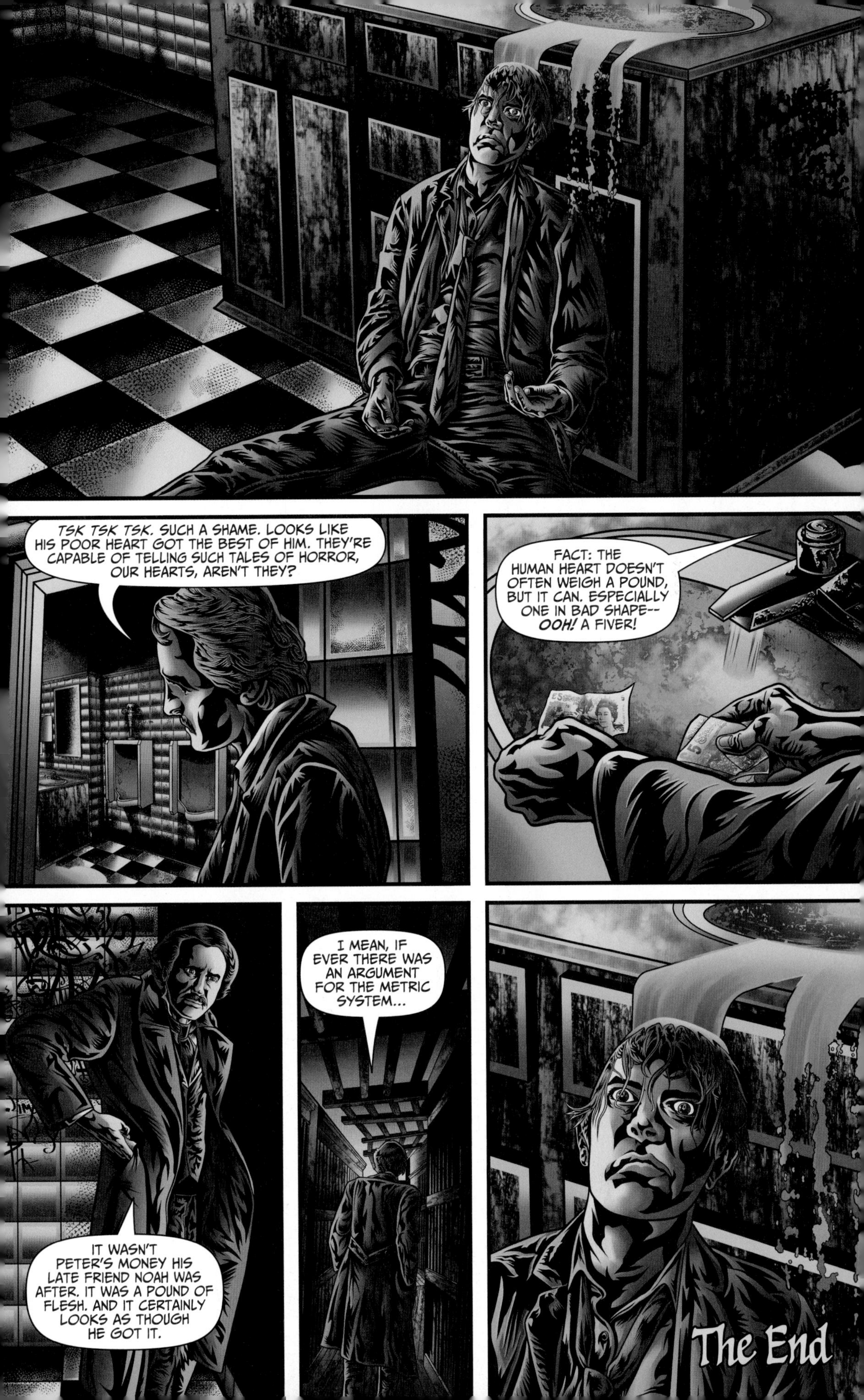
TSK TSK TSK. SUCH A SHAME. LOOKS LIKE HIS POOR HEART GOT THE BEST OF HIM. THEY'RE CAPABLE OF TELLING SUCH TALES OF HORROR, OUR HEARTS, AREN'T THEY?
FACT: THE HUMAN HEART DOESN'T OFTEN WEIGH A POUND, BUT IT CAN. ESPECIALLY ONE IN BAD SHAPE-- OOH! A FIVER!
IT WASN'T PETER'S MONEY HIS LATE FRIEND NOAH WAS AFTER. IT WAS A POUND OF FLESH. AND IT CERTAINLY LOOKS AS THOUGH HE GOT IT.
I MEAN, IF EVER THERE WAS AN ARGUMENT FOR THE METRIC SYSTEM...
The End

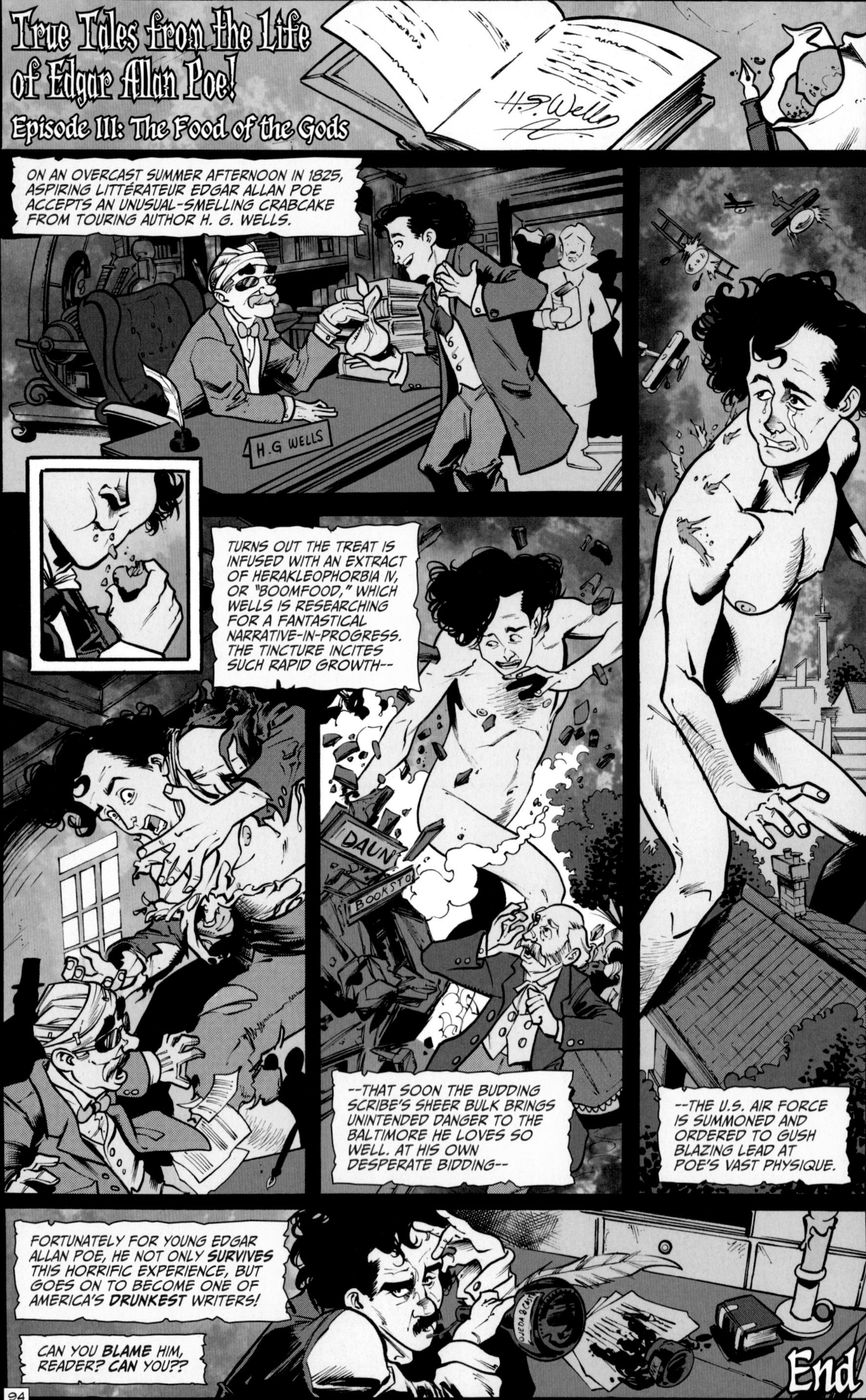
True Tales from the Life of Edgar Allan Poe!
Episode III: The Food of the Gods
H. G. Wells
ON AN OVERCAST SUMMER AFTERNOON IN 1825, ASPIRING LITTÉRATEUR EDGAR ALLAN POE ACCEPTS AN UNUSUAL-SMELLING CRABCAKE FROM TOURING AUTHOR H. G. WELLS.
H.G WELLS
TURNS OUT THE TREAT IS INFUSED WITH AN EXTRACT OF HERAKLEOPHORBIA IV, OR "BOOMFOOD," WHICH WELLS IS RESEARCHING FOR A FANTASTICAL NARRATIVE-IN-PROGRESS. THE TINCTURE INCITES SUCH RAPID GROWTH--
DAUN
BOOKSTO
--THAT SOON THE BUDDING SCRIBE'S SHEER BULK BRINGS UNINTENDED DANGER TO THE BALTIMORE HE LOVES SO WELL. AT HIS OWN DESPERATE BIDDING--
--THE U.S. AIR FORCE IS SUMMONED AND ORDERED TO GUSH BLAZING LEAD AT POE'S VAST PHYSIQUE.
FORTUNATELY FOR YOUNG EDGAR ALLAN POE, HE NOT ONLY SURVIVES THIS HORRIFIC EXPERIENCE, BUT GOES ON TO BECOME ONE OF AMERICA'S DRUNKEST WRITERS!
CAN YOU BLAME HIM, READER? CAN YOU??
End

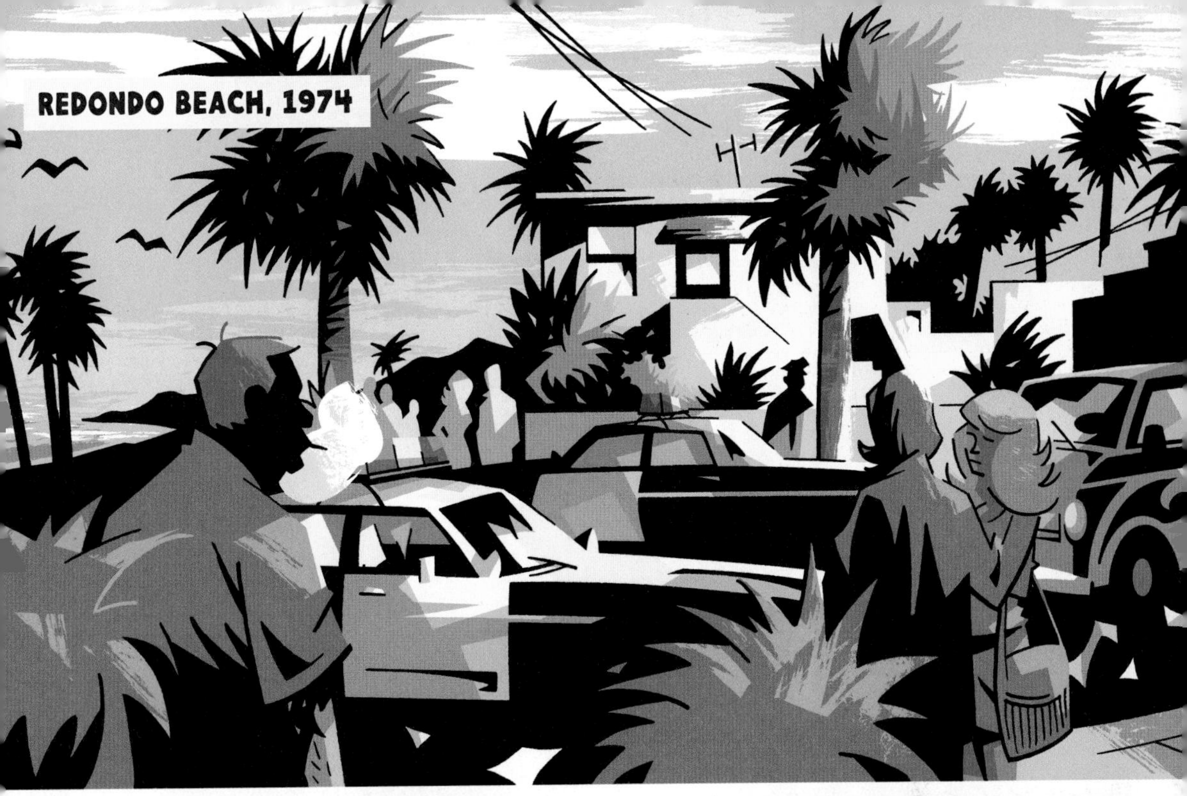
REDONDO BEACH, 1974

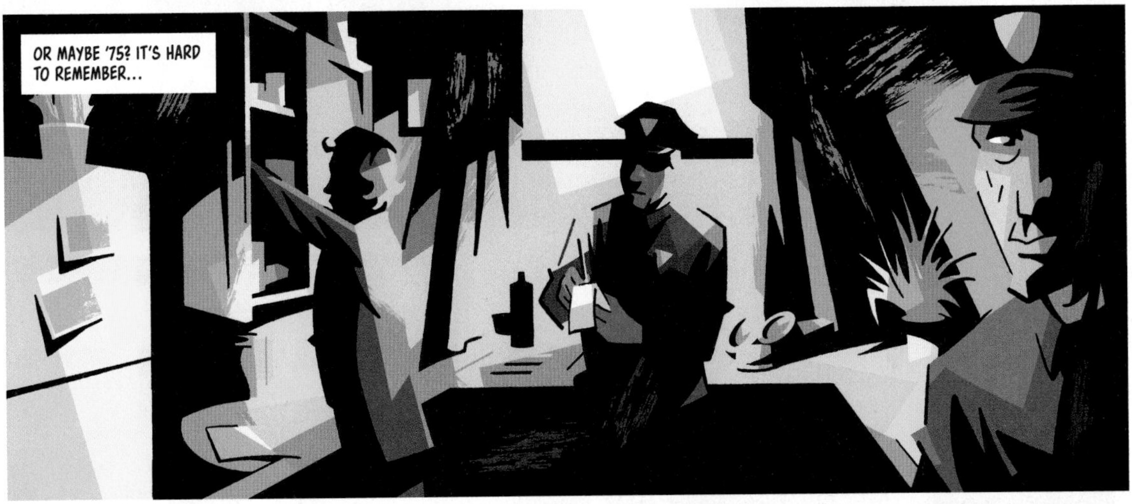
OR MAYBE '75? IT'S HARD TO REMEMBER...

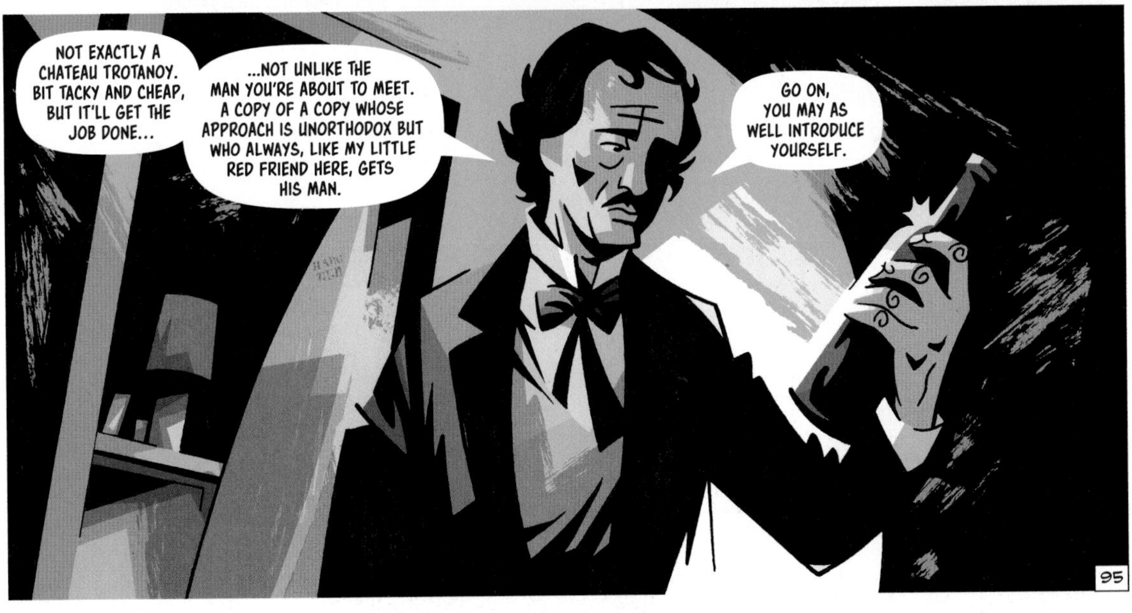
NOT EXACTLY A CHATEAU TROTANOY. BIT TACKY AND CHEAP, BUT IT'LL GET THE JOB DONE...
...NOT UNLIKE THE MAN YOU'RE ABOUT TO MEET. A COPY OF A COPY WHOSE APPROACH IS UNORTHODOX BUT WHO ALWAYS, LIKE MY LITTLE RED FRIEND HERE, GETS HIS MAN.
GO ON, YOU MAY AS WELL INTRODUCE YOURSELF.

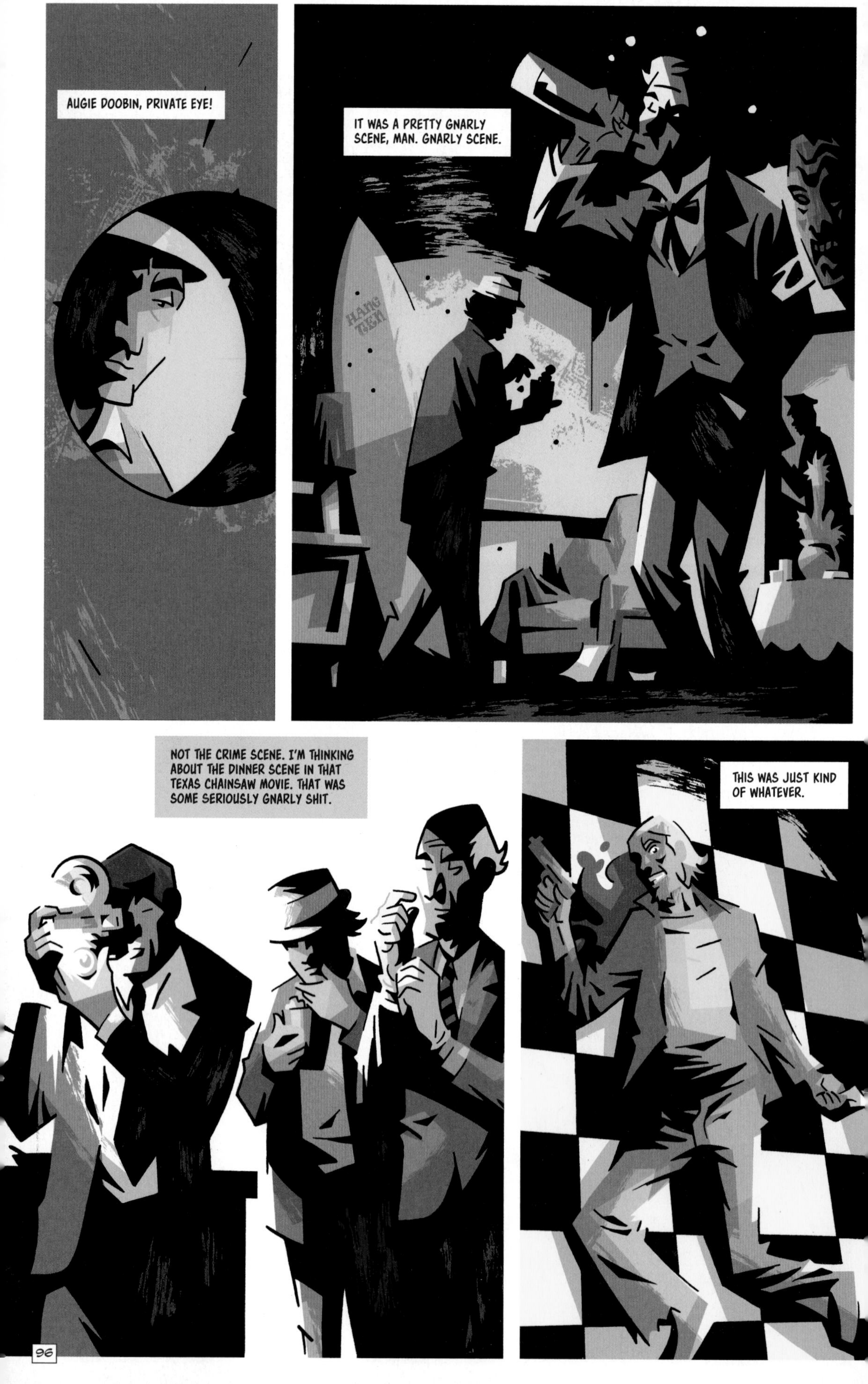
AUGIE DOOBIN, PRIVATE EYE!
IT WAS A PRETTY GNARLY SCENE, MAN. GNARLY SCENE.
HANG TEN
NOT THE CRIME SCENE. I'M THINKING ABOUT THE DINNER SCENE IN THAT TEXAS CHAINSAW MOVIE. THAT WAS SOME SERIOUSLY GNARLY SHIT.
THIS WAS JUST KIND OF WHATEVER.

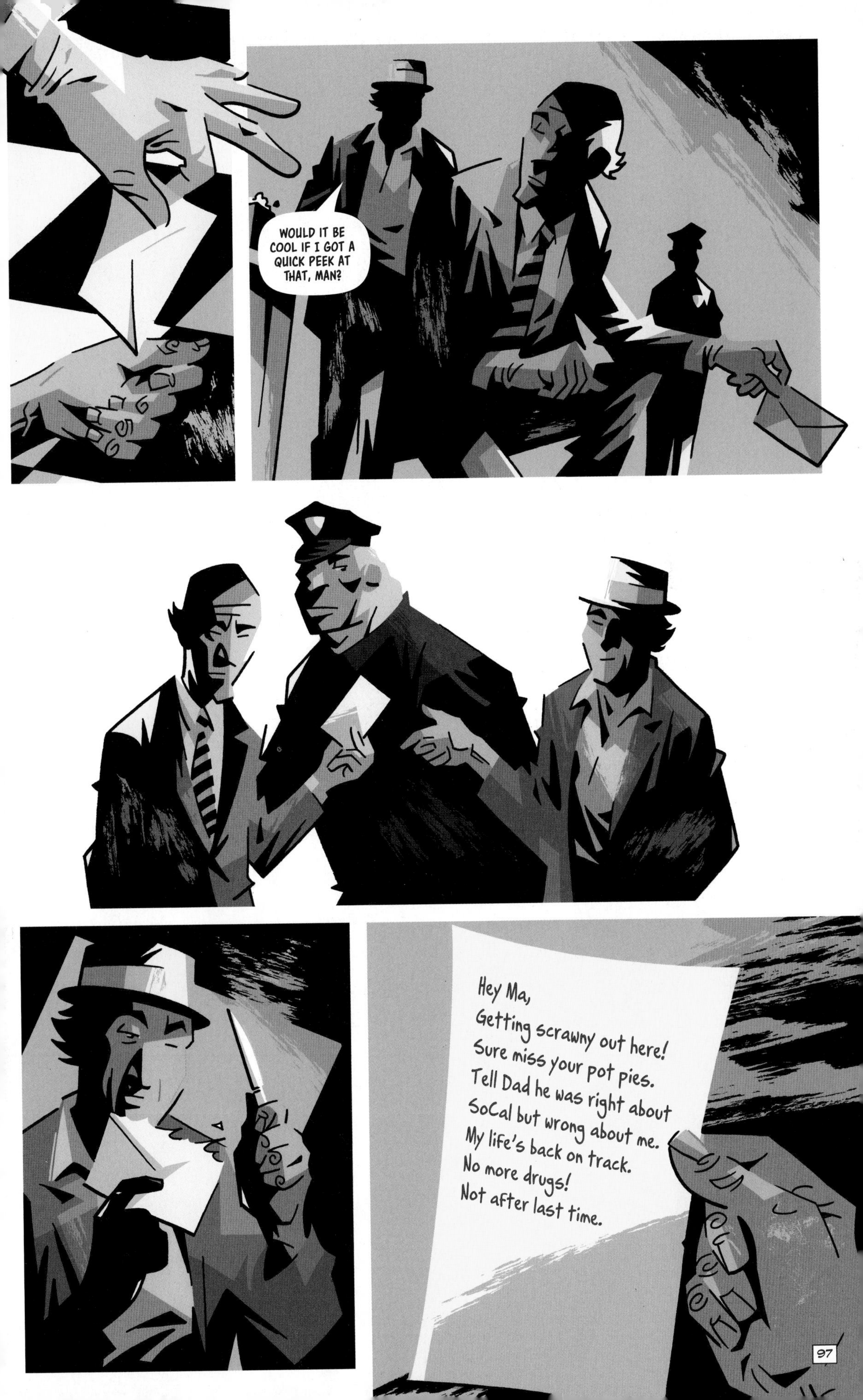
WOULD IT BE COOL IF I GOT A QUICK PEEK AT THAT, MAN?
Hey Ma,
Getting scrawny out here!
Sure miss your pot pies.
Tell Dad he was right about
SoCal but wrong about me.
My life's back on track.
No more drugs!
Not after last time.

AND JUST WHAT IN THE SWEET POSTAL FUCK DO WE HAVE HERE?

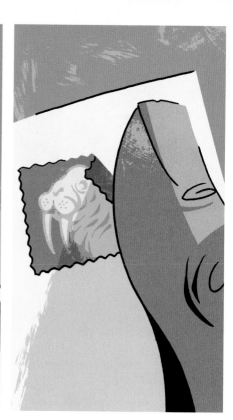

WELL, THERE'S ONLY ONE WAY TO SEE A HUNCH THROUGH TO THE OTHER SIDE. DIVE STRAIGHT INTO THE DEEP END, BABY. GET YOUR BRAIN WET.

LICK

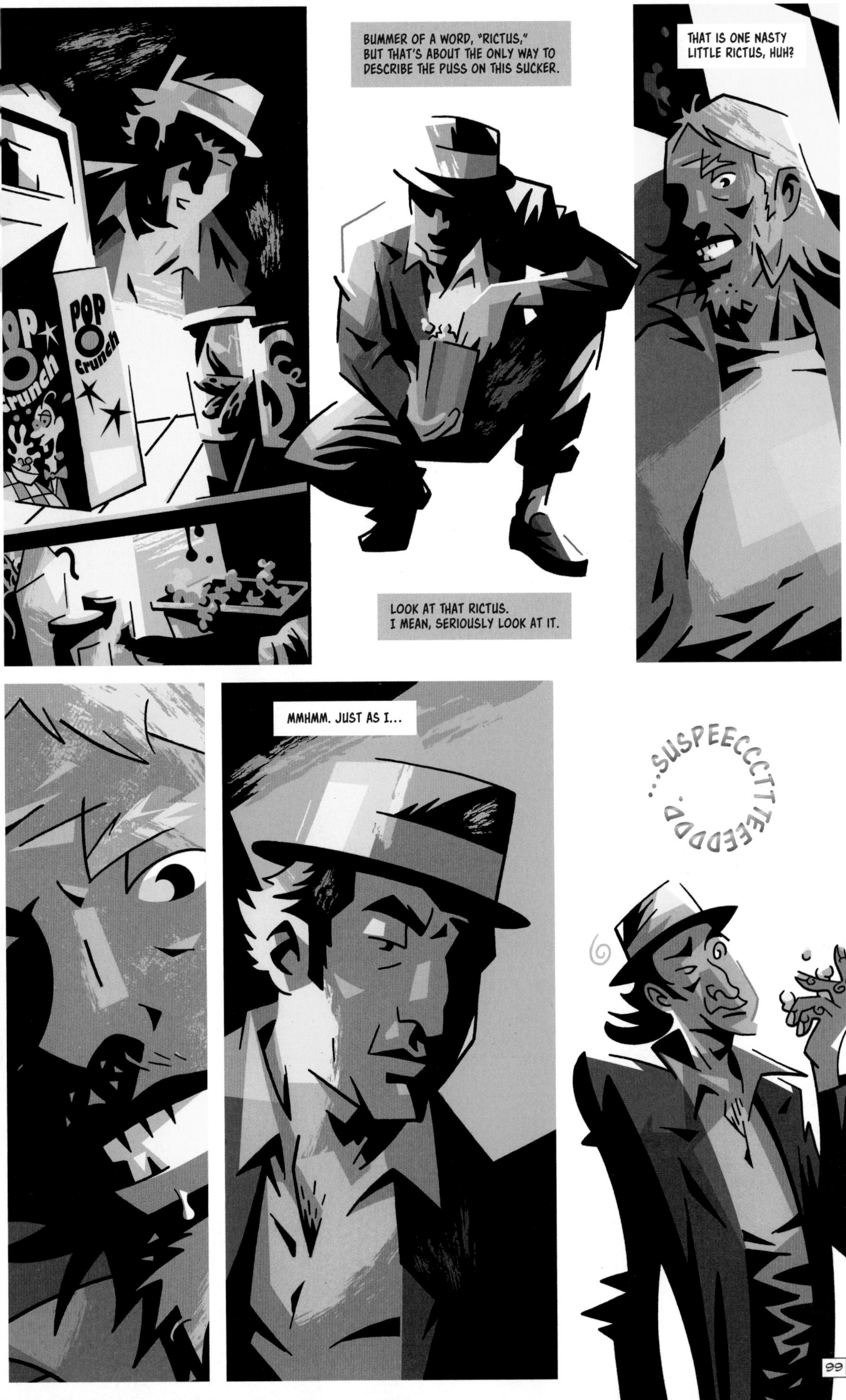
POP Crunch
POP Crunch
BUMMER OF A WORD, "RICTUS," BUT THAT'S ABOUT THE ONLY WAY TO DESCRIBE THE PUSS ON THIS SUCKER.
LOOK AT THAT RICTUS. I MEAN, SERIOUSLY LOOK AT IT.
THAT IS ONE NASTY LITTLE RICTUS, HUH?
MMHMM. JUST AS I...
...SUSPEECCCTTIEEEDDD.

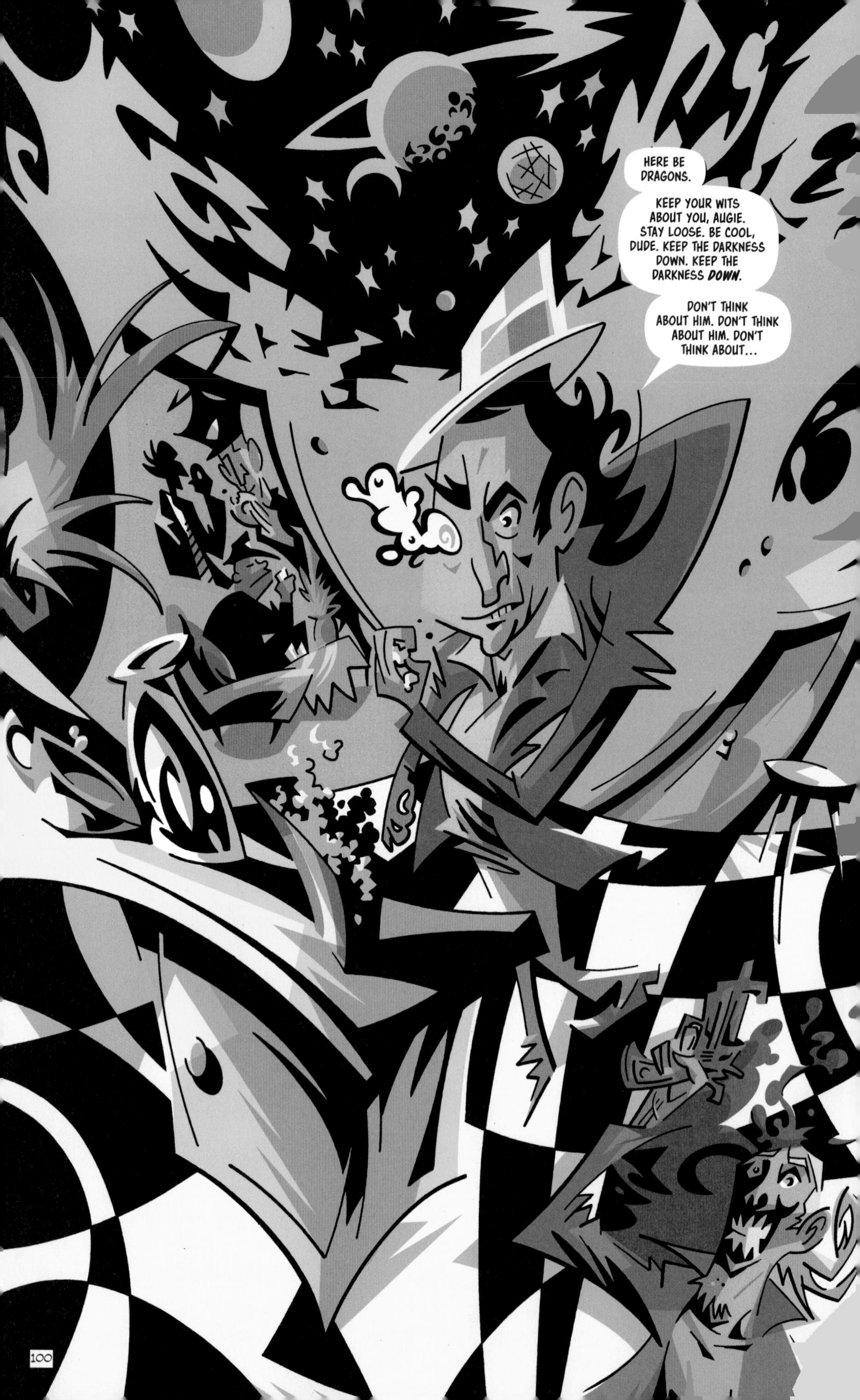
HERE BE DRAGONS.
KEEP YOUR WITS ABOUT YOU, AUGIE. STAY LOOSE. BE COOL, DUDE. KEEP THE DARKNESS DOWN. KEEP THE DARKNESS ***DOWN***.
DON'T THINK ABOUT HIM. DON'T THINK ABOUT HIM. DON'T THINK ABOUT...

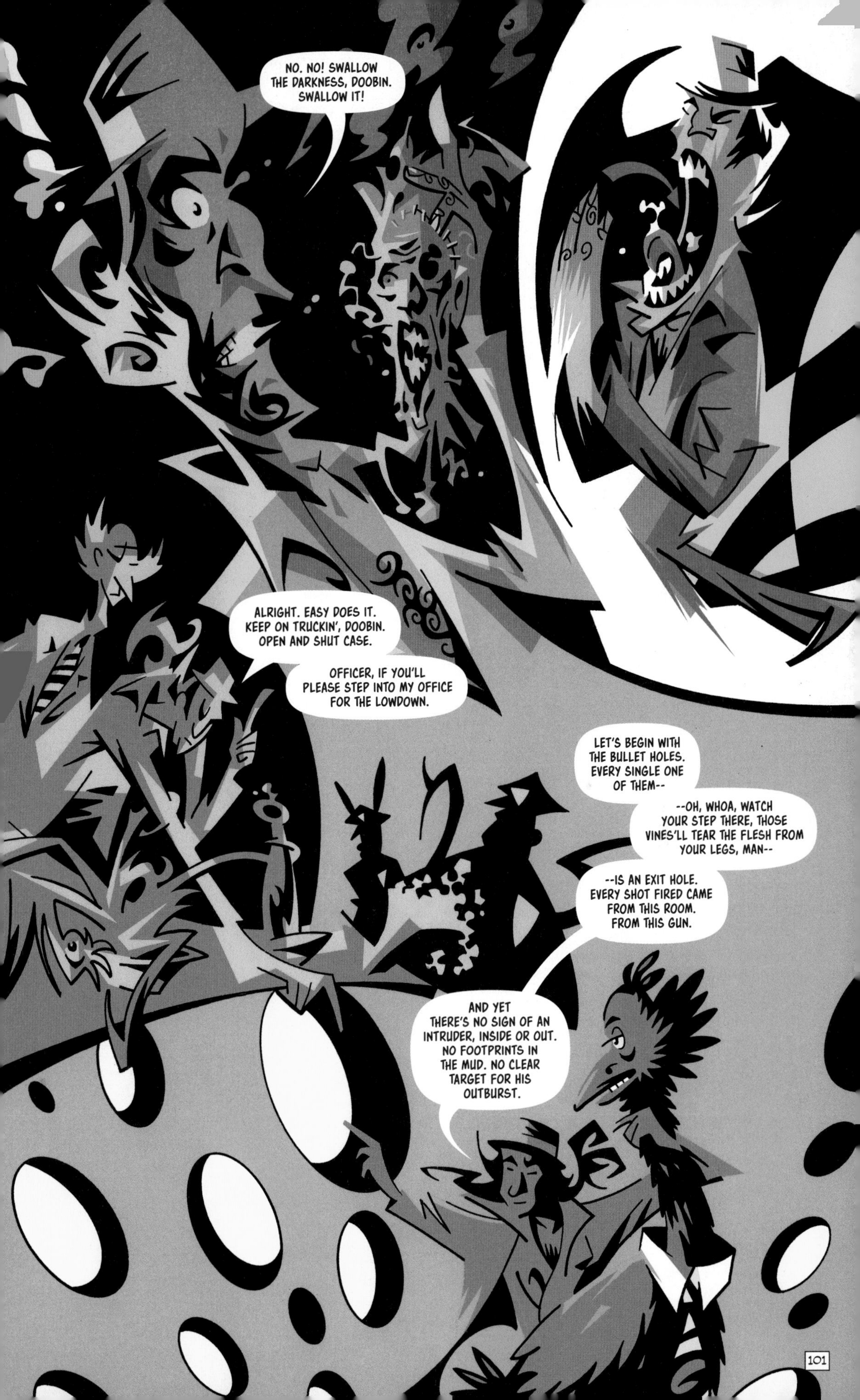
NO. NO! SWALLOW THE DARKNESS, DOOBIN. SWALLOW IT!
ALRIGHT. EASY DOES IT. KEEP ON TRUCKIN', DOOBIN. OPEN AND SHUT CASE.
OFFICER, IF YOU'LL PLEASE STEP INTO MY OFFICE FOR THE LOWDOWN.
LET'S BEGIN WITH THE BULLET HOLES. EVERY SINGLE ONE OF THEM--
--OH, WHOA, WATCH YOUR STEP THERE, THOSE VINES'LL TEAR THE FLESH FROM YOUR LEGS, MAN--
--IS AN EXIT HOLE. EVERY SHOT FIRED CAME FROM THIS ROOM. FROM THIS GUN.
AND YET THERE'S NO SIGN OF AN INTRUDER, INSIDE OR OUT. NO FOOTPRINTS IN THE MUD. NO CLEAR TARGET FOR HIS OUTBURST.

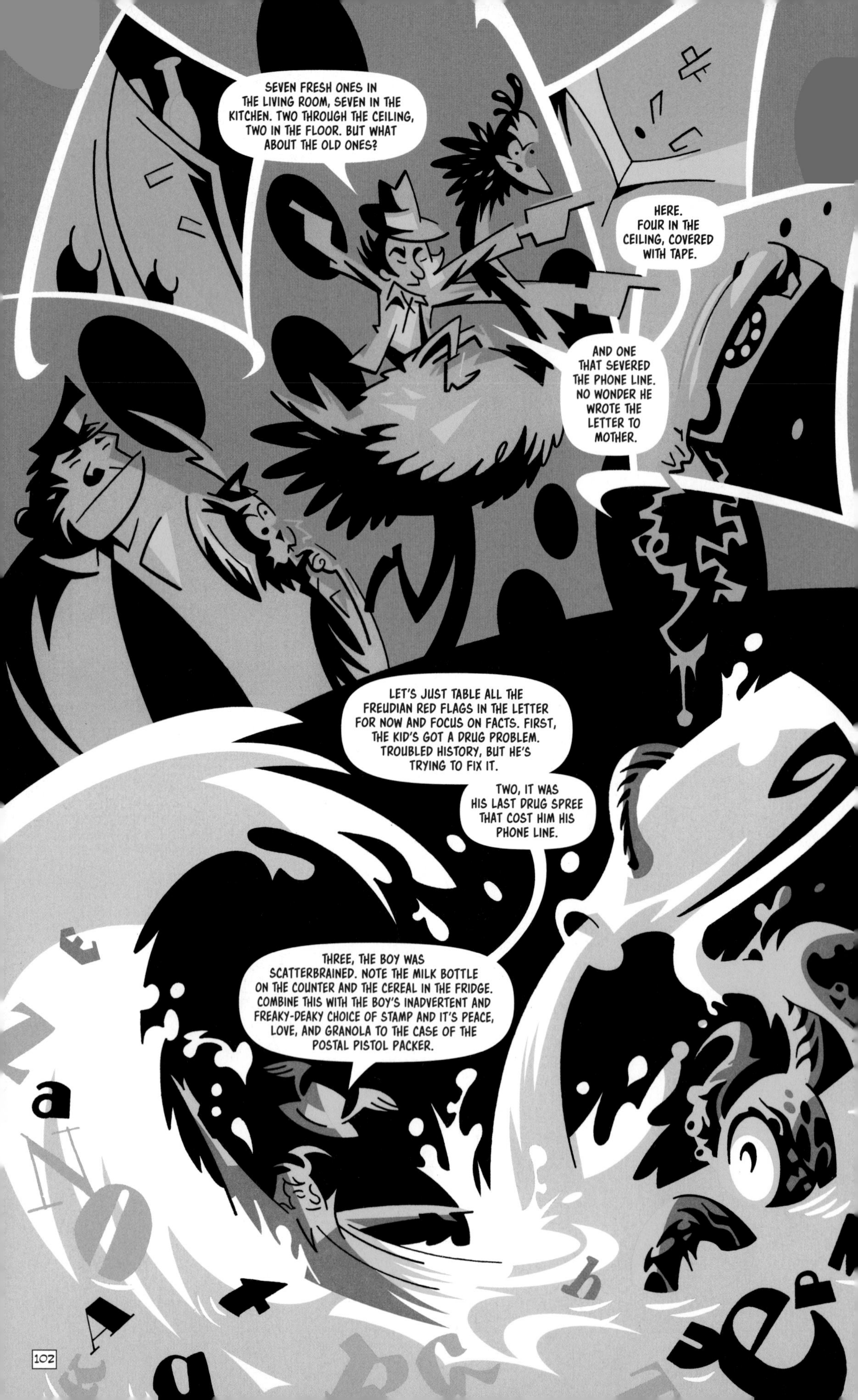

SEVEN FRESH ONES IN THE LIVING ROOM, SEVEN IN THE KITCHEN. TWO THROUGH THE CEILING, TWO IN THE FLOOR. BUT WHAT ABOUT THE OLD ONES?
HERE. FOUR IN THE CEILING, COVERED WITH TAPE.
AND ONE THAT SEVERED THE PHONE LINE. NO WONDER HE WROTE THE LETTER TO MOTHER.
LET'S JUST TABLE ALL THE FREUDIAN RED FLAGS IN THE LETTER FOR NOW AND FOCUS ON FACTS. FIRST, THE KID'S GOT A DRUG PROBLEM. TROUBLED HISTORY, BUT HE'S TRYING TO FIX IT.
TWO, IT WAS HIS LAST DRUG SPREE THAT COST HIM HIS PHONE LINE.
THREE, THE BOY WAS SCATTERBRAINED. NOTE THE MILK BOTTLE ON THE COUNTER AND THE CEREAL IN THE FRIDGE. COMBINE THIS WITH THE BOY'S INADVERTENT AND FREAKY-DEAKY CHOICE OF STAMP AND IT'S PEACE, LOVE, AND GRANOLA TO THE CASE OF THE POSTAL PISTOL PACKER.

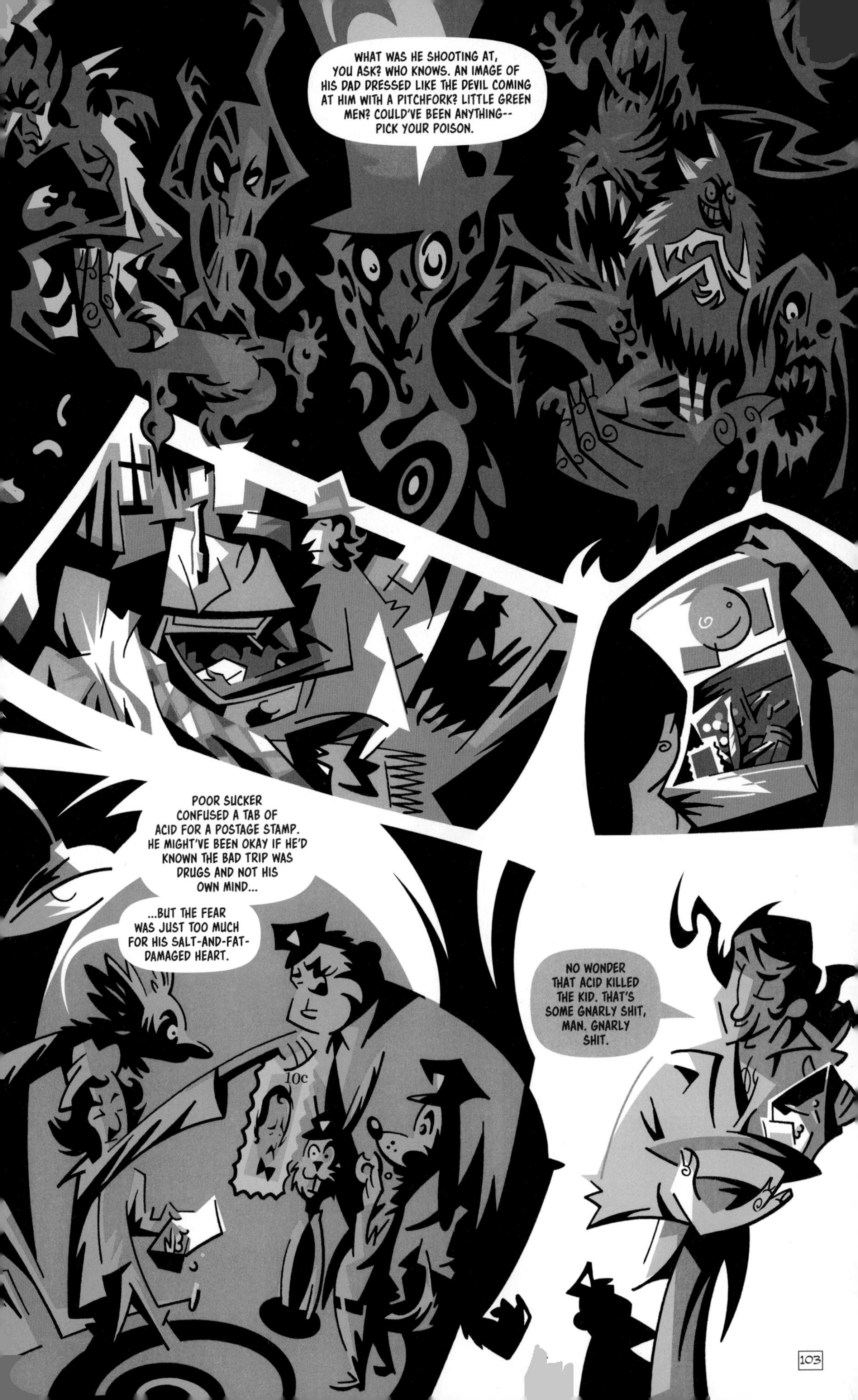
WHAT WAS HE SHOOTING AT, YOU ASK? WHO KNOWS. AN IMAGE OF HIS DAD DRESSED LIKE THE DEVIL COMING AT HIM WITH A PITCHFORK? LITTLE GREEN MEN? COULD'VE BEEN ANYTHING-- PICK YOUR POISON.
POOR SUCKER CONFUSED A TAB OF ACID FOR A POSTAGE STAMP. HE MIGHT'VE BEEN OKAY IF HE'D KNOWN THE BAD TRIP WAS DRUGS AND NOT HIS OWN MIND...
...BUT THE FEAR WAS JUST TOO MUCH FOR HIS SALT-AND-FAT-DAMAGED HEART.
10c
NO WONDER THAT ACID KILLED THE KID. THAT'S SOME GNARLY SHIT, MAN. GNARLY SHIT.

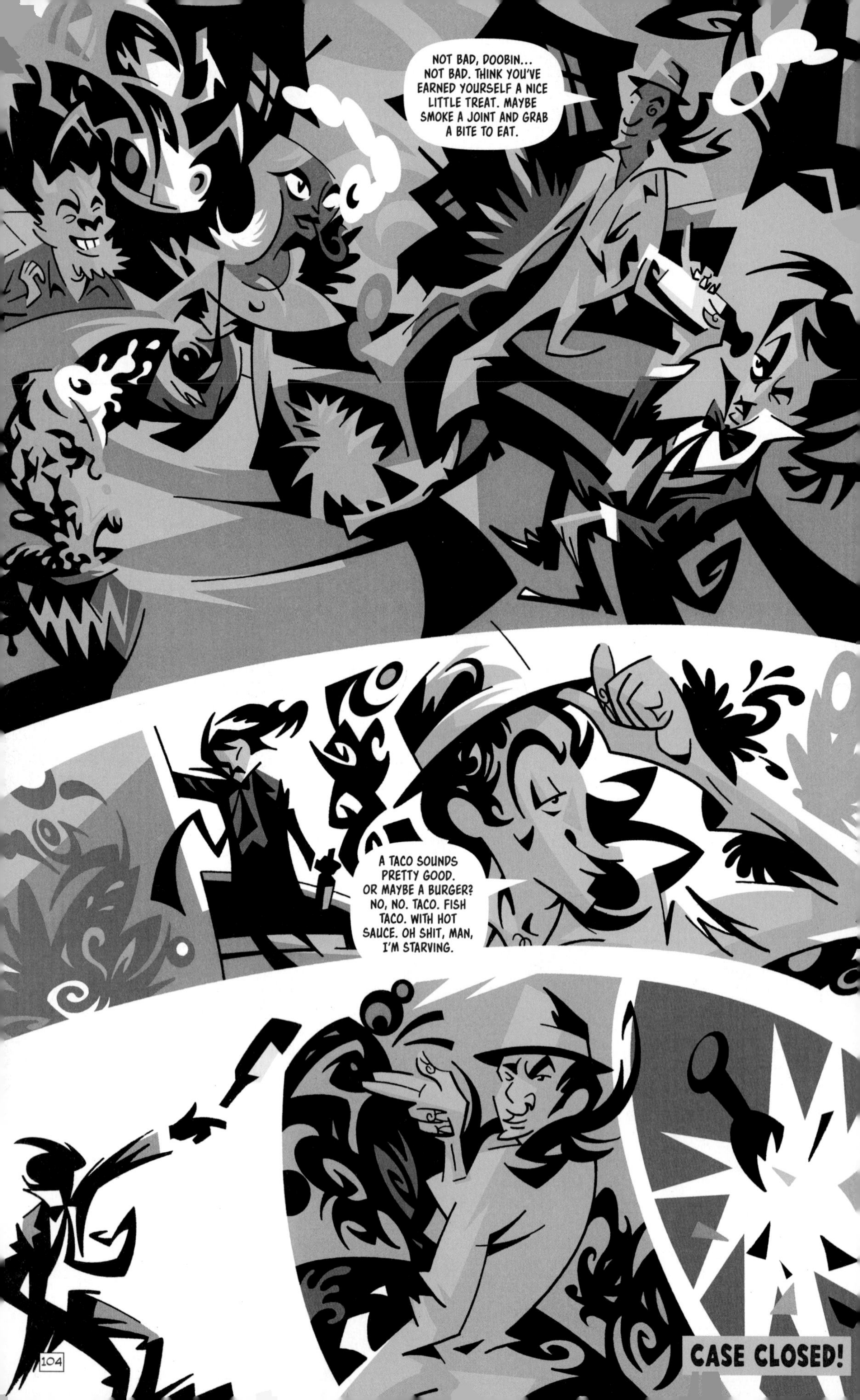
NOT BAD, DOOBIN... NOT BAD. THINK YOU'VE EARNED YOURSELF A NICE LITTLE TREAT. MAYBE SMOKE A JOINT AND GRAB A BITE TO EAT.
A TACO SOUNDS PRETTY GOOD. OR MAYBE A BURGER? NO, NO. TACO. FISH TACO. WITH HOT SAUCE. OH SHIT, MAN, I'M STARVING.
CASE CLOSED!

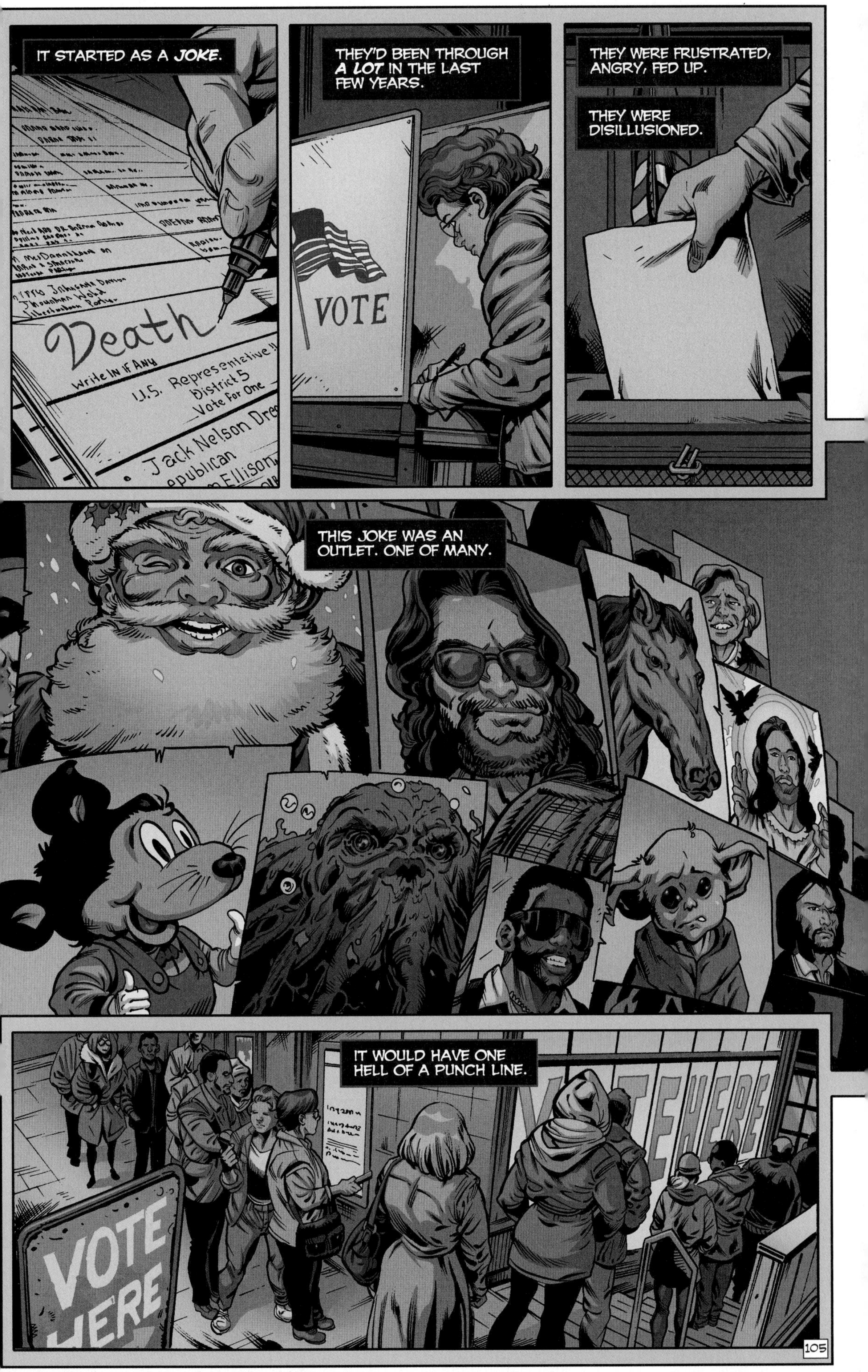
IT STARTED AS A ***JOKE***.
Death
Write IN if Any
U.S. Representative!!
District 5
Vote for One
THEY'D BEEN THROUGH ***A LOT*** IN THE LAST FEW YEARS.
VOTE
THEY WERE FRUSTRATED, ANGRY, FED UP.
THEY WERE DISILLUSIONED.
THIS JOKE WAS AN OUTLET. ONE OF MANY.
IT WOULD HAVE ONE HELL OF A PUNCH LINE.
VOTE HERE

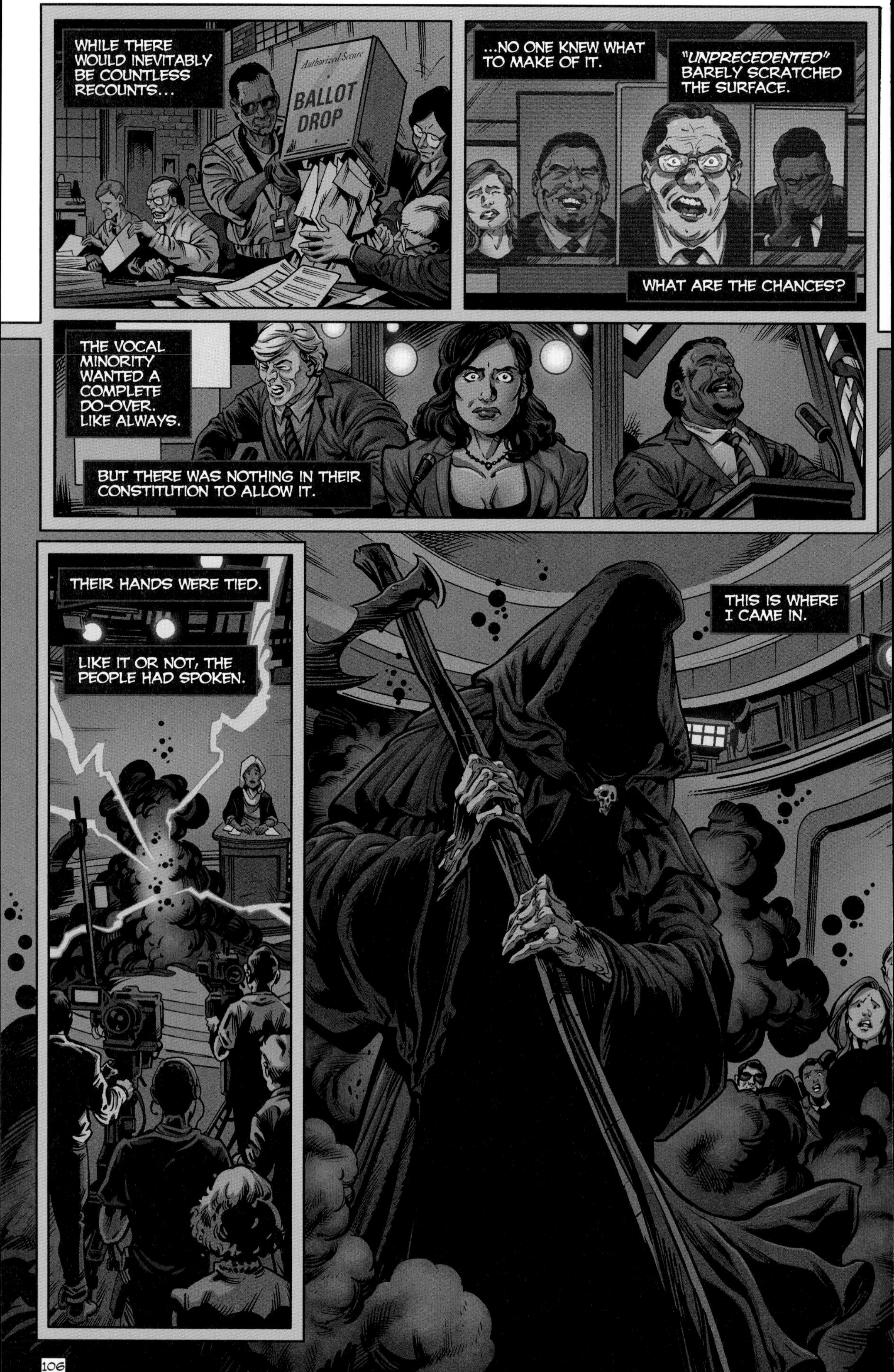
WHILE THERE WOULD INEVITABLY BE COUNTLESS RECOUNTS...
Authorized Secure
BALLOT DROP
...NO ONE KNEW WHAT TO MAKE OF IT.
"UNPRECEDENTED" BARELY SCRATCHED THE SURFACE.
WHAT ARE THE CHANCES?
THE VOCAL MINORITY WANTED A COMPLETE DO-OVER. LIKE ALWAYS.
BUT THERE WAS NOTHING IN THEIR CONSTITUTION TO ALLOW IT.
THEIR HANDS WERE TIED.
LIKE IT OR NOT, THE PEOPLE HAD SPOKEN.
THIS IS WHERE I CAME IN.

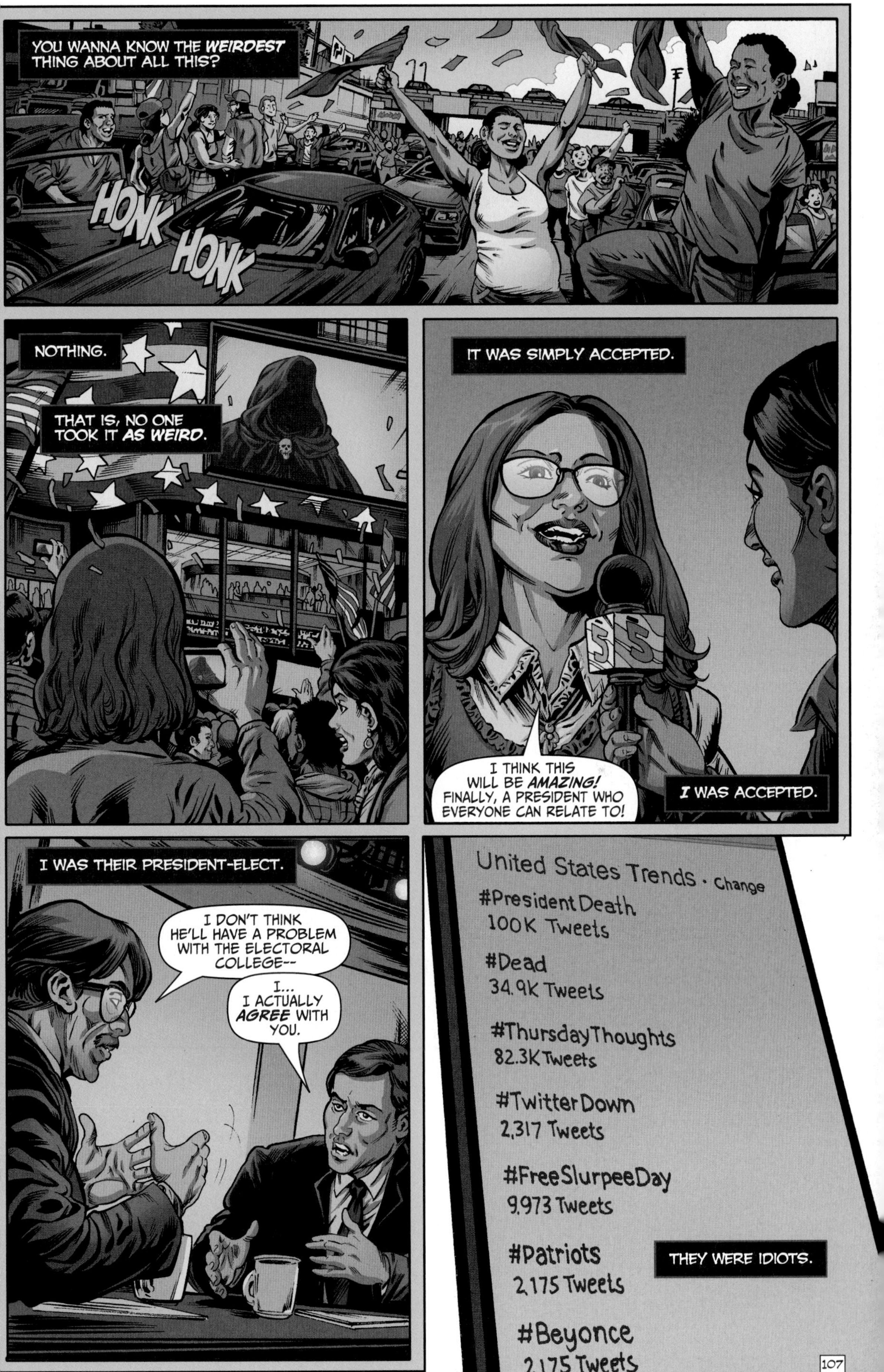
YOU WANNA KNOW THE WEIRDEST THING ABOUT ALL THIS?
HONK
HONK
NOTHING.
THAT IS, NO ONE TOOK IT AS WEIRD.
IT WAS SIMPLY ACCEPTED.
I THINK THIS WILL BE AMAZING! FINALLY, A PRESIDENT WHO EVERYONE CAN RELATE TO!
I WAS ACCEPTED.
I WAS THEIR PRESIDENT-ELECT.
I DON'T THINK HE'LL HAVE A PROBLEM WITH THE ELECTORAL COLLEGE--
I... I ACTUALLY AGREE WITH YOU.
United States Trends · Change
#PresidentDeath
100K Tweets
#Dead
34.9K Tweets
#ThursdayThoughts
82.3K Tweets
#TwitterDown
2,317 Tweets
#FreeSlurpeeDay
9,973 Tweets
#Patriots
2,175 Tweets
THEY WERE IDIOTS.
#Beyonce
2,175 Tweets

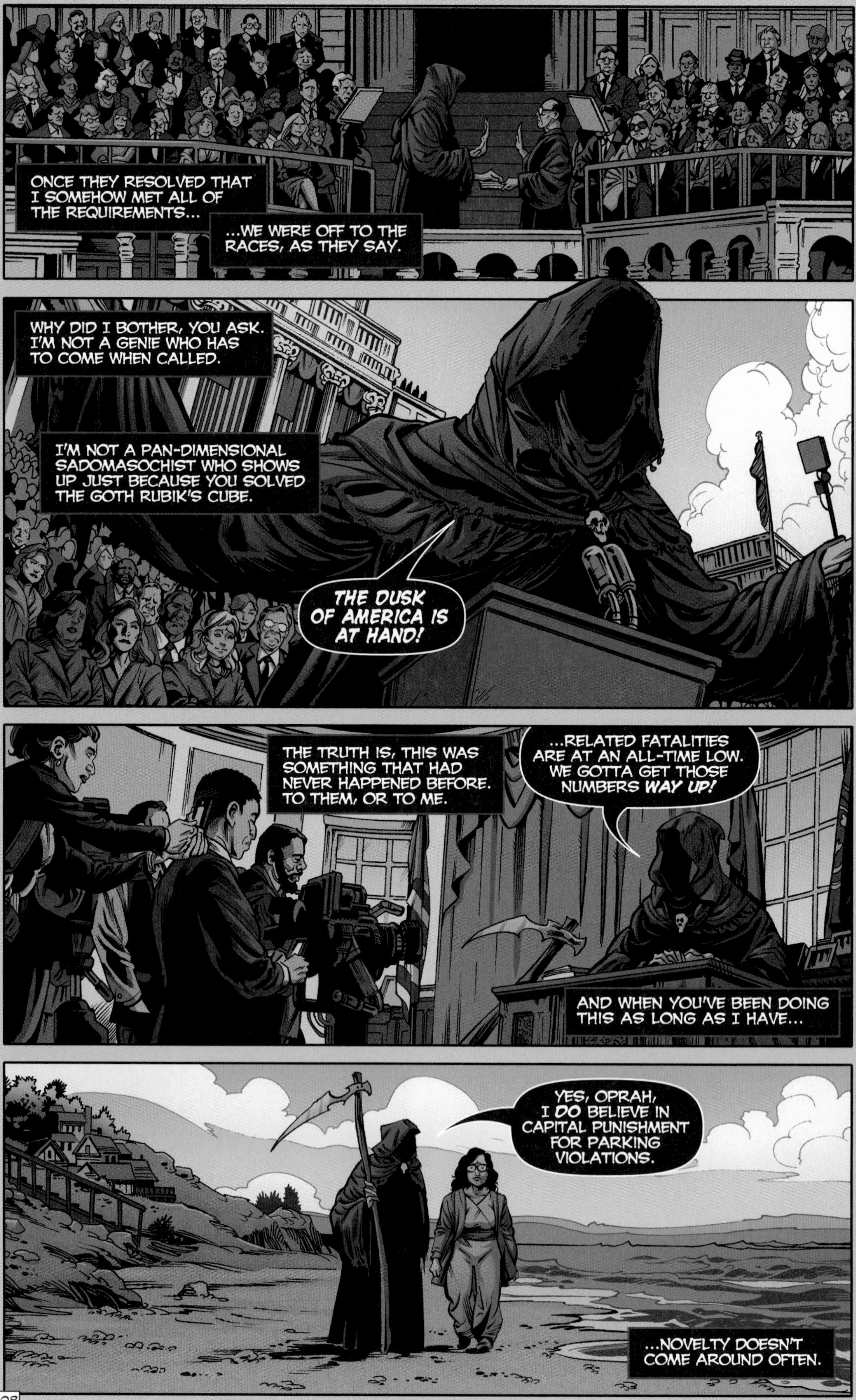
ONCE THEY RESOLVED THAT I SOMEHOW MET ALL OF THE REQUIREMENTS...
...WE WERE OFF TO THE RACES, AS THEY SAY.
WHY DID I BOTHER, YOU ASK. I'M NOT A GENIE WHO HAS TO COME WHEN CALLED.
I'M NOT A PAN-DIMENSIONAL SADOMASOCHIST WHO SHOWS UP JUST BECAUSE YOU SOLVED THE GOTH RUBIK'S CUBE.
THE DUSK OF AMERICA IS AT HAND!
THE TRUTH IS, THIS WAS SOMETHING THAT HAD NEVER HAPPENED BEFORE. TO THEM, OR TO ME.
...RELATED FATALITIES ARE AT AN ALL-TIME LOW. WE GOTTA GET THOSE NUMBERS WAY UP!
AND WHEN YOU'VE BEEN DOING THIS AS LONG AS I HAVE...
YES, OPRAH, I DO BELIEVE IN CAPITAL PUNISHMENT FOR PARKING VIOLATIONS.
...NOVELTY DOESN'T COME AROUND OFTEN.

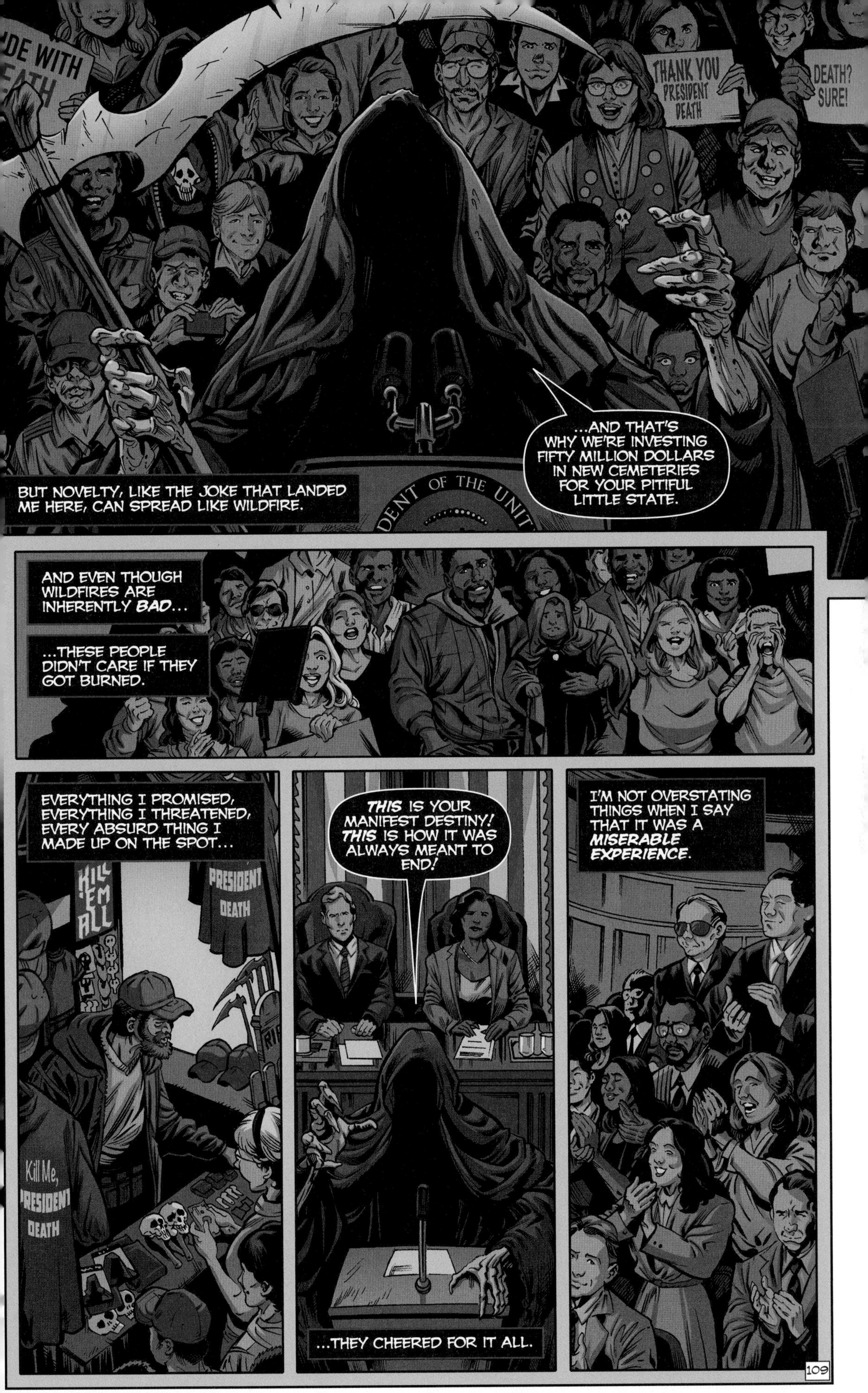
DE WITH
EATH
THANK YOU
PRESIDENT
DEATH
DEATH?
SURE!
...AND THAT'S WHY WE'RE INVESTING FIFTY MILLION DOLLARS IN NEW CEMETERIES FOR YOUR PITIFUL LITTLE STATE.
BUT NOVELTY, LIKE THE JOKE THAT LANDED ME HERE, CAN SPREAD LIKE WILDFIRE.
AND EVEN THOUGH WILDFIRES ARE INHERENTLY *BAD*...
...THESE PEOPLE DIDN'T CARE IF THEY GOT BURNED.
EVERYTHING I PROMISED, EVERYTHING I THREATENED, EVERY ABSURD THING I MADE UP ON THE SPOT...
KILL 'EM ALL
PRESIDENT DEATH
Kill Me, PRESIDENT DEATH
THIS IS YOUR MANIFEST DESTINY! *THIS* IS HOW IT WAS ALWAYS MEANT TO END!
...THEY CHEERED FOR IT ALL.
I'M NOT OVERSTATING THINGS WHEN I SAY THAT IT WAS A *MISERABLE EXPERIENCE*.

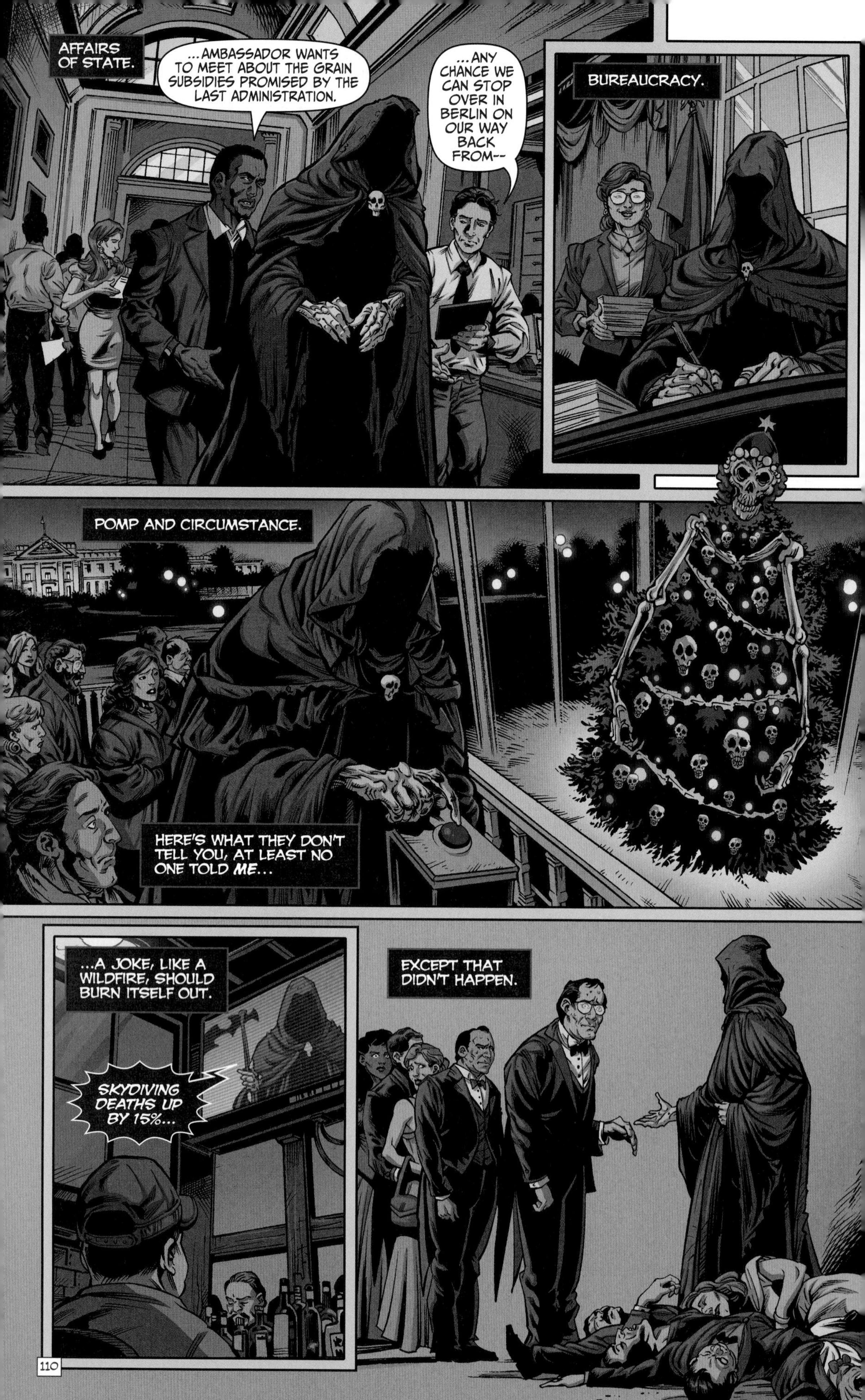
AFFAIRS OF STATE.
...AMBASSADOR WANTS TO MEET ABOUT THE GRAIN SUBSIDIES PROMISED BY THE LAST ADMINISTRATION.
...ANY CHANCE WE CAN STOP OVER IN BERLIN ON OUR WAY BACK FROM--
BUREAUCRACY.
POMP AND CIRCUMSTANCE.
HERE'S WHAT THEY DON'T TELL YOU, AT LEAST NO ONE TOLD *ME*...
...A JOKE, LIKE A WILDFIRE, SHOULD BURN ITSELF OUT.
SKYDIVING DEATHS UP BY 15%...
EXCEPT THAT DIDN'T HAPPEN.

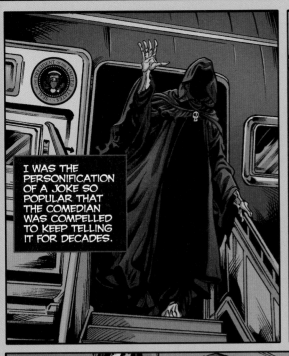

I WAS THE PERSONIFICATION OF A JOKE SO POPULAR THAT THE COMEDIAN WAS COMPELLED TO KEEP TELLING IT FOR DECADES.

IT DIDN'T MATTER THAT THE NOVELTY HAD WORN OFF FOR ME.

THE AUDIENCES STILL SHOWED UP, DEMANDING THE SAME OLD JOKE.

I SUPPOSE IT WASN'T ALL BAD. BUT YOU'RE PROBABLY WONDERING...

THE BOMBING OF BERLIN WAS A HUGE HIT FOR US!

WHY DIDN'T I JUST RESIGN?

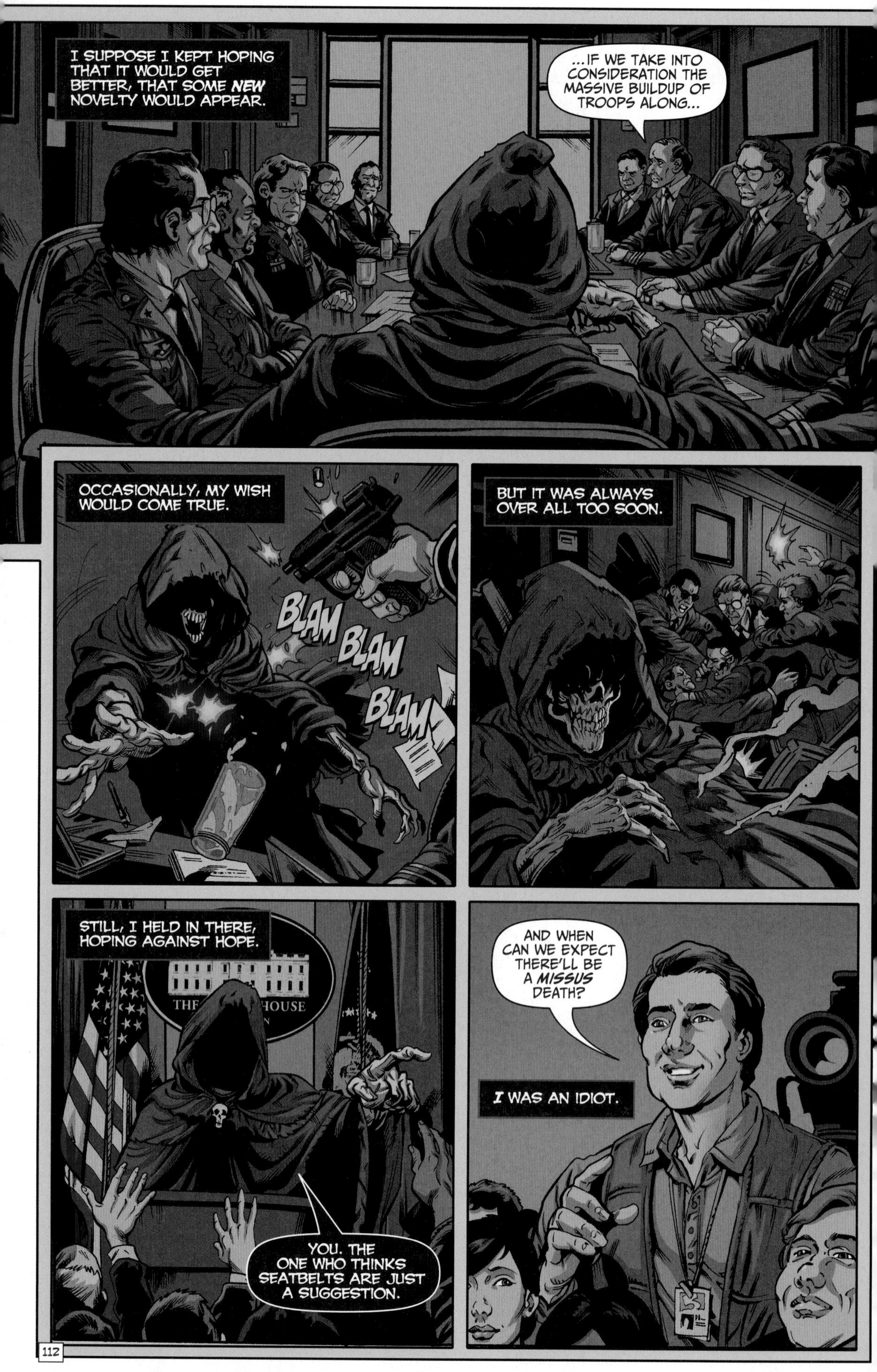
I SUPPOSE I KEPT HOPING THAT IT WOULD GET BETTER, THAT SOME NEW NOVELTY WOULD APPEAR.
...IF WE TAKE INTO CONSIDERATION THE MASSIVE BUILDUP OF TROOPS ALONG...
OCCASIONALLY, MY WISH WOULD COME TRUE.
BLAM BLAM BLAM
BUT IT WAS ALWAYS OVER ALL TOO SOON.
STILL, I HELD IN THERE, HOPING AGAINST HOPE.
YOU. THE ONE WHO THINKS SEATBELTS ARE JUST A SUGGESTION.
AND WHEN CAN WE EXPECT THERE'LL BE A MISSUS DEATH?
I WAS AN IDIOT.

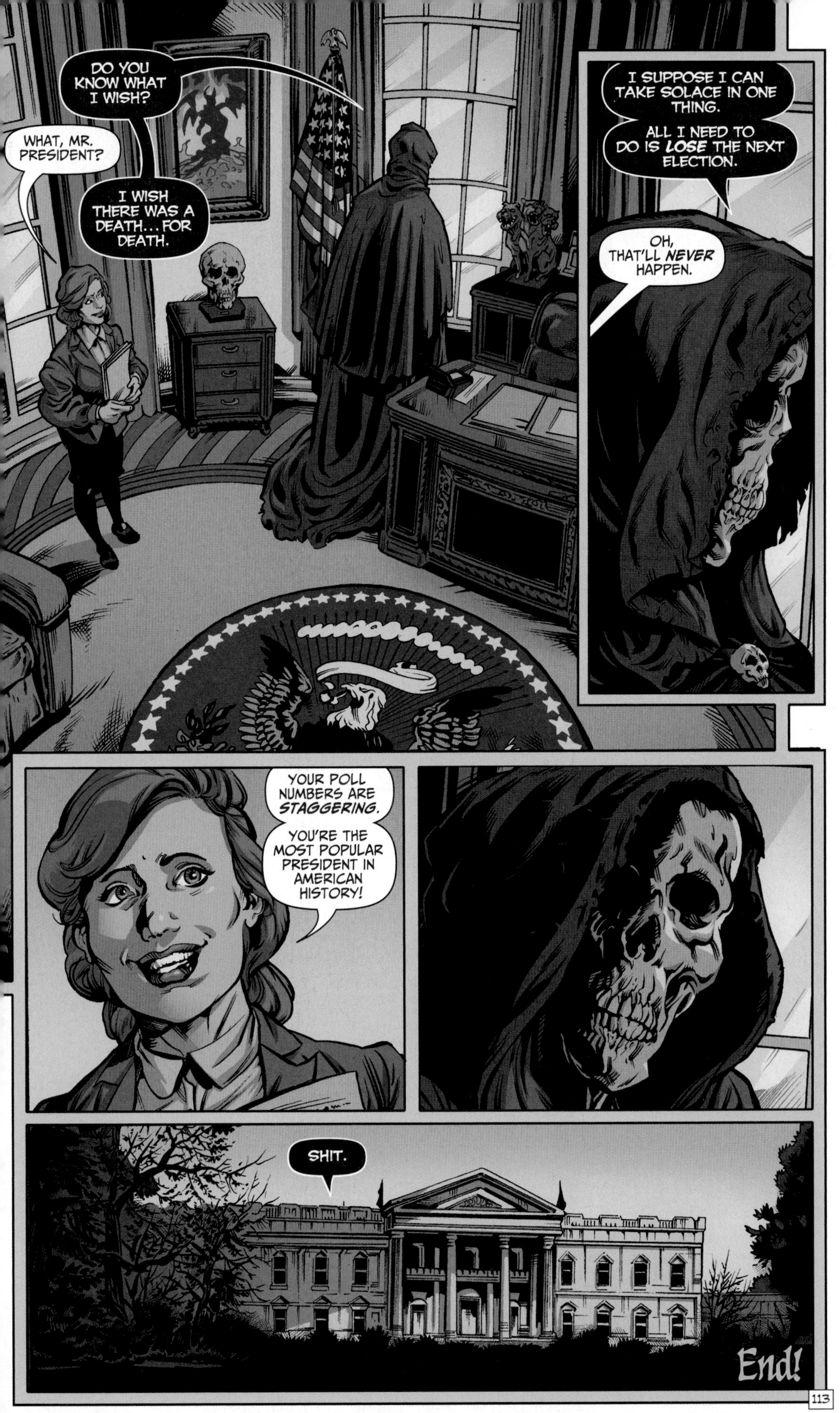
DO YOU KNOW WHAT I WISH?
WHAT, MR. PRESIDENT?
I WISH THERE WAS A DEATH... FOR DEATH.
I SUPPOSE I CAN TAKE SOLACE IN ONE THING.
ALL I NEED TO DO IS *LOSE* THE NEXT ELECTION.
OH, THAT'LL *NEVER* HAPPEN.
YOUR POLL NUMBERS ARE *STAGGERING*.
YOU'RE THE MOST POPULAR PRESIDENT IN AMERICAN HISTORY!
SHIT.
End!

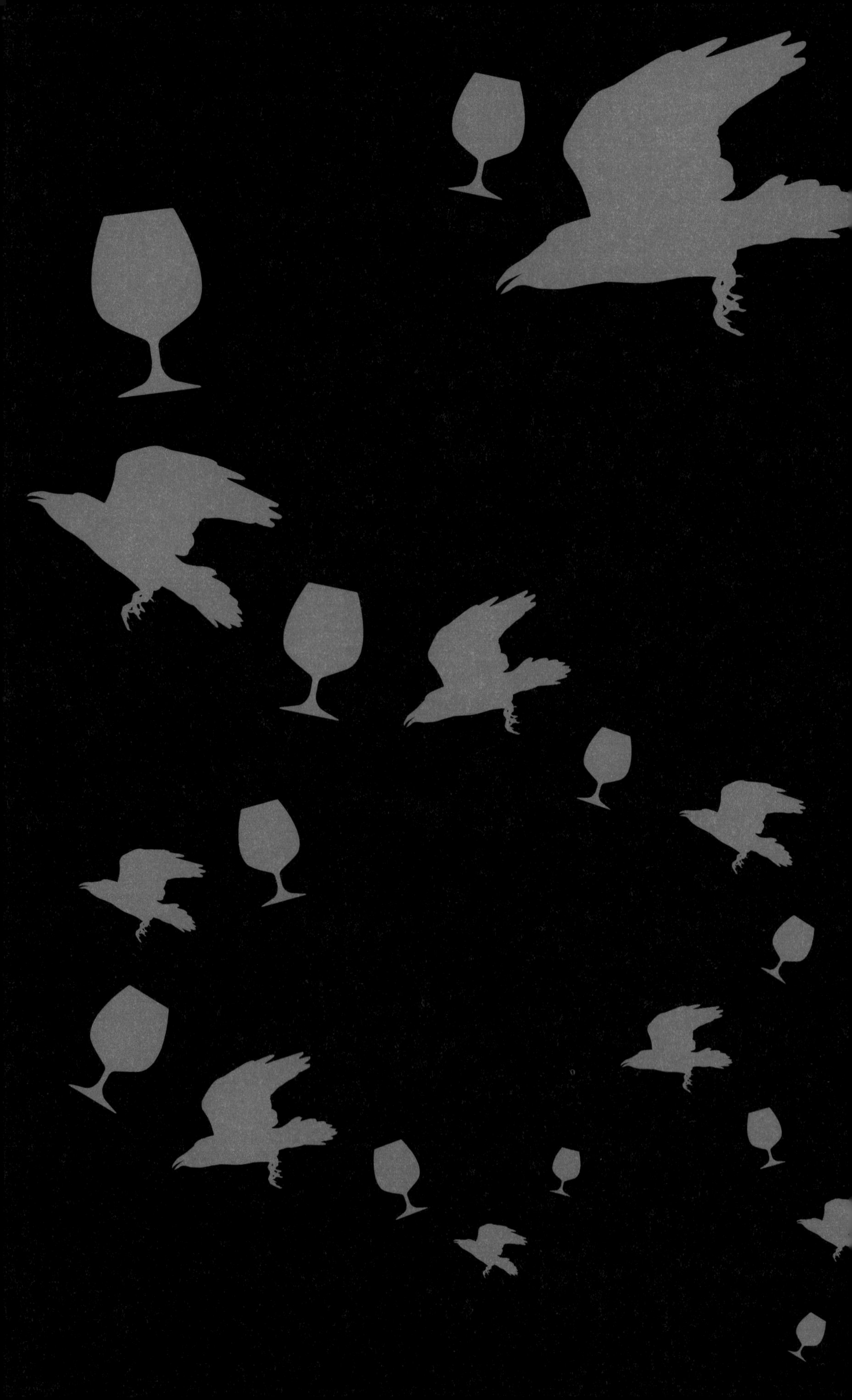

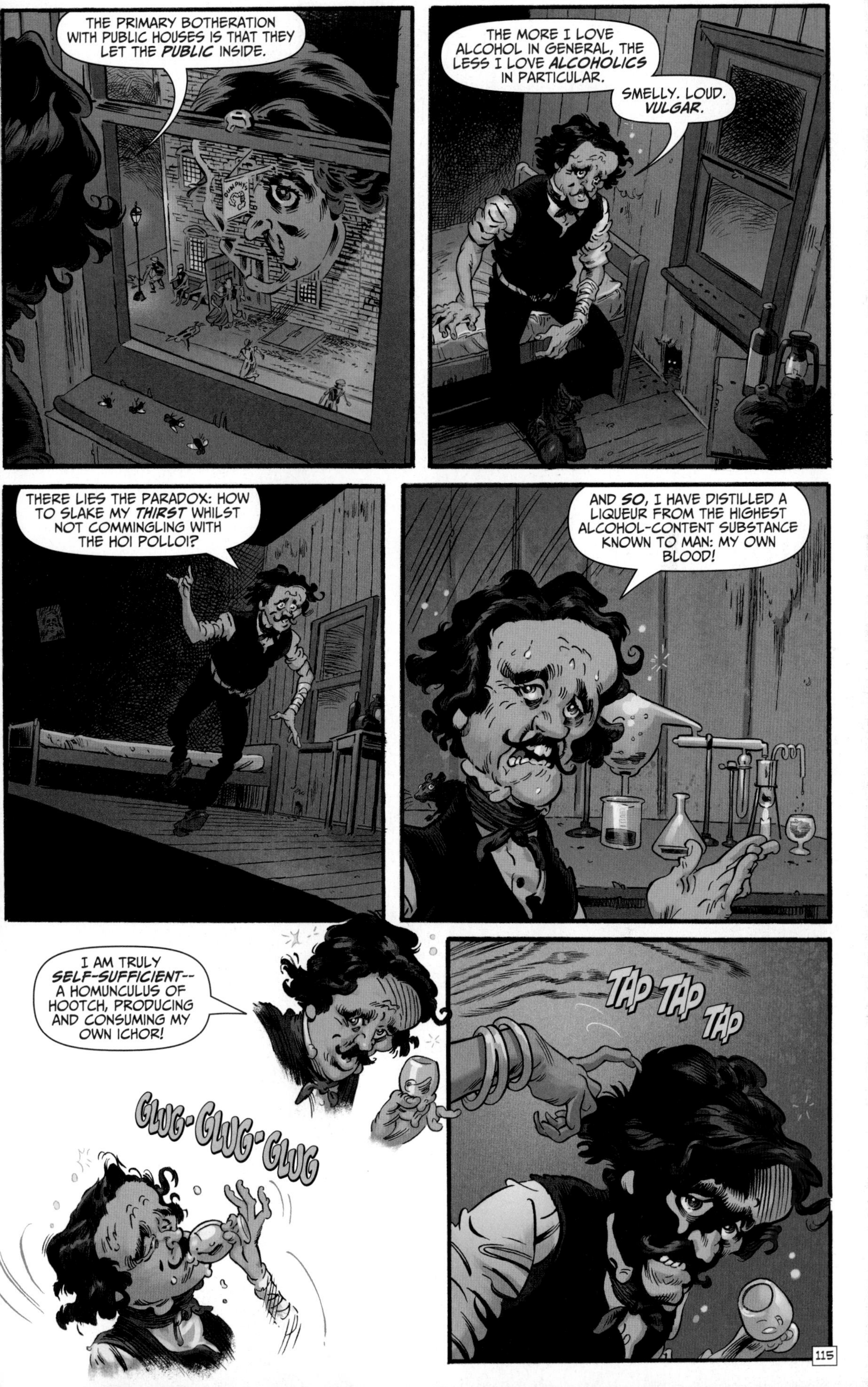

THE PRIMARY BOTHERATION WITH PUBLIC HOUSES IS THAT THEY LET THE *PUBLIC* INSIDE.
DUMPHY'S
THE MORE I LOVE ALCOHOL IN GENERAL, THE LESS I LOVE *ALCOHOLICS* IN PARTICULAR.
SMELLY. LOUD. *VULGAR*.
THERE LIES THE PARADOX: HOW TO SLAKE MY *THIRST* WHILST NOT COMMINGLING WITH THE HOI POLLOI?
AND *SO*, I HAVE DISTILLED A LIQUEUR FROM THE HIGHEST ALCOHOL-CONTENT SUBSTANCE KNOWN TO MAN: MY OWN BLOOD!
I AM TRULY *SELF-SUFFICIENT*--A HOMUNCULUS OF HOOTCH, PRODUCING AND CONSUMING MY OWN ICHOR!
TAP TAP TAP
GLUG-GLUG-GLUG

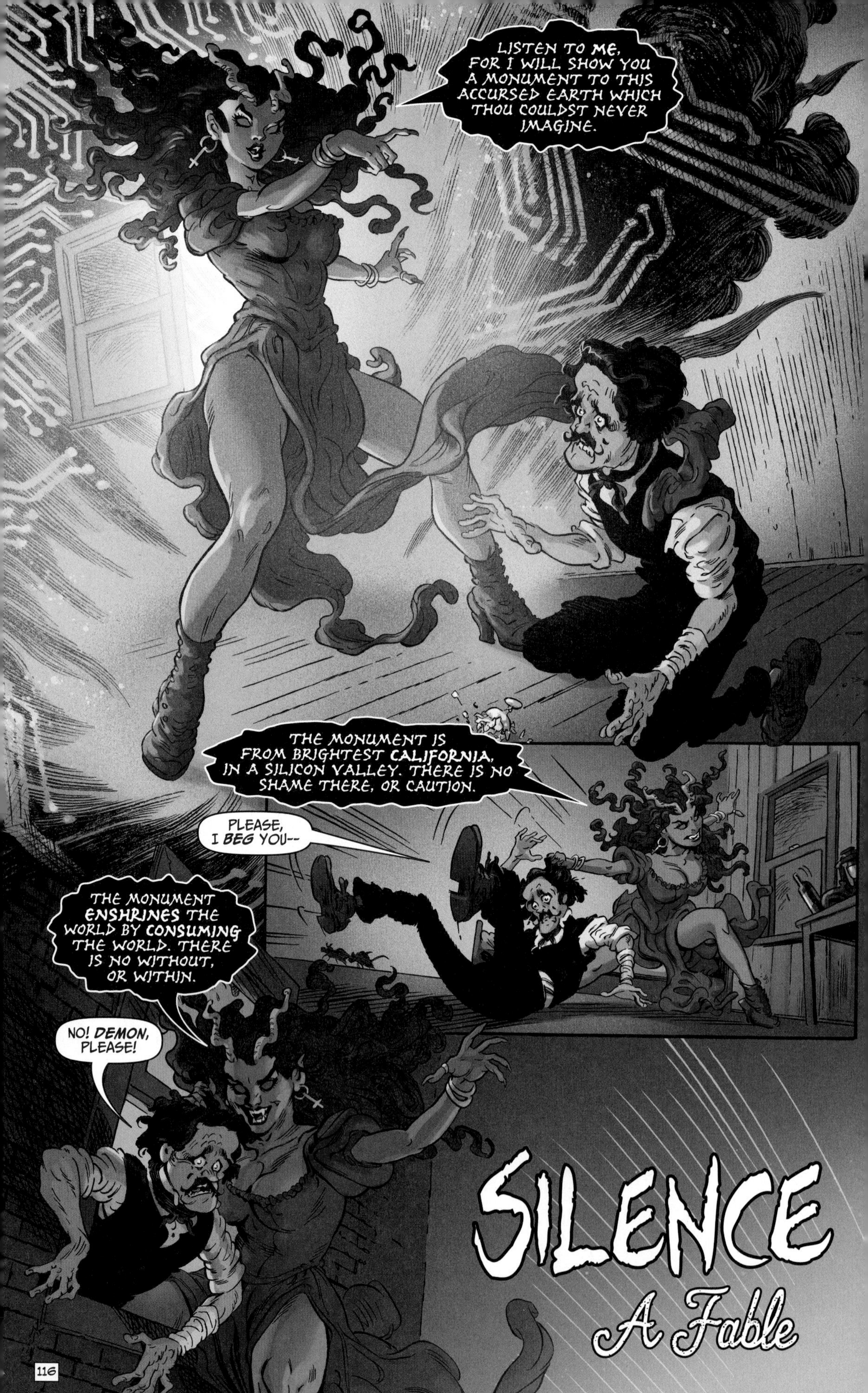
LISTEN TO ME, FOR I WILL SHOW YOU A MONUMENT TO THIS ACCURSED EARTH WHICH THOU COULDST NEVER IMAGINE.
THE MONUMENT IS FROM BRIGHTEST CALIFORNIA, IN A SILICON VALLEY. THERE IS NO SHAME THERE, OR CAUTION.
PLEASE, I BEG YOU--
THE MONUMENT ENSHRINES THE WORLD BY CONSUMING THE WORLD. THERE IS NO WITHOUT, OR WITHIN.
NO! DEMON, PLEASE!
SILENCE
A Fable

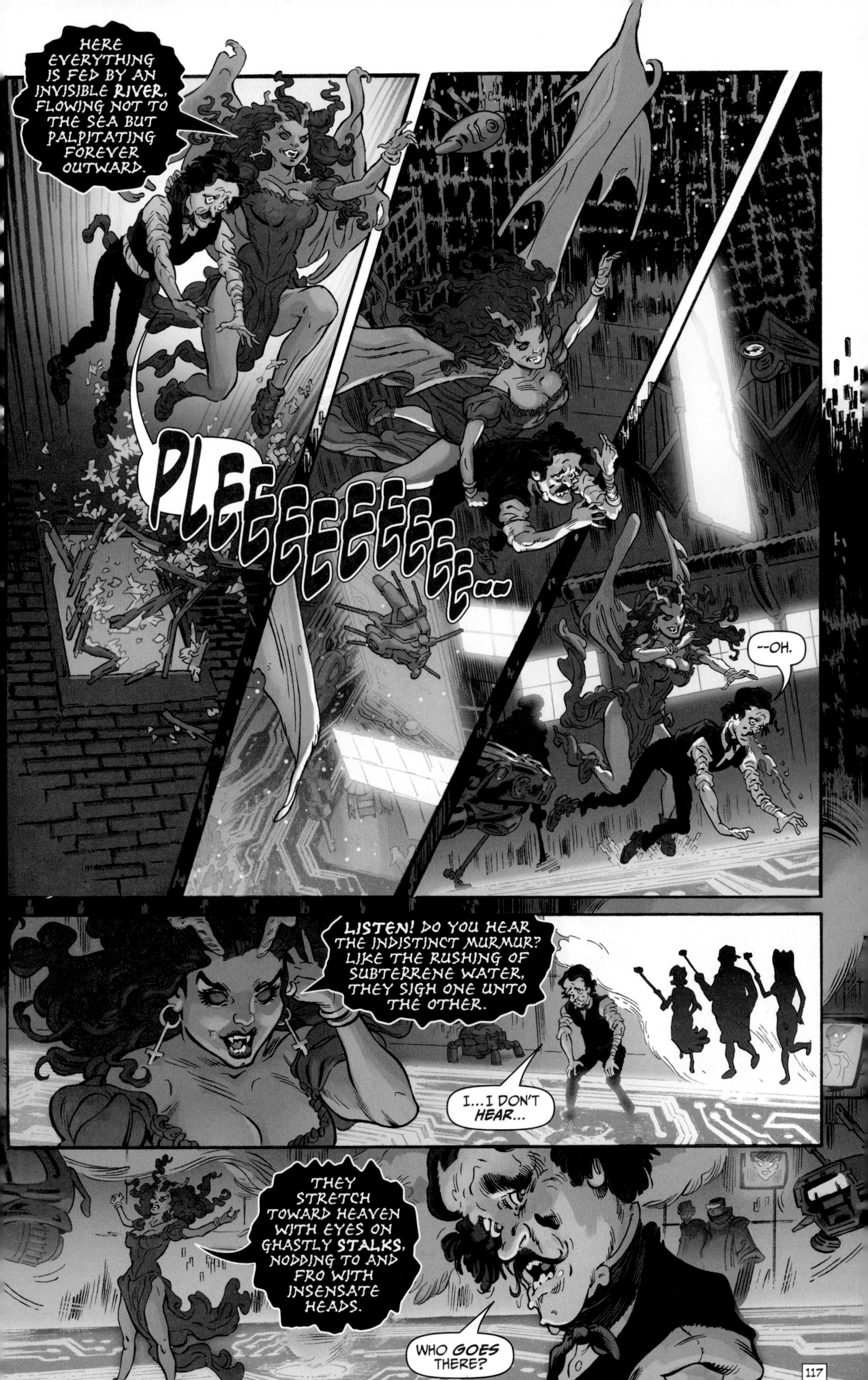
HERE EVERYTHING IS FED BY AN INVISIBLE RIVER, FLOWING NOT TO THE SEA BUT PALPITATING FOREVER OUTWARD.
PLEEEEEEEEEE...
--OH.
LISTEN! DO YOU HEAR THE INDISTINCT MURMUR? LIKE THE RUSHING OF SUBTERRENE WATER, THEY SIGH ONE UNTO THE OTHER.
I...I DON'T HEAR...
THEY STRETCH TOWARD HEAVEN WITH EYES ON GHASTLY STALKS, NODDING TO AND FRO WITH INSENSATE HEADS.
WHO GOES THERE?

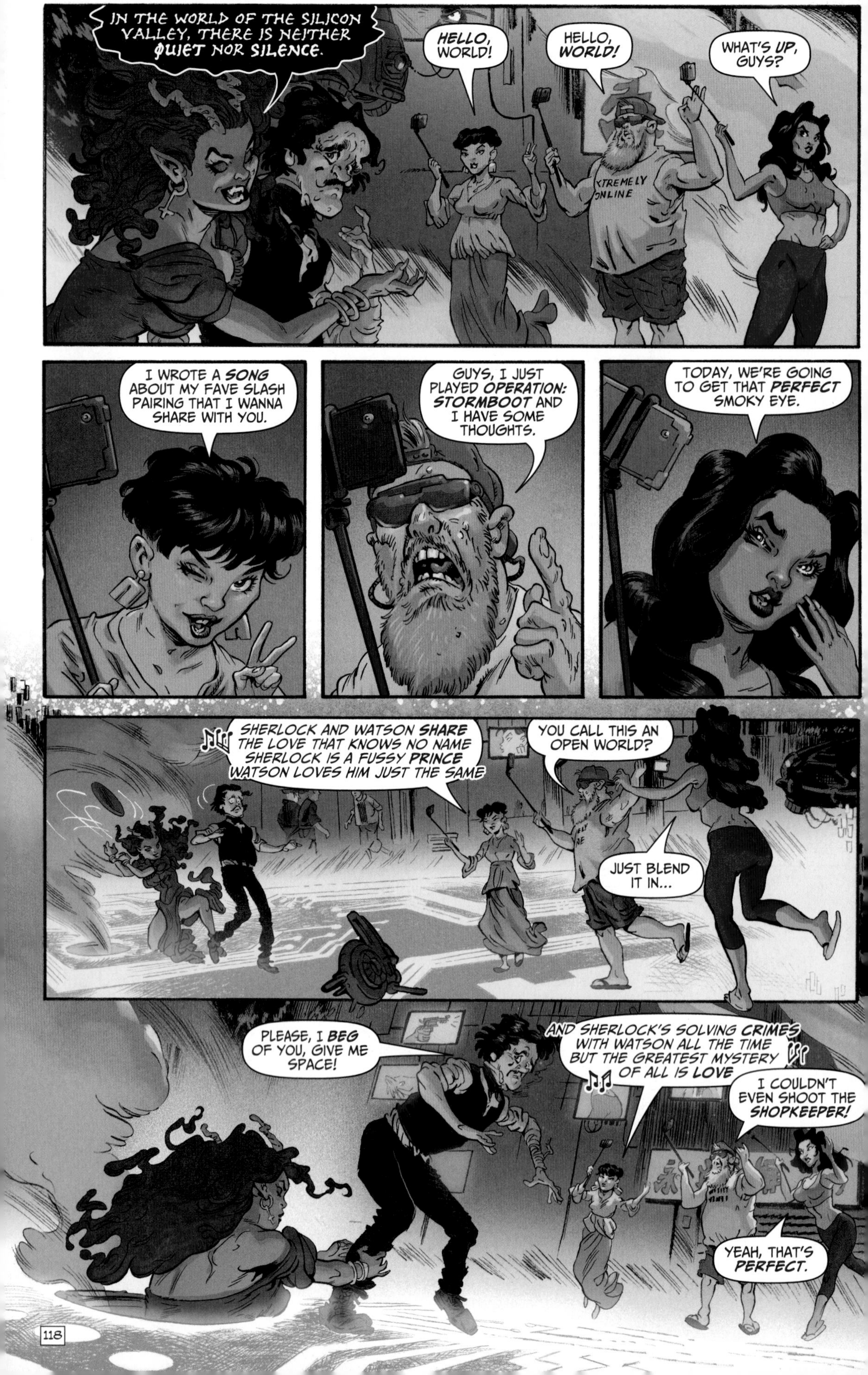
IN THE WORLD OF THE SILICON VALLEY, THERE IS NEITHER QUIET NOR SILENCE.
HELLO, WORLD!
HELLO, WORLD!
WHAT'S UP, GUYS?
XTREMELY ONLINE
I WROTE A SONG ABOUT MY FAVE SLASH PAIRING THAT I WANNA SHARE WITH YOU.
GUYS, I JUST PLAYED OPERATION: STORMBOOT AND I HAVE SOME THOUGHTS.
TODAY, WE'RE GOING TO GET THAT PERFECT SMOKY EYE.
SHERLOCK AND WATSON SHARE THE LOVE THAT KNOWS NO NAME SHERLOCK IS A FUSSY PRINCE WATSON LOVES HIM JUST THE SAME
YOU CALL THIS AN OPEN WORLD?
JUST BLEND IT IN...
PLEASE, I BEG OF YOU, GIVE ME SPACE!
AND SHERLOCK'S SOLVING CRIMES WITH WATSON ALL THE TIME BUT THE GREATEST MYSTERY OF ALL IS LOVE
I COULDN'T EVEN SHOOT THE SHOPKEEPER!
YEAH, THAT'S PERFECT.

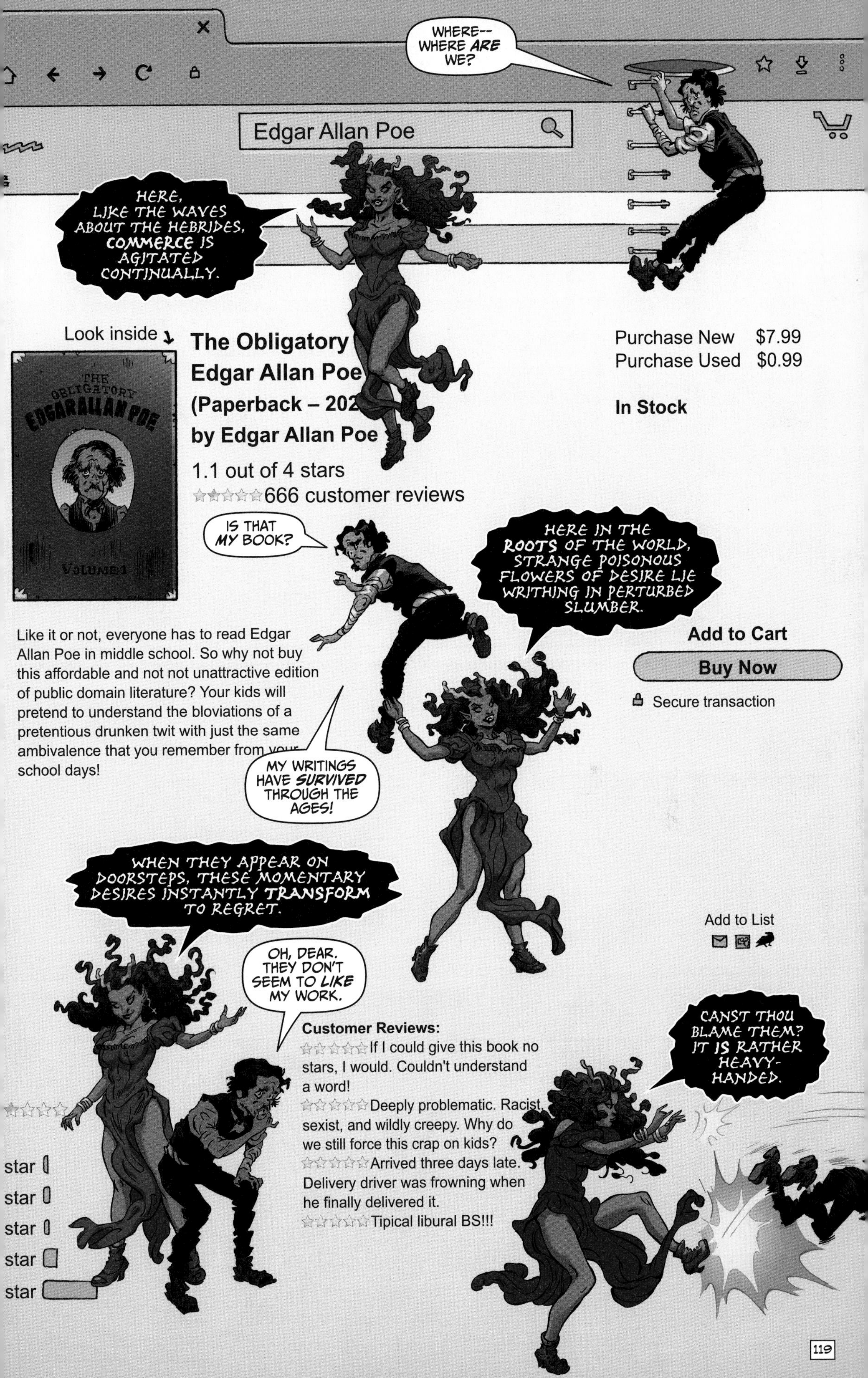

WHERE-- WHERE ARE WE?
Edgar Allan Poe
HERE, LIKE THE WAVES ABOUT THE HEBRIDES, COMMERCE IS AGITATED CONTINUALLY.
Look inside
THE OBLIGATORY EDGAR ALLAN POE VOLUME 1
The Obligatory Edgar Allan Poe (Paperback – 202
by Edgar Allan Poe
1.1 out of 4 stars
666 customer reviews
Purchase New $7.99
Purchase Used $0.99
In Stock
IS THAT MY BOOK?
HERE IN THE ROOTS OF THE WORLD, STRANGE POISONOUS FLOWERS OF DESIRE LIE WRITHING IN PERTURBED SLUMBER.
Like it or not, everyone has to read Edgar Allan Poe in middle school. So why not buy this affordable and not not unattractive edition of public domain literature? Your kids will pretend to understand the bloviations of a pretentious drunken twit with just the same ambivalence that you remember from your school days!
Add to Cart
Buy Now
Secure transaction
MY WRITINGS HAVE SURVIVED THROUGH THE AGES!
WHEN THEY APPEAR ON DOORSTEPS, THESE MOMENTARY DESIRES INSTANTLY TRANSFORM TO REGRET.
Add to List
OH, DEAR. THEY DON'T SEEM TO LIKE MY WORK.
Customer Reviews:
If I could give this book no stars, I would. Couldn't understand a word!
Deeply problematic. Racist, sexist, and wildly creepy. Why do we still force this crap on kids?
Arrived three days late. Delivery driver was frowning when he finally delivered it.
Tipical libural BS!!!
CANST THOU BLAME THEM? IT IS RATHER HEAVY-HANDED.
star
star
star
star
star

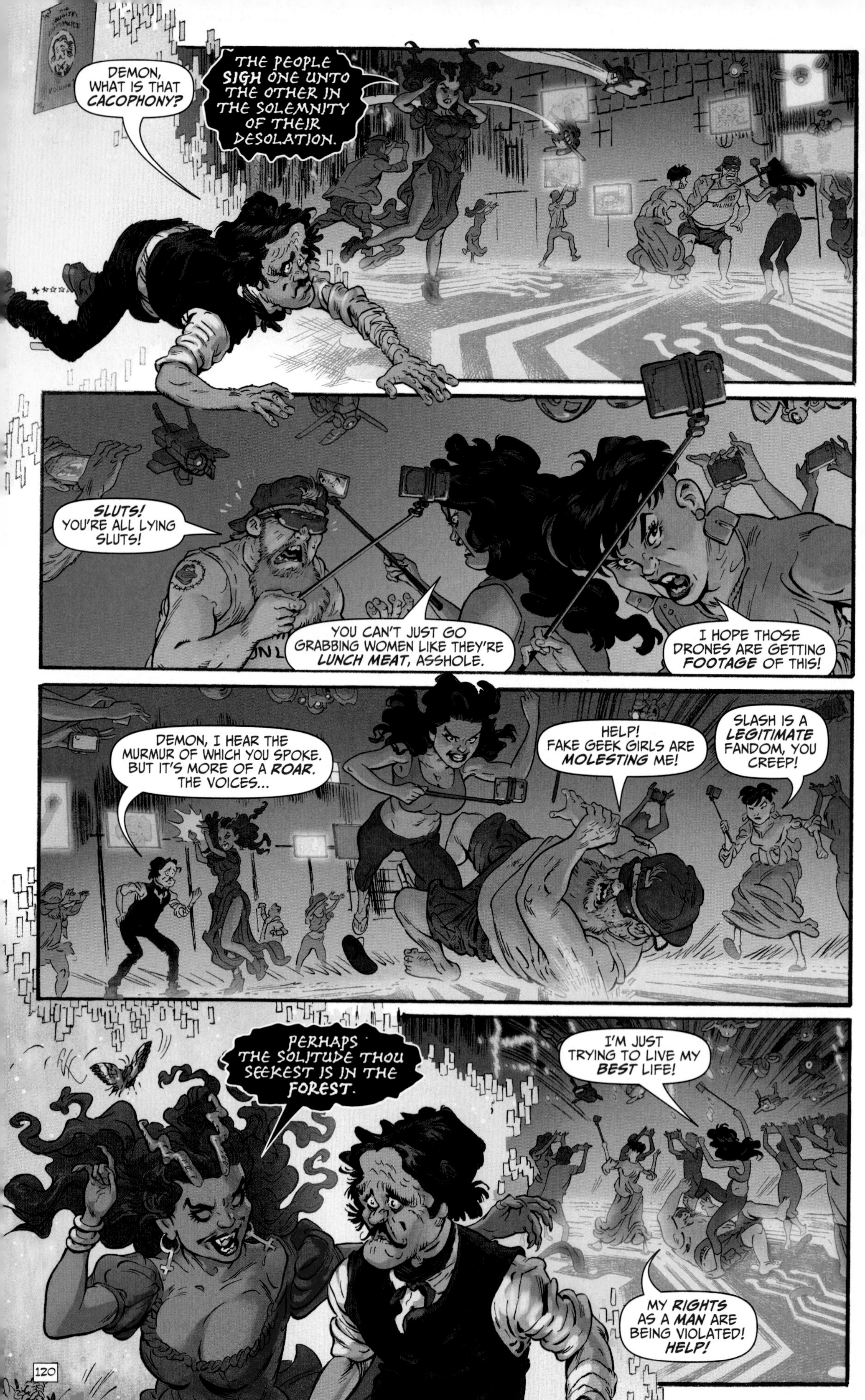
DEMON, WHAT IS THAT CACOPHONY?
THE PEOPLE SIGH ONE UNTO THE OTHER IN THE SOLEMNITY OF THEIR DESOLATION.
SLUTS! YOU'RE ALL LYING SLUTS!
YOU CAN'T JUST GO GRABBING WOMEN LIKE THEY'RE LUNCH MEAT, ASSHOLE.
I HOPE THOSE DRONES ARE GETTING FOOTAGE OF THIS!
DEMON, I HEAR THE MURMUR OF WHICH YOU SPOKE. BUT IT'S MORE OF A ROAR. THE VOICES...
HELP! FAKE GEEK GIRLS ARE MOLESTING ME!
SLASH IS A LEGITIMATE FANDOM, YOU CREEP!
PERHAPS THE SOLITUDE THOU SEEKEST IS IN THE FOREST.
I'M JUST TRYING TO LIVE MY BEST LIFE!
MY RIGHTS AS A MAN ARE BEING VIOLATED! HELP!

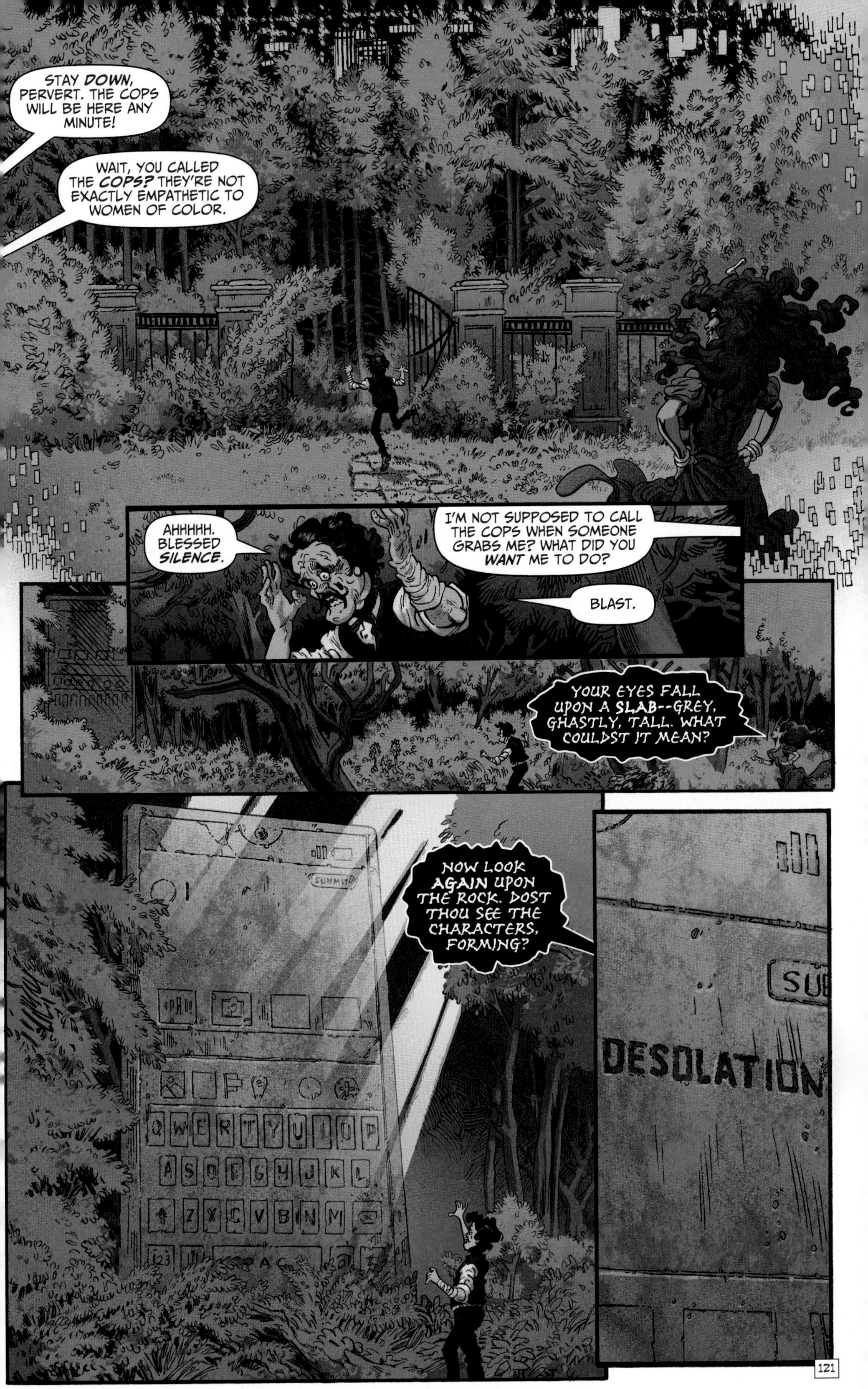
STAY DOWN, PERVERT. THE COPS WILL BE HERE ANY MINUTE!
WAIT, YOU CALLED THE COPS? THEY'RE NOT EXACTLY EMPATHETIC TO WOMEN OF COLOR.
AHHHHH. BLESSED SILENCE.
I'M NOT SUPPOSED TO CALL THE COPS WHEN SOMEONE GRABS ME? WHAT DID YOU WANT ME TO DO?
BLAST.
YOUR EYES FALL UPON A SLAB--GREY, GHASTLY, TALL. WHAT COULDST IT MEAN?
SUBMIT
QWERTYUIOP
ASDFGHJKL
ZXCVBNM
123
NOW LOOK AGAIN UPON THE ROCK. DOST THOU SEE THE CHARACTERS, FORMING?
SU
DESOLATION

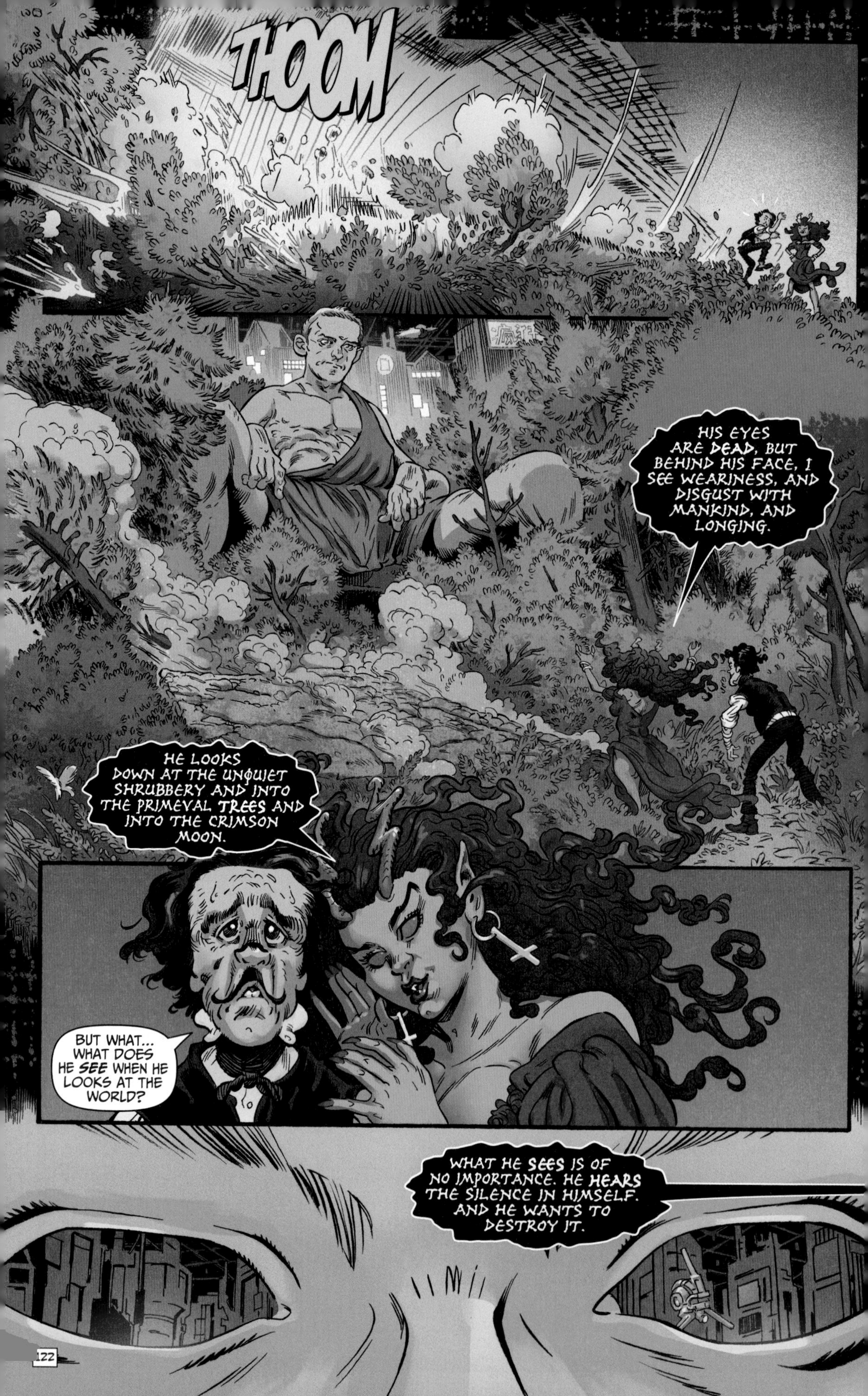
THOOM
HIS EYES ARE DEAD, BUT BEHIND HIS FACE, I SEE WEARINESS, AND DISGUST WITH MANKIND, AND LONGING.
HE LOOKS DOWN AT THE UNQUIET SHRUBBERY AND INTO THE PRIMEVAL TREES AND INTO THE CRIMSON MOON.
BUT WHAT... WHAT DOES HE SEE WHEN HE LOOKS AT THE WORLD?
WHAT HE SEES IS OF NO IMPORTANCE. HE HEARS THE SILENCE IN HIMSELF. AND HE WANTS TO DESTROY IT.

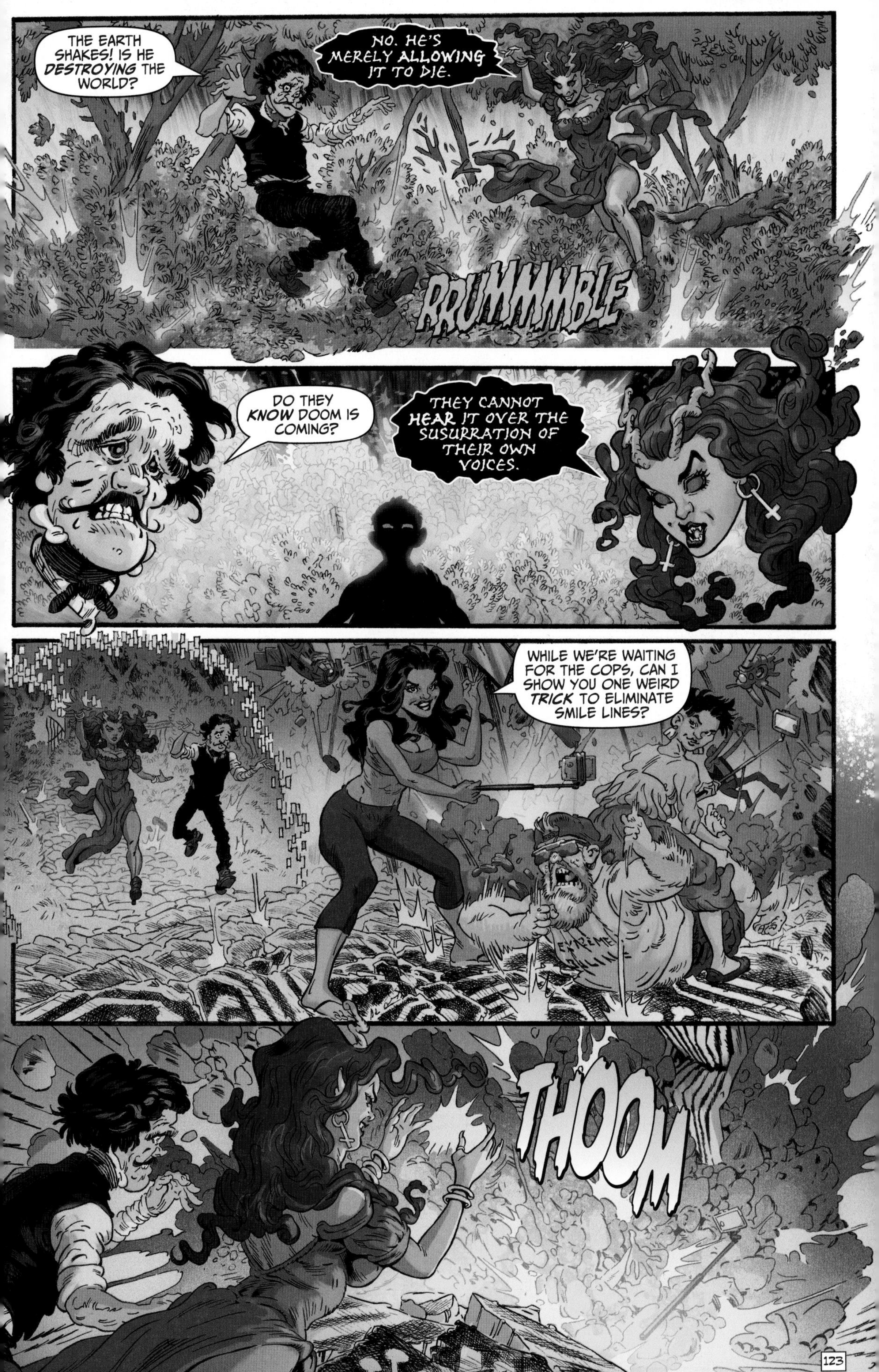
THE EARTH SHAKES! IS HE DESTROYING THE WORLD?
NO. HE'S MERELY ALLOWING IT TO DIE.
RRUMMMBLE
DO THEY KNOW DOOM IS COMING?
THEY CANNOT HEAR IT OVER THE SUSURRATION OF THEIR OWN VOICES.
WHILE WE'RE WAITING FOR THE COPS, CAN I SHOW YOU ONE WEIRD TRICK TO ELIMINATE SMILE LINES?
EXTREME
THOOM

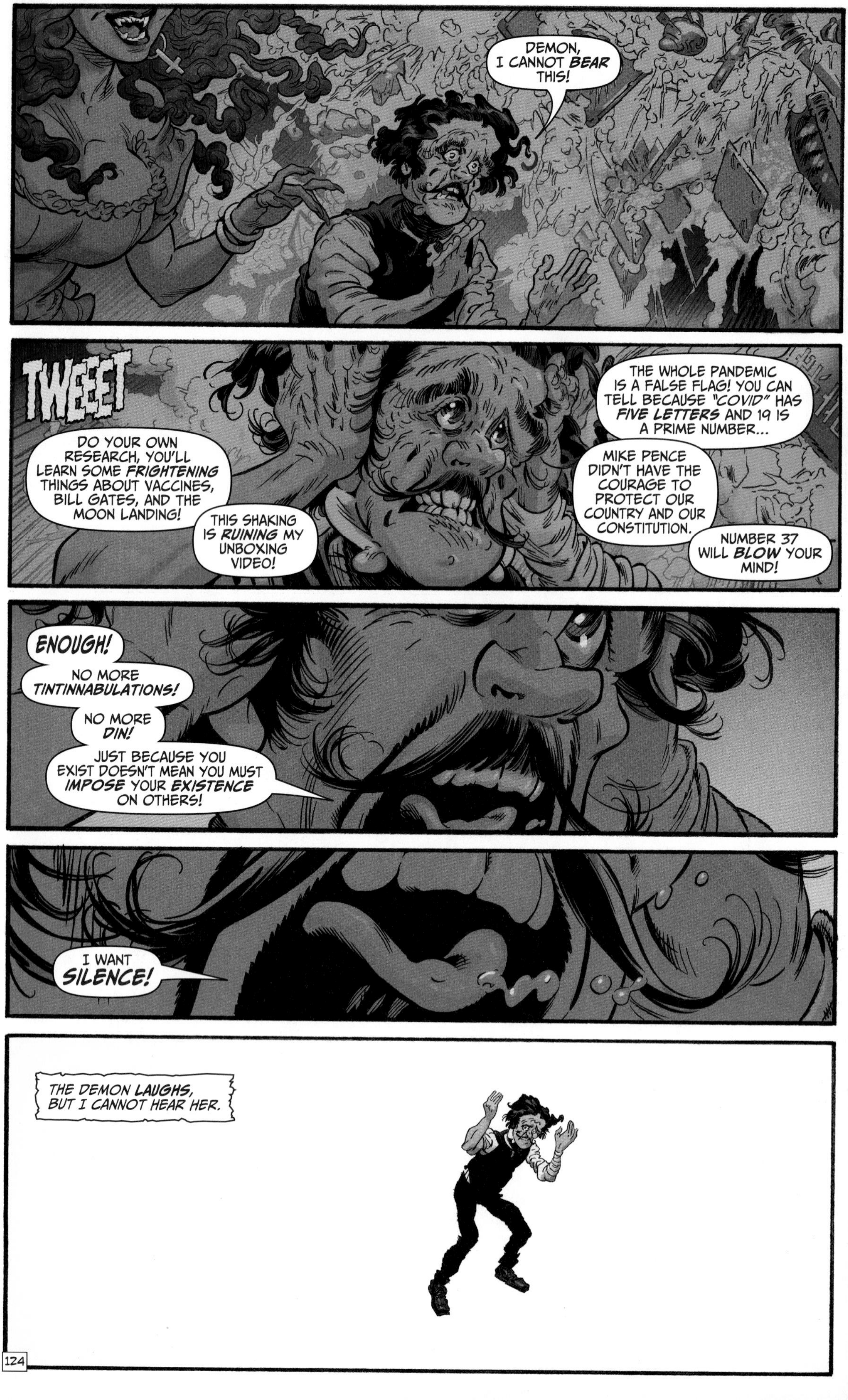
DEMON, I CANNOT BEAR THIS!
TWEEET
DO YOUR OWN RESEARCH, YOU'LL LEARN SOME FRIGHTENING THINGS ABOUT VACCINES, BILL GATES, AND THE MOON LANDING!
THIS SHAKING IS RUINING MY UNBOXING VIDEO!
THE WHOLE PANDEMIC IS A FALSE FLAG! YOU CAN TELL BECAUSE "COVID" HAS FIVE LETTERS AND 19 IS A PRIME NUMBER...
MIKE PENCE DIDN'T HAVE THE COURAGE TO PROTECT OUR COUNTRY AND OUR CONSTITUTION.
NUMBER 37 WILL BLOW YOUR MIND!
ENOUGH!
NO MORE TINTINNABULATIONS!
NO MORE DIN!
JUST BECAUSE YOU EXIST DOESN'T MEAN YOU MUST IMPOSE YOUR EXISTENCE ON OTHERS!
I WANT SILENCE!
THE DEMON LAUGHS, BUT I CANNOT HEAR HER.

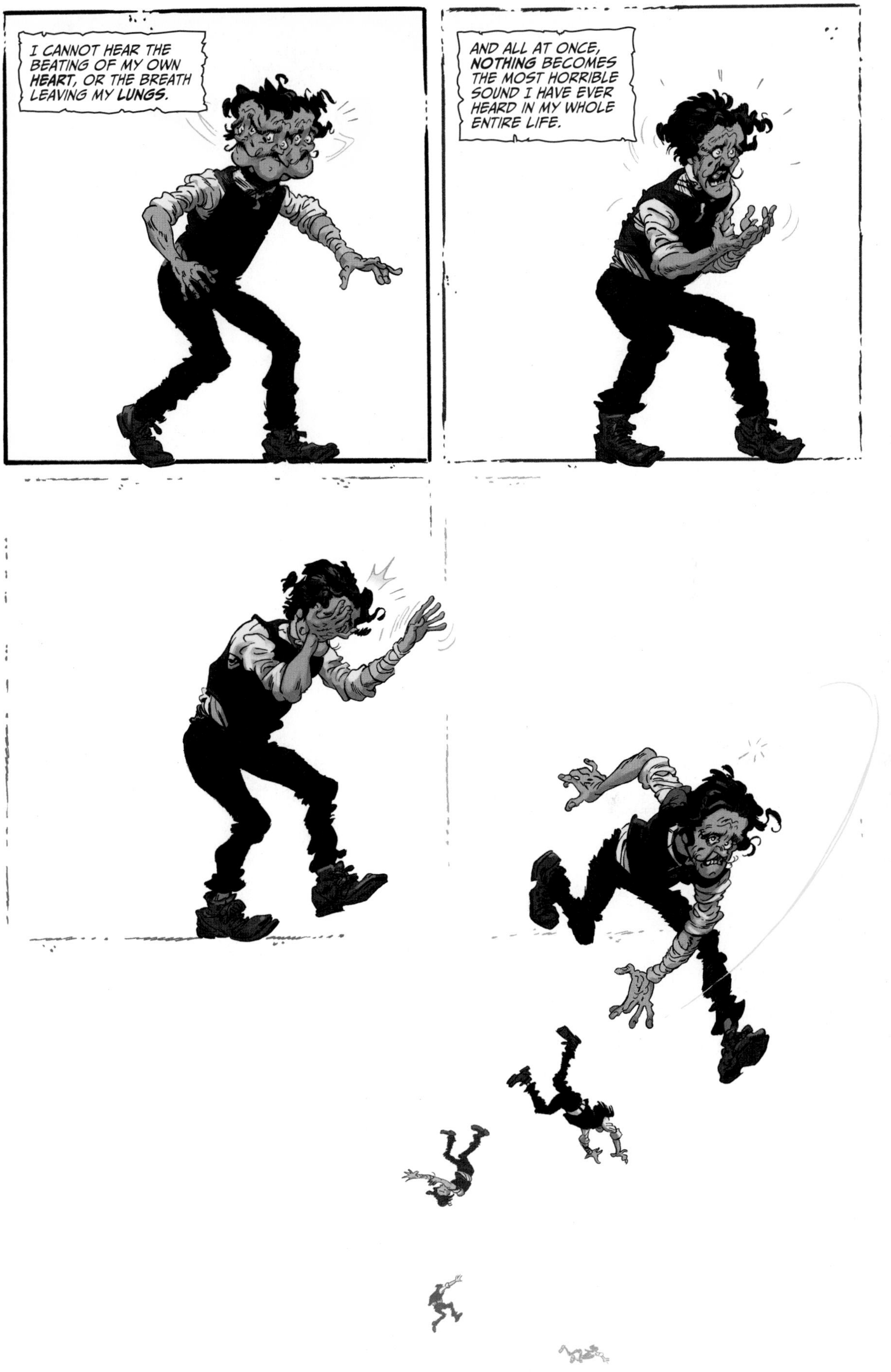
I CANNOT HEAR THE BEATING OF MY OWN **HEART**, OR THE BREATH LEAVING MY **LUNGS**.
AND ALL AT ONCE, **NOTHING** BECOMES THE MOST HORRIBLE SOUND I HAVE EVER HEARD IN MY WHOLE ENTIRE LIFE.

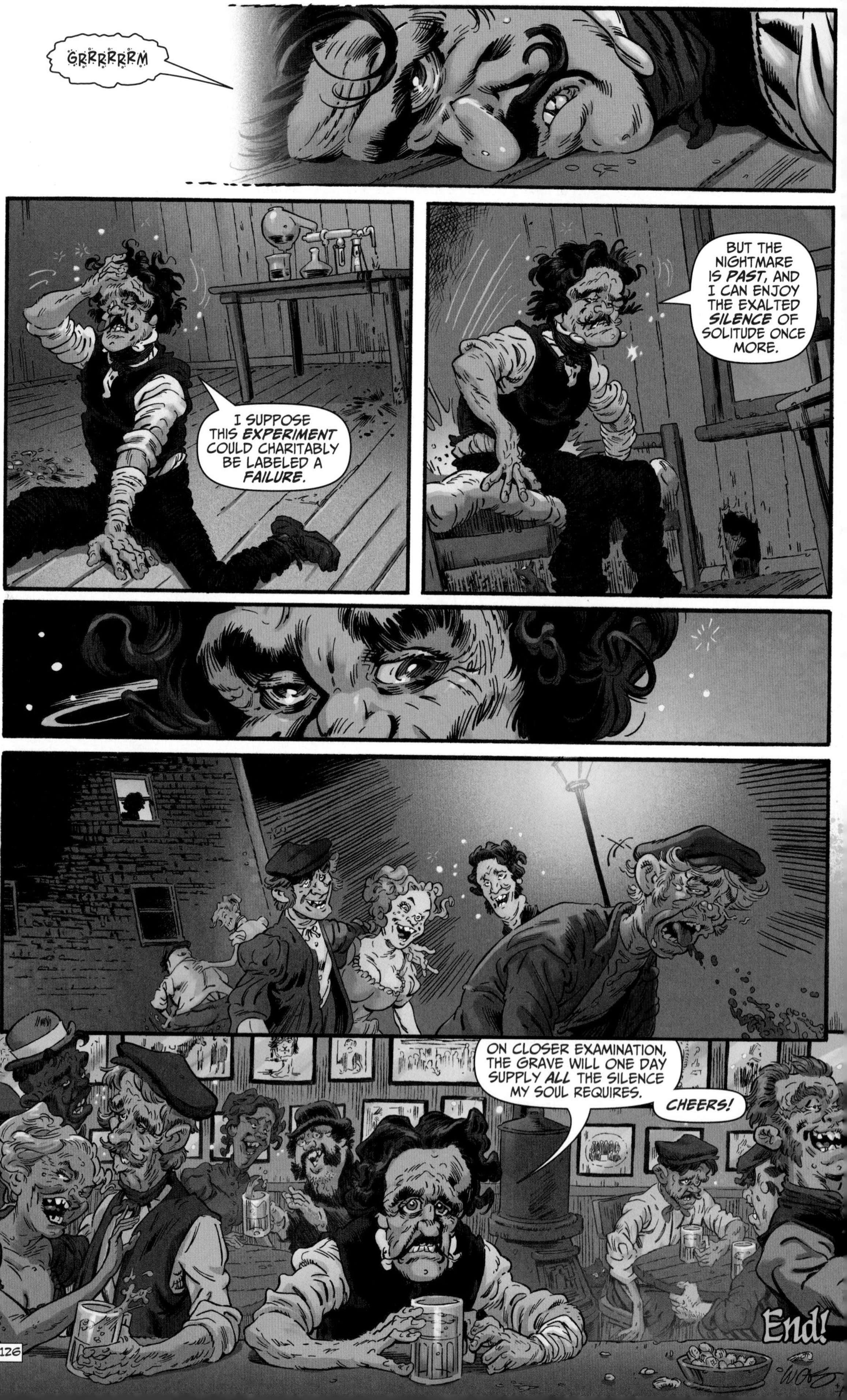
GRRRRRRM
I SUPPOSE THIS EXPERIMENT COULD CHARITABLY BE LABELED A FAILURE.
BUT THE NIGHTMARE IS PAST, AND I CAN ENJOY THE EXALTED SILENCE OF SOLITUDE ONCE MORE.
ON CLOSER EXAMINATION, THE GRAVE WILL ONE DAY SUPPLY ALL THE SILENCE MY SOUL REQUIRES.
CHEERS!
End!

As a teenager I devoured the stories of Edgar Allan Poe, but when I came to "The Sphinx" I remember being decidedly put off. How could someone mistake an object very close for one very far away? This seemed unlikely on a simple ocular level, and my teenage mind rebelled. I had failed, of course, to recognize the author's mastery of the depiction of *fear* and how, in its most drastic form, it can distort our perception of physical reality. The fear in this story is of the cholera plague that ravaged New York in 1832, driving the protagonist, a self-described "nervous" type, to a refuge north of the city. I felt an obvious parallel to today's "plague," Covid-19, and people's varying reactions to the prospect of total quarantine. And so the "monster" becomes a giant version of the virus itself, and the difference in scale is even more extreme than in the original.

— **RICK GEARY**

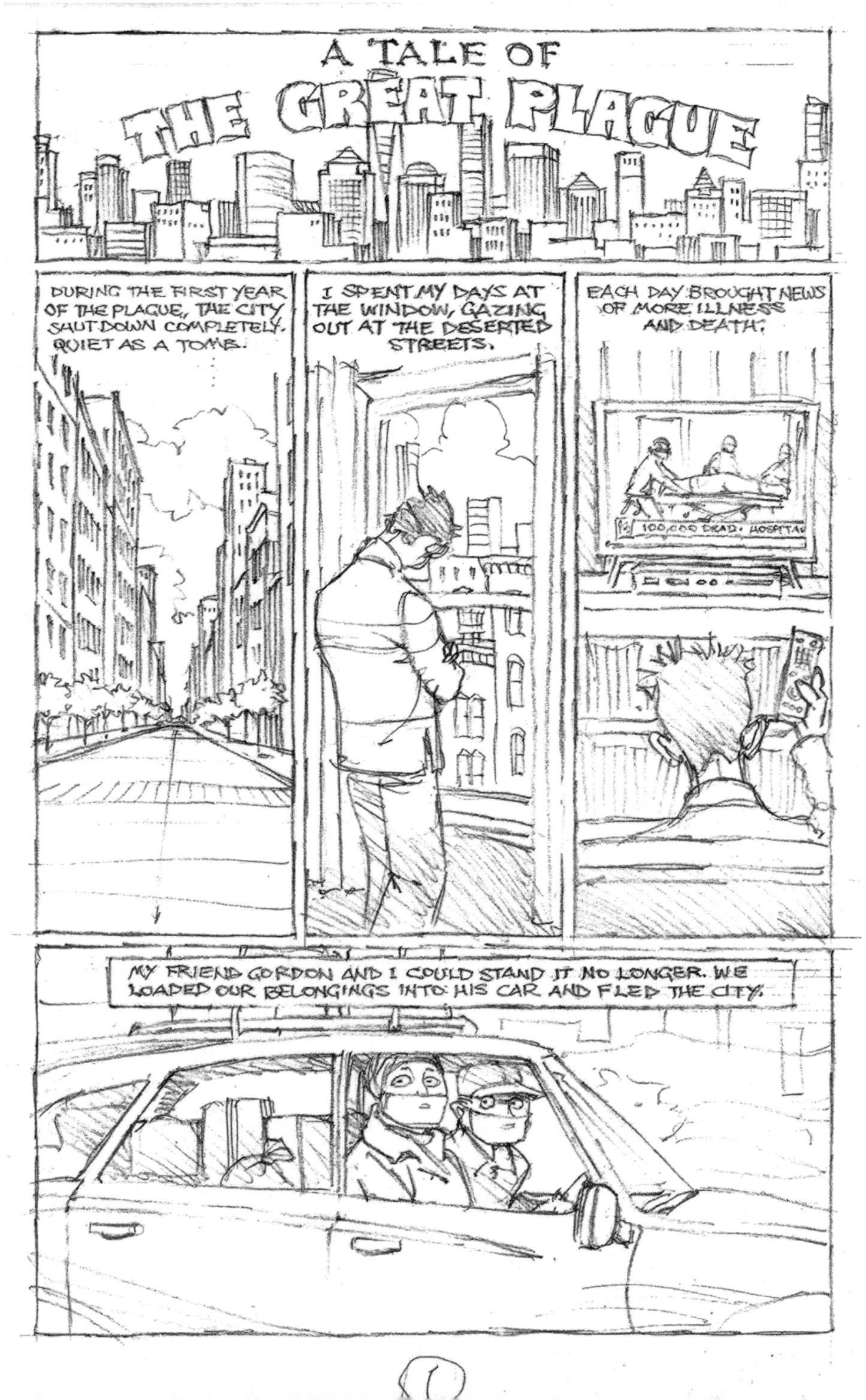
A TALE OF
THE GREAT PLAGUE
DURING THE FIRST YEAR OF THE PLAGUE, THE CITY SHUT DOWN COMPLETELY. QUIET AS A TOMB.
I SPENT MY DAYS AT THE WINDOW, GAZING OUT AT THE DESERTED STREETS.
EACH DAY BROUGHT NEWS OF MORE ILLNESS AND DEATH.
100,000 DEAD. HOSPITA
MY FRIEND GORDON AND I COULD STAND IT NO LONGER. WE LOADED OUR BELONGINGS INTO HIS CAR AND FLED THE CITY.
1

"A TALE OF THE GREAT PLAGUE," Pages 2-5 pencil art by Rick Geary

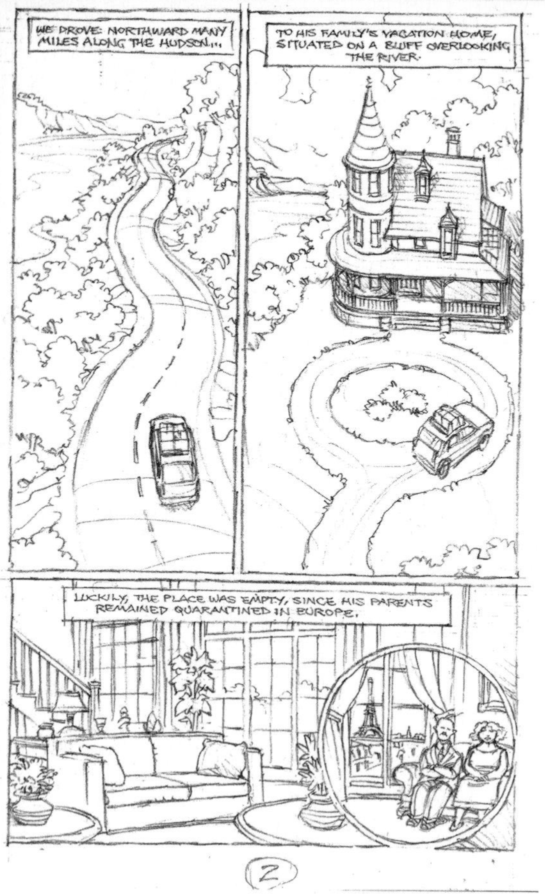

WE DROVE NORTHWARD MANY MILES ALONG THE HUDSON...
TO HIS FAMILY'S VACATION HOME, SITUATED ON A BLUFF OVERLOOKING THE RIVER.
LUCKILY, THE PLACE WAS EMPTY, SINCE HIS PARENTS REMAINED QUARANTINED IN EUROPE.
2

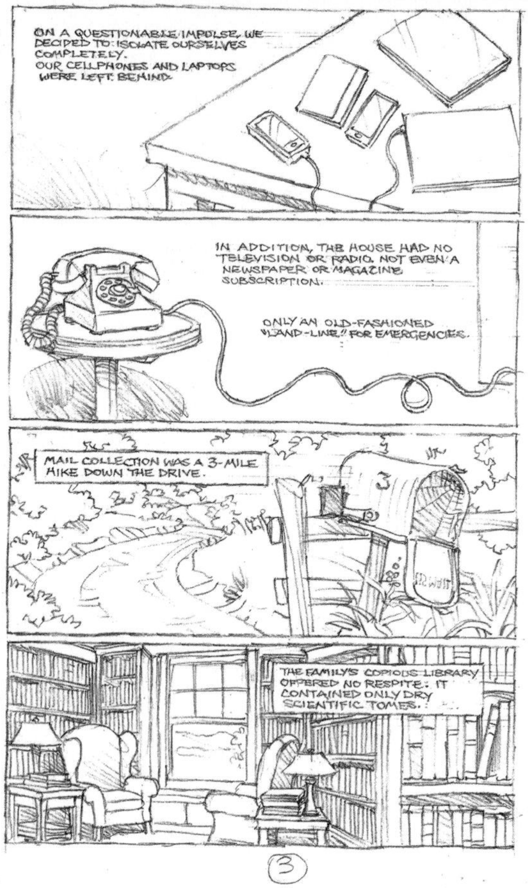

ON A QUESTIONABLE IMPULSE, WE DECIDED TO ISOLATE OURSELVES COMPLETELY. OUR CELLPHONES AND LAPTOPS WERE LEFT BEHIND.
IN ADDITION, THE HOUSE HAD NO TELEVISION OR RADIO. NOT EVEN A NEWSPAPER OR MAGAZINE SUBSCRIPTION.
ONLY AN OLD-FASHIONED "LAND-LINE" FOR EMERGENCIES.
MAIL COLLECTION WAS A 3-MILE HIKE DOWN THE DRIVE.
THE FAMILY'S COPIOUS LIBRARY OFFERED NO RESPITE: IT CONTAINED ONLY DRY SCIENTIFIC TOMES.
3

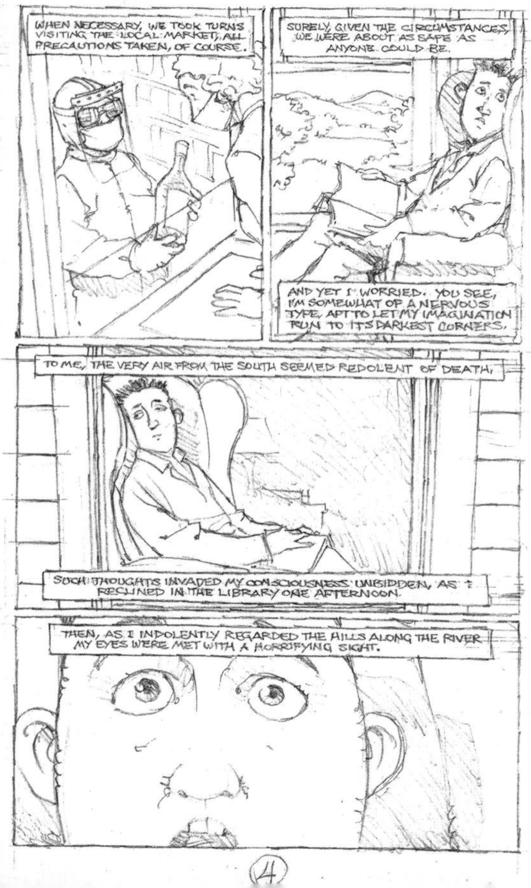

WHEN NECESSARY, WE TOOK TURNS VISITING THE LOCAL MARKET, ALL PRECAUTIONS TAKEN, OF COURSE.
SURELY, GIVEN THE CIRCUMSTANCES, WE WERE ABOUT AS SAFE AS ANYONE COULD BE.
AND YET I WORRIED. YOU SEE, I'M SOMEWHAT OF A NERVOUS TYPE, APT TO LET MY IMAGINATION RUN TO ITS DARKEST CORNERS.
TO ME, THE VERY AIR FROM THE SOUTH SEEMED REDOLENT OF DEATH.
SUCH THOUGHTS INVADED MY CONSCIOUSNESS UNBIDDEN, AS I RECLINED IN THE LIBRARY ONE AFTERNOON.
THEN, AS I INDOLENTLY REGARDED THE HILLS ALONG THE RIVER MY EYES WERE MET WITH A HORRIFYING SIGHT.
4

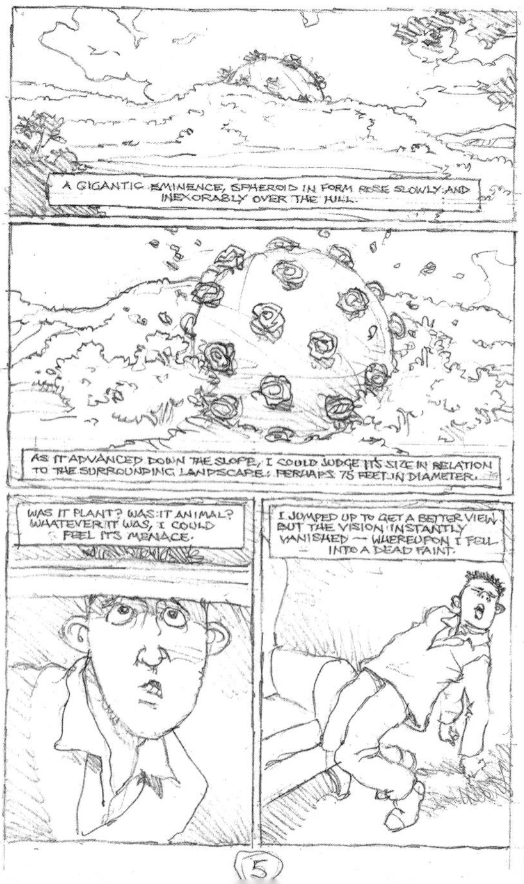

A GIGANTIC EMINENCE, SPHEROID IN FORM ROSE SLOWLY AND INEXORABLY OVER THE HILL.
AS IT ADVANCED DOWN THE SLOPE, I COULD JUDGE ITS SIZE IN RELATION TO THE SURROUNDING LANDSCAPE: PERHAPS 75 FEET IN DIAMETER.
WAS IT PLANT? WAS IT ANIMAL? WHATEVER IT WAS, I COULD FEEL ITS MENACE.
I JUMPED UP TO GET A BETTER VIEW, BUT THE VISION INSTANTLY VANISHED — WHEREUPON I FELL INTO A DEAD FAINT.
5

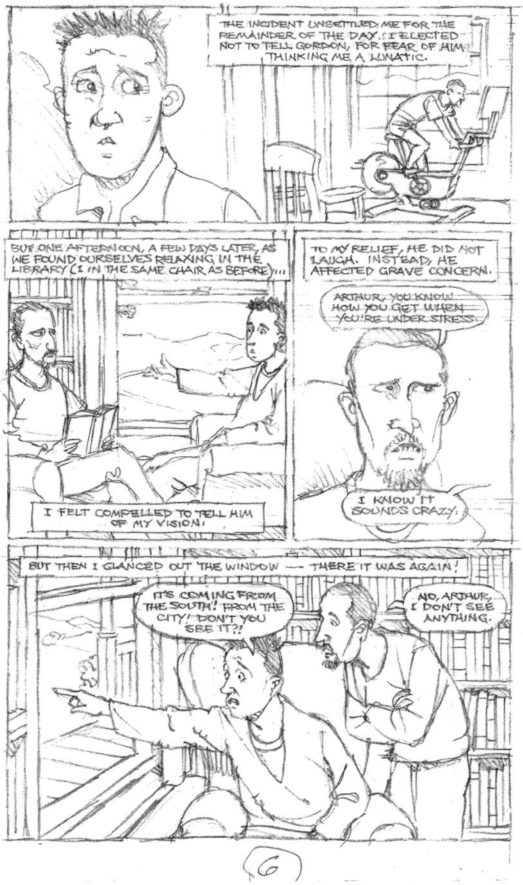
THE INCIDENT UNSETTLED ME FOR THE REMAINDER OF THE DAY. I ELECTED NOT TO TELL GORDON, FOR FEAR OF HIM THINKING ME A LUNATIC.
BUT ONE AFTERNOON, A FEW DAYS LATER, AS WE FOUND OURSELVES RELAXING IN THE LIBRARY (I IN THE SAME CHAIR AS BEFORE)...
I FELT COMPELLED TO TELL HIM OF MY VISION.
TO MY RELIEF, HE DID NOT LAUGH. INSTEAD, HE AFFECTED GRAVE CONCERN.
ARTHUR, YOU KNOW HOW YOU GET WHEN YOU'RE UNDER STRESS.
I KNOW IT SOUNDS CRAZY.
BUT THEN I GLANCED OUT THE WINDOW — THERE IT WAS AGAIN!
IT'S COMING FROM THE SOUTH! FROM THE CITY! DON'T YOU SEE IT?!
NO, ARTHUR, I DON'T SEE ANYTHING.
6

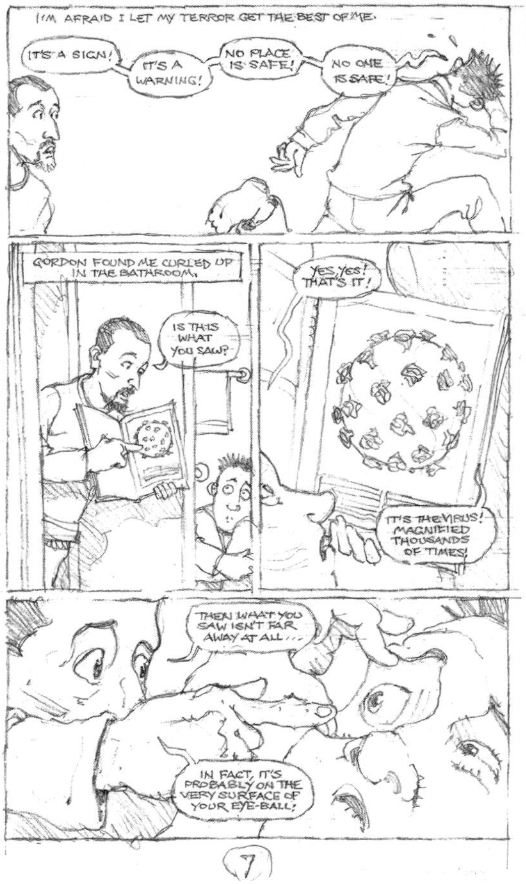
I'M AFRAID I LET MY TERROR GET THE BEST OF ME.
IT'S A SIGN!
IT'S A WARNING!
NO PLACE IS SAFE!
NO ONE IS SAFE!
GORDON FOUND ME CURLED UP IN THE BATHROOM.
IS THIS WHAT YOU SAW?
YES, YES! THAT'S IT!
IT'S THE VIRUS! MAGNIFIED THOUSANDS OF TIMES!
THEN WHAT YOU SAW ISN'T FAR AWAY AT ALL...
IN FACT, IT'S PROBABLY ON THE VERY SURFACE OF YOUR EYE-BALL!
7

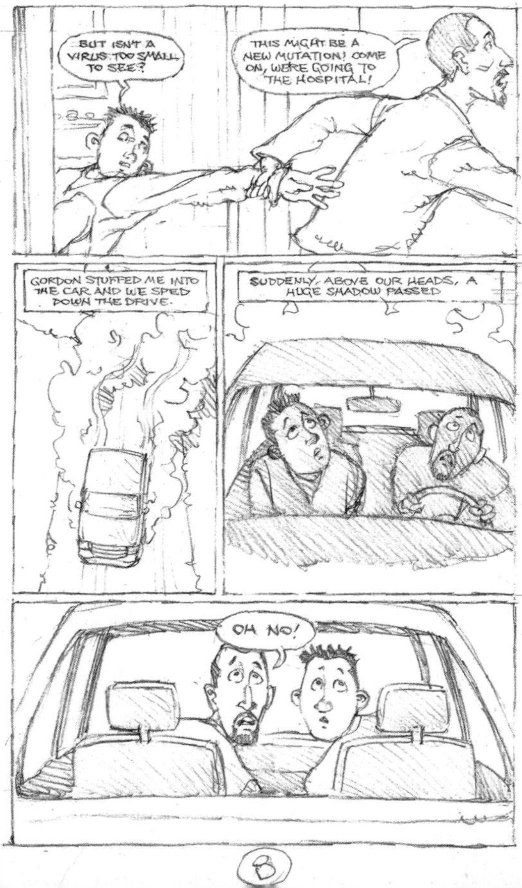
BUT ISN'T A VIRUS TOO SMALL TO SEE?
THIS MIGHT BE A NEW MUTATION! COME ON, WE'RE GOING TO THE HOSPITAL!
GORDON STUFFED ME INTO THE CAR AND WE SPED DOWN THE DRIVE.
SUDDENLY, ABOVE OUR HEADS, A HUGE SHADOW PASSED
OH NO!
8

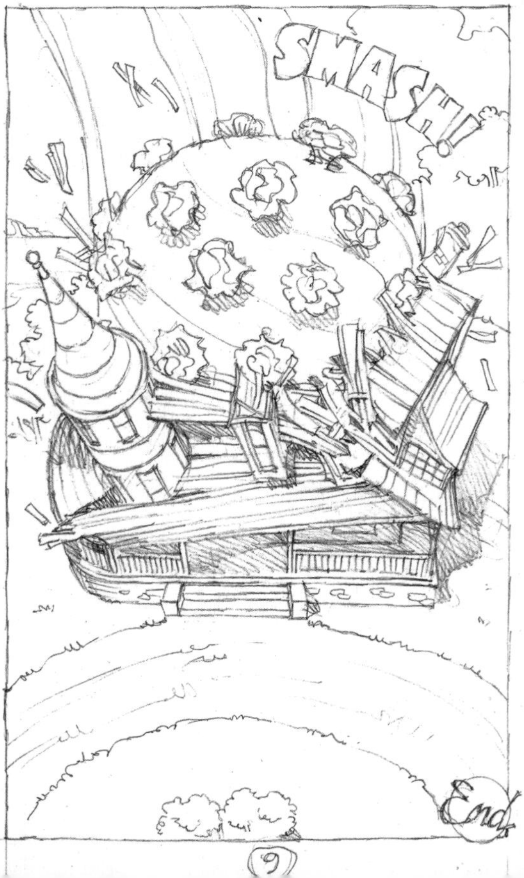
SMASH!
End
9

EDGAR ALLAN POE'S SNIFTER OF DEATH #1 COVER by Richard Williams

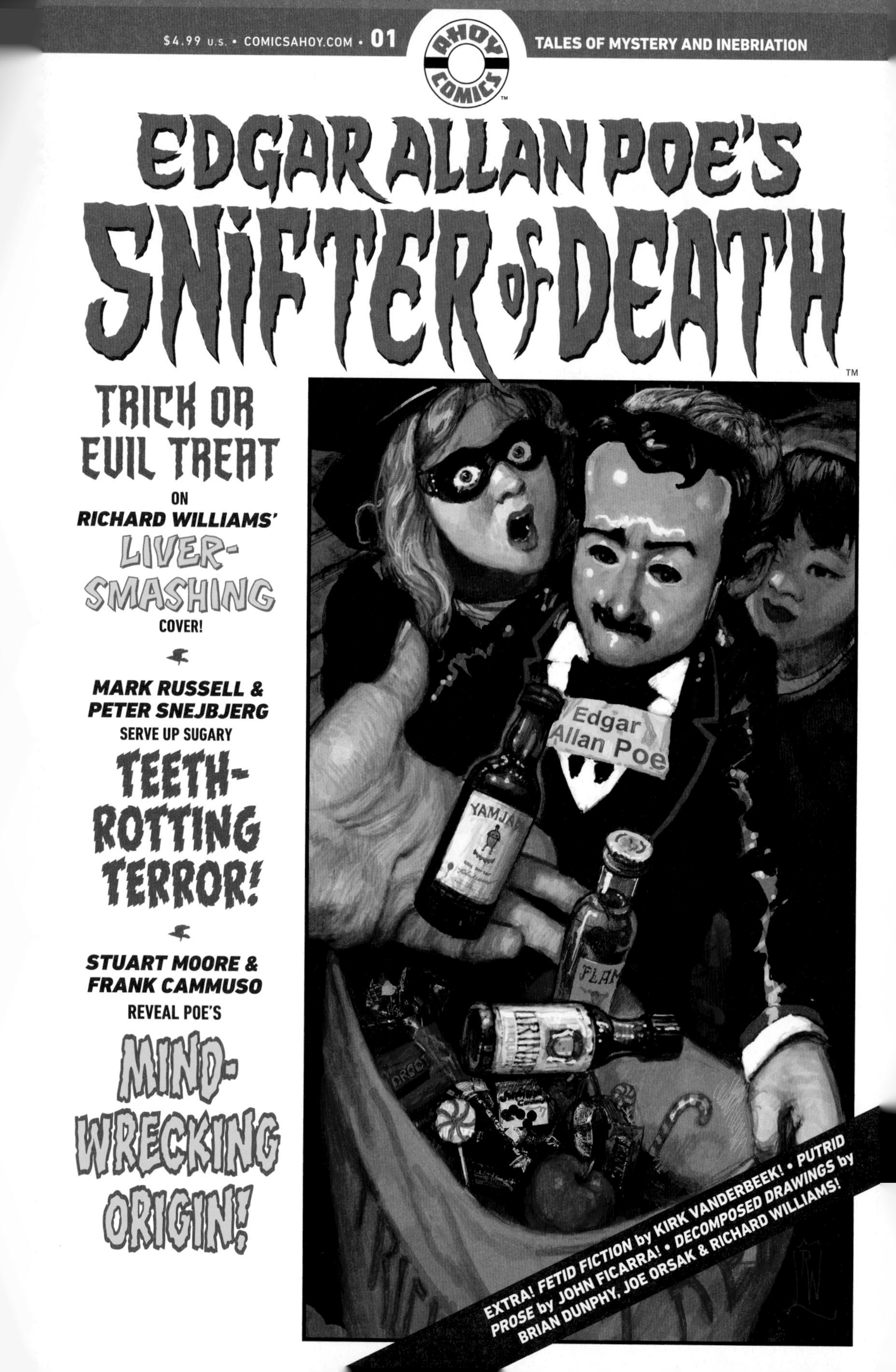
$4.99 U.S. • COMICSAHOY.COM • 01
AHOY COMICS
TALES OF MYSTERY AND INEBRIATION
EDGAR ALLAN POE'S
SNIFTER of DEATH
TRICK OR EVIL TREAT
ON RICHARD WILLIAMS' LIVER-SMASHING COVER!
MARK RUSSELL & PETER SNEJBJERG
SERVE UP SUGARY
TEETH-ROTTING TERROR!
STUART MOORE & FRANK CAMMUSO
REVEAL POE'S
MIND-WRECKING ORIGIN!
Edgar Allan Poe
YAMJAR
EXTRA! FETID FICTION by KIRK VANDERBEEK! • PUTRID PROSE by JOHN FICARRA! • DECOMPOSED DRAWINGS by BRIAN DUNPHY, JOE ORSAK & RICHARD WILLIAMS!

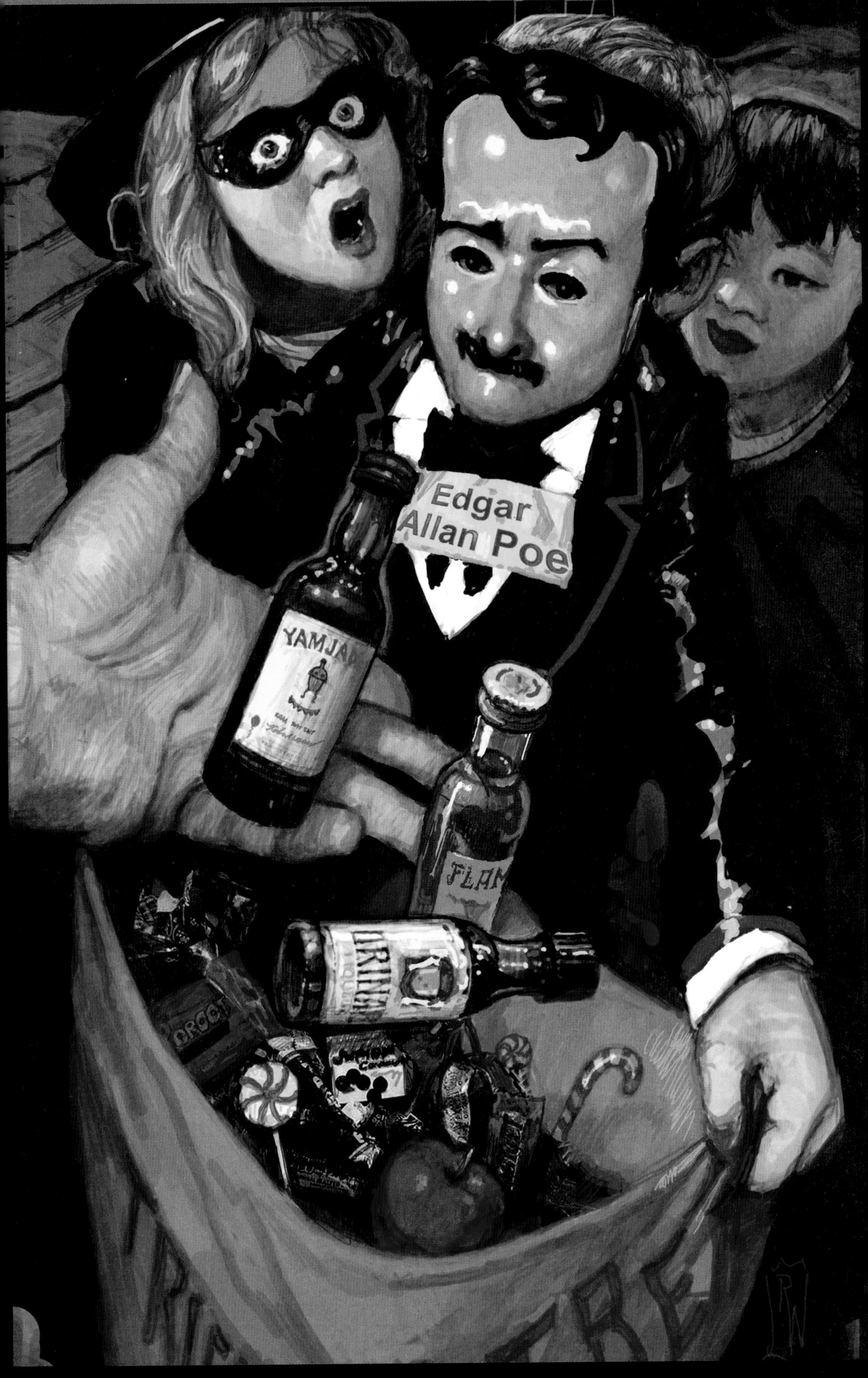
Edgar Allan Poe

EDGAR ALLAN POE'S SNIFTER OF DEATH #2 COVER by Richard Williams

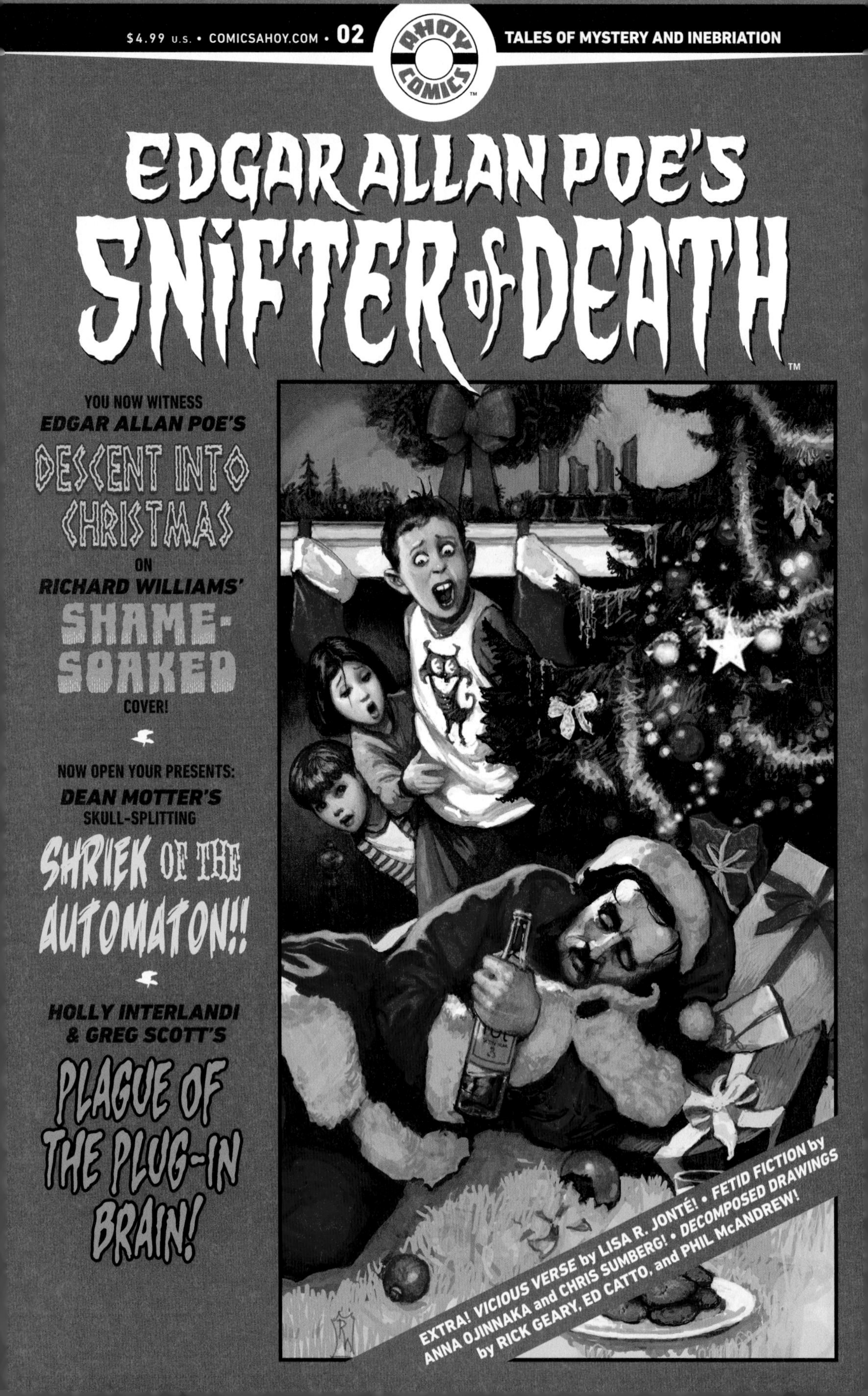
$4.99 U.S. • COMICSAHOY.COM • 02
AHOY COMICS
TALES OF MYSTERY AND INEBRIATION
EDGAR ALLAN POE'S
SNIFTER of DEATH
YOU NOW WITNESS
EDGAR ALLAN POE'S
DESCENT INTO CHRISTMAS
ON
RICHARD WILLIAMS'
SHAME-SOAKED
COVER!
NOW OPEN YOUR PRESENTS:
DEAN MOTTER'S
SKULL-SPLITTING
SHRIEK OF THE AUTOMATON!!
HOLLY INTERLANDI
& GREG SCOTT'S
PLAGUE OF THE PLUG-IN BRAIN!
EXTRA! VICIOUS VERSE by LISA R. JONTÉ! • FETID FICTION by
ANNA OJINNAKA and CHRIS SUMBERG! • DECOMPOSED DRAWINGS
by RICK GEARY, ED CATTO, and PHIL McANDREW!

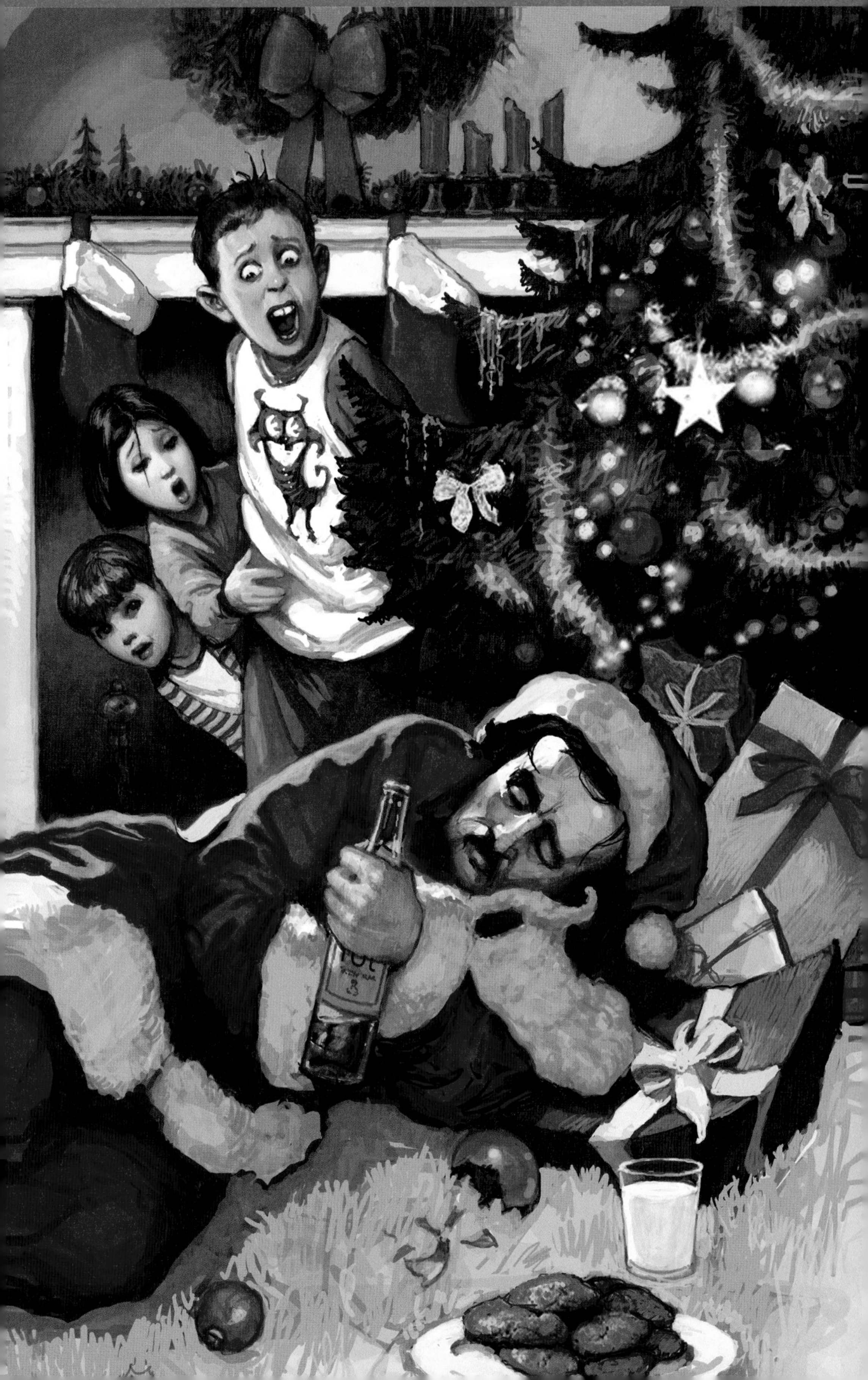

EDGAR ALLAN POE'S SNIFTER OF DEATH #3 COVER by Richard Williams

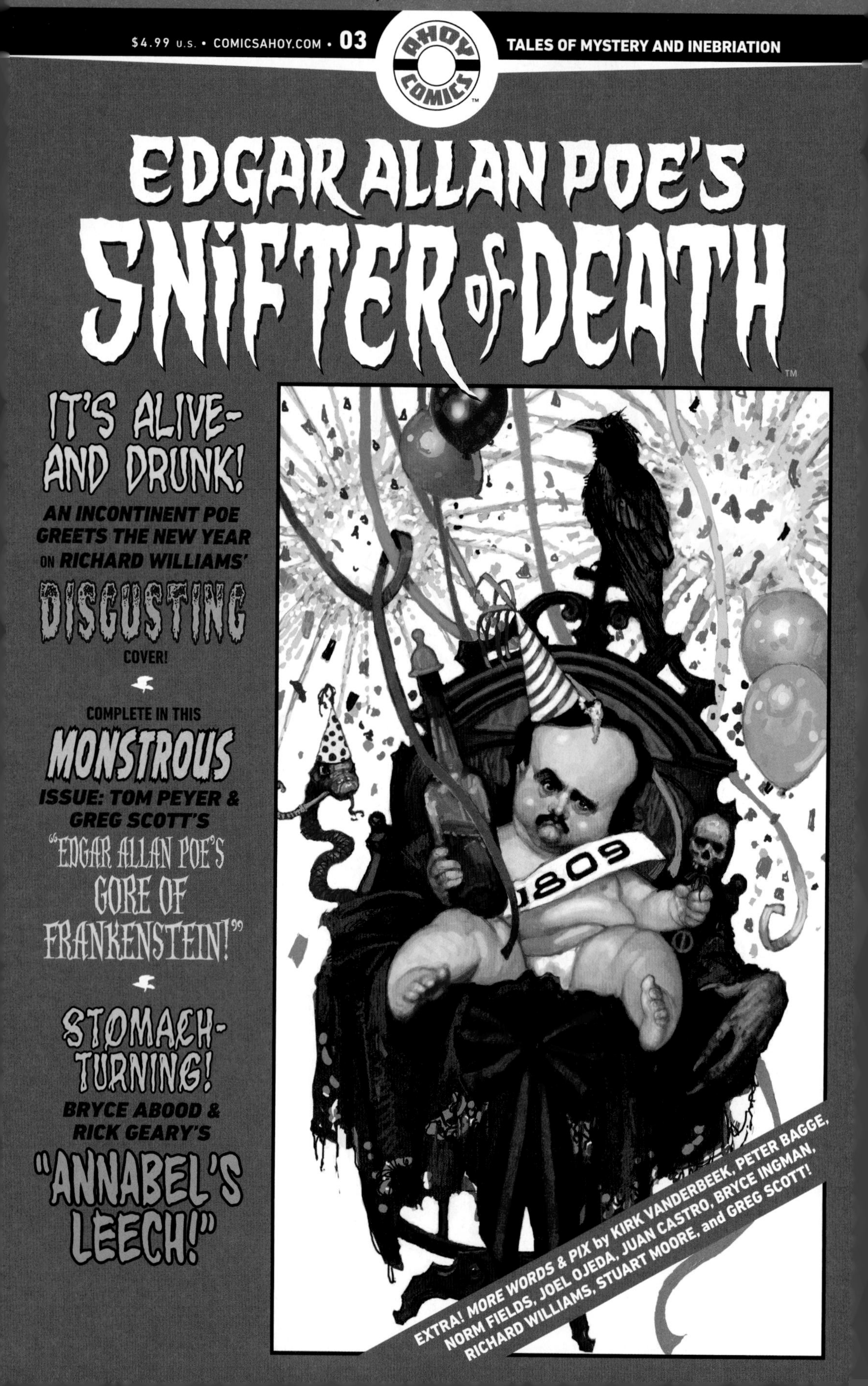

$4.99 U.S. • COMICSAHOY.COM • 03
AHOY COMICS
TALES OF MYSTERY AND INEBRIATION
EDGAR ALLAN POE'S SNIFTER OF DEATH
IT'S ALIVE- AND DRUNK!
AN INCONTINENT POE GREETS THE NEW YEAR ON RICHARD WILLIAMS' DISGUSTING COVER!
COMPLETE IN THIS MONSTROUS ISSUE: TOM PEYER & GREG SCOTT'S "EDGAR ALLAN POE'S GORE OF FRANKENSTEIN!"
STOMACH-TURNING! BRYCE ABOOD & RICK GEARY'S "ANNABEL'S LEECH!"
1809
EXTRA! MORE WORDS & PIX by KIRK VANDERBEEK, PETER BAGGE, NORM FIELDS, JOEL OJEDA, JUAN CASTRO, BRYCE INGMAN, RICHARD WILLIAMS, STUART MOORE, and GREG SCOTT!

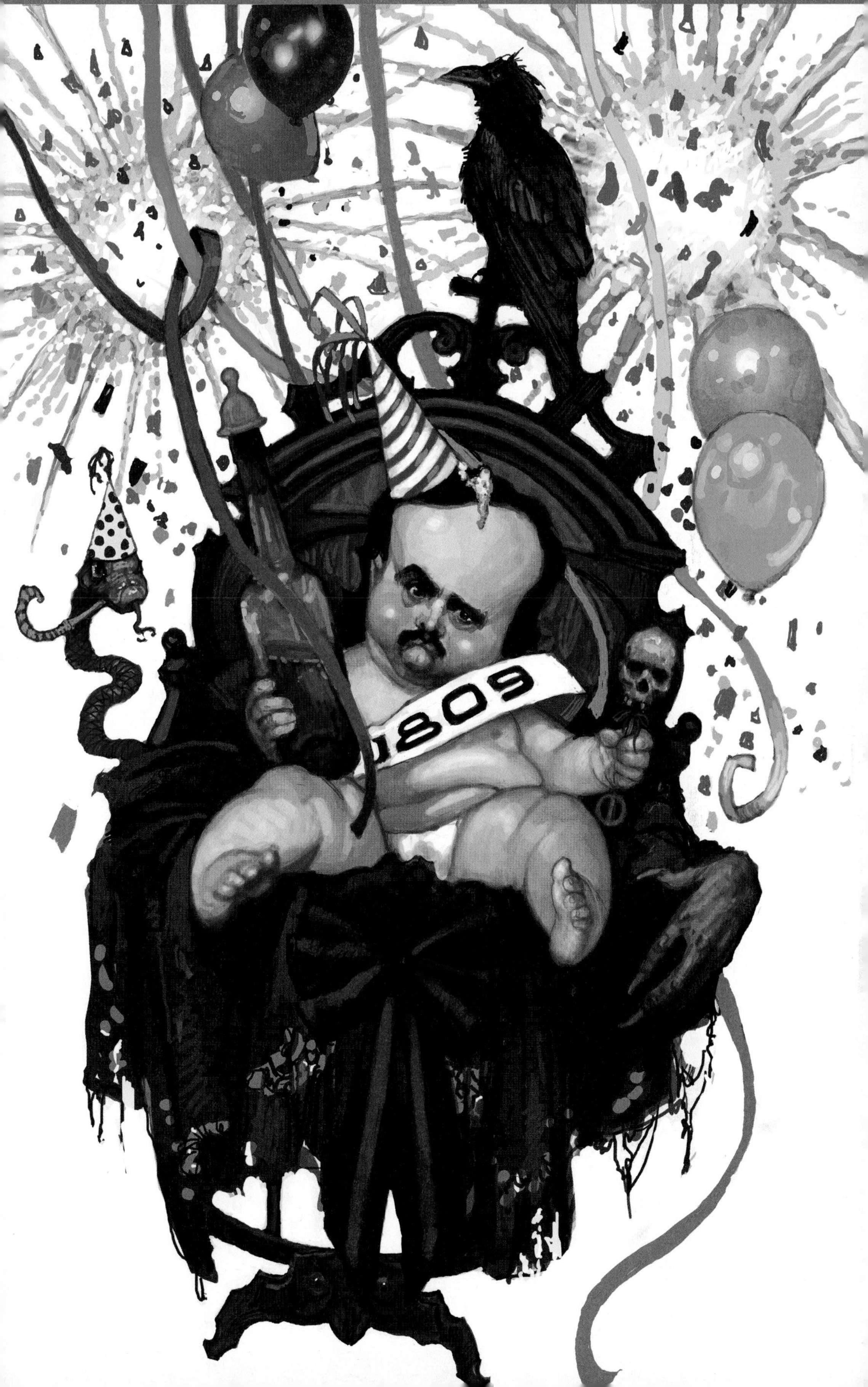
1809

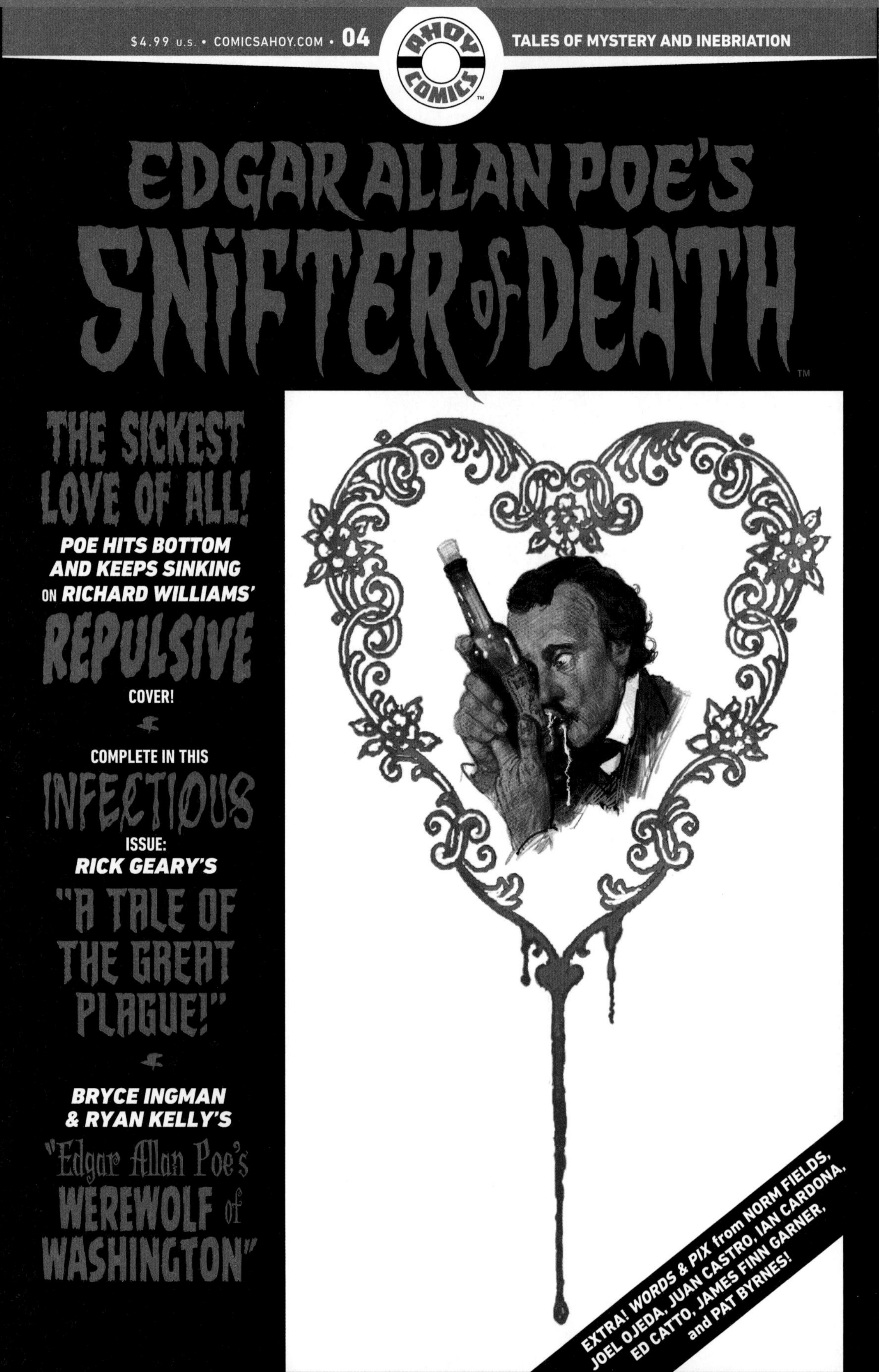
$4.99 U.S. • COMICSAHOY.COM • 04
AHOY COMICS
TALES OF MYSTERY AND INEBRIATION
EDGAR ALLAN POE'S
SNIFTER of DEATH
THE SICKEST LOVE OF ALL!
POE HITS BOTTOM AND KEEPS SINKING ON RICHARD WILLIAMS' REPULSIVE COVER!
COMPLETE IN THIS INFECTIOUS ISSUE:
RICK GEARY'S "A TALE OF THE GREAT PLAGUE!"
BRYCE INGMAN & RYAN KELLY'S "Edgar Allan Poe's WEREWOLF of WASHINGTON"
EXTRA! WORDS & PIX from NORM FIELDS, JOEL OJEDA, JUAN CASTRO, IAN CARDONA, ED CATTO, JAMES FINN GARNER, and PAT BYRNES!

EDGAR ALLAN POE'S SNIFTER OF DEATH #4 COVER by Richard Williams

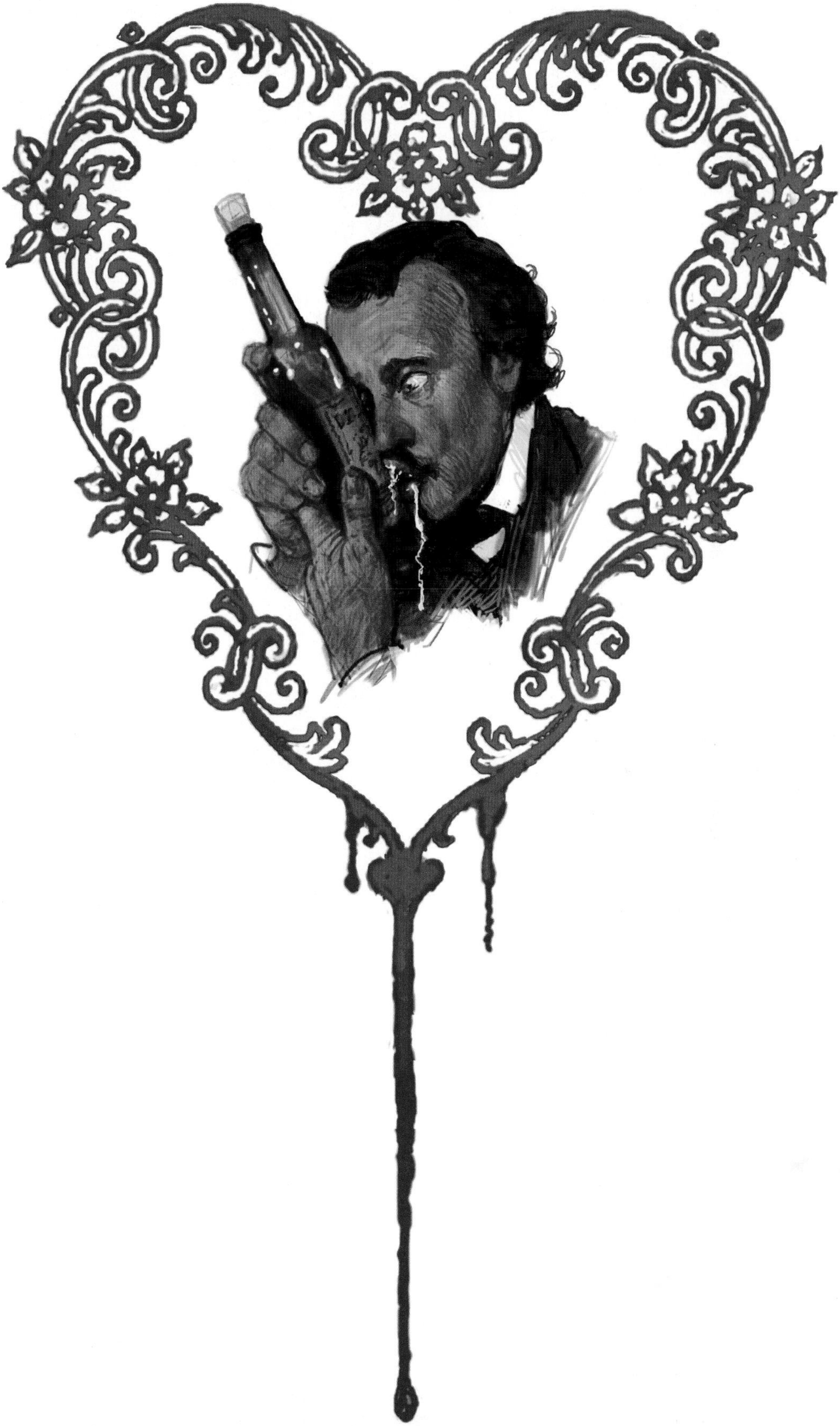

EDGAR ALLAN POE'S SNIFTER OF DEATH #5 COVER by Richard Williams

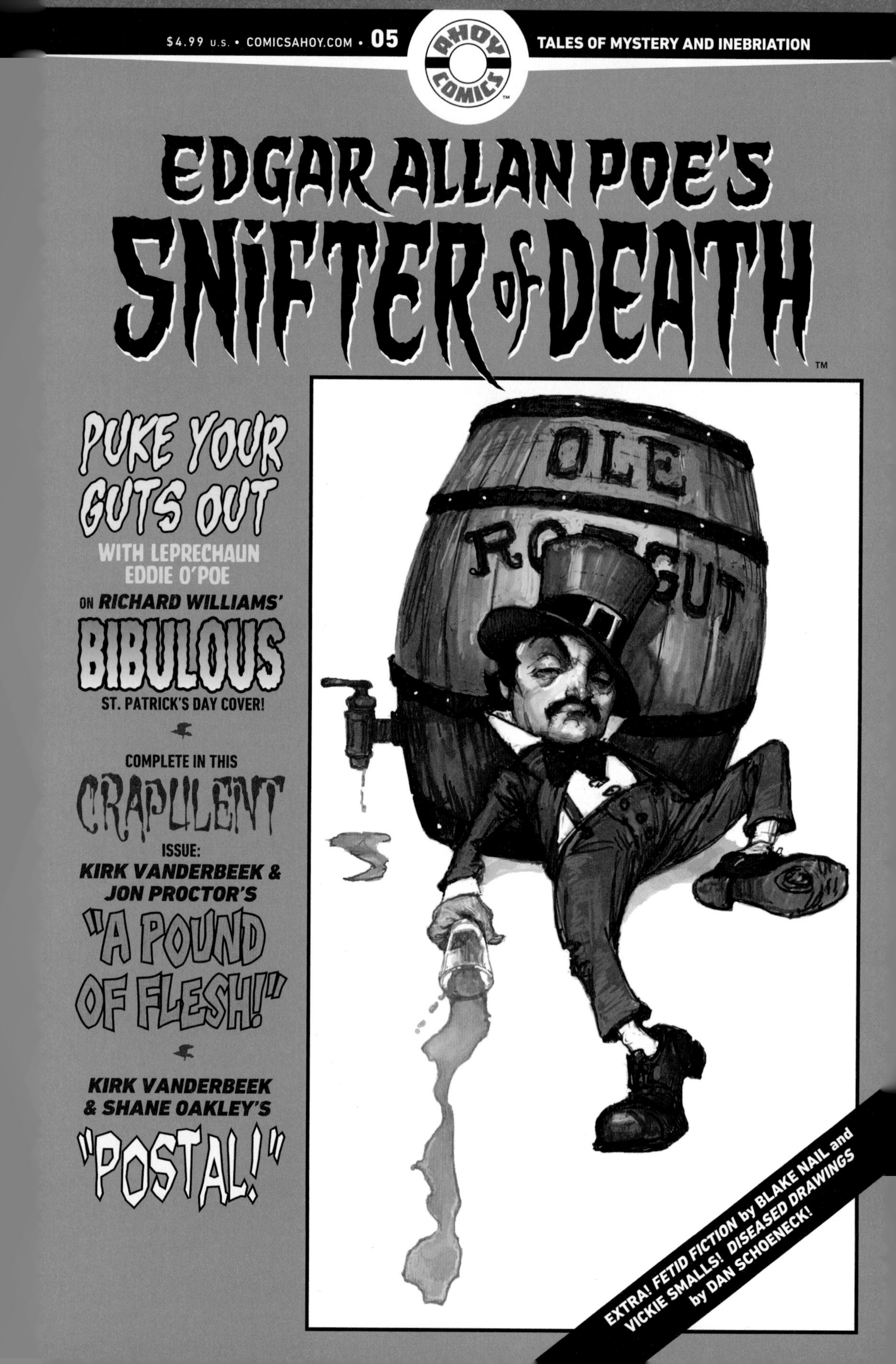

$4.99 U.S. • COMICSAHOY.COM • 05
AHOY COMICS
TALES OF MYSTERY AND INEBRIATION
EDGAR ALLAN POE'S
SNIFTER of DEATH
PUKE YOUR GUTS OUT
WITH LEPRECHAUN EDDIE O'POE
ON RICHARD WILLIAMS'
BIBULOUS
ST. PATRICK'S DAY COVER!
COMPLETE IN THIS
CRAPULENT
ISSUE:
KIRK VANDERBEEK & JON PROCTOR'S
"A POUND OF FLESH!"
KIRK VANDERBEEK & SHANE OAKLEY'S
"POSTAL!"
OLE
EXTRA! FETID FICTION by BLAKE NAIL and VICKIE SMALLS! DISEASED DRAWINGS by DAN SCHOENECK!

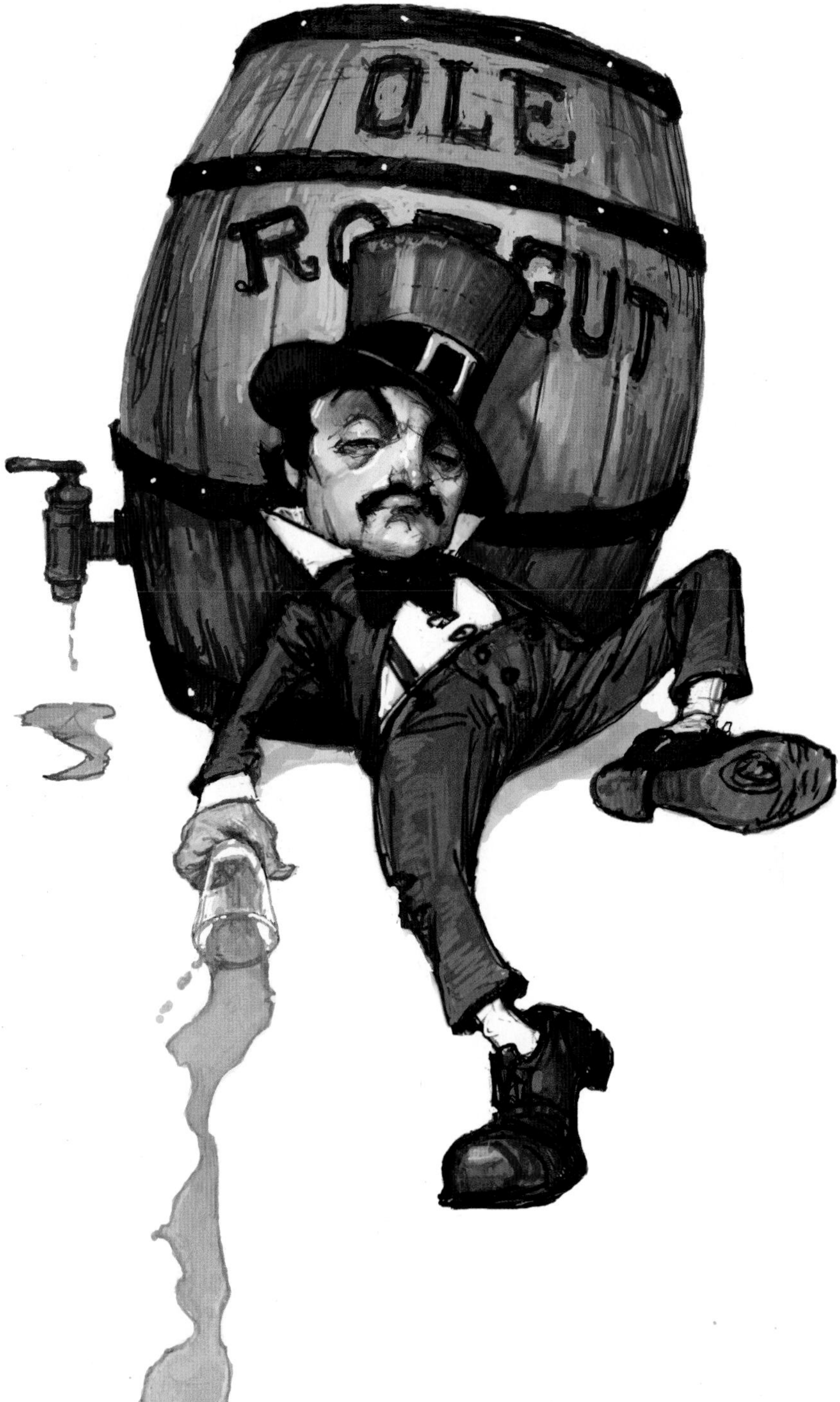
OLE

EDGAR ALLAN POE'S SNIFTER OF DEATH #6 COVER by Richard Williams

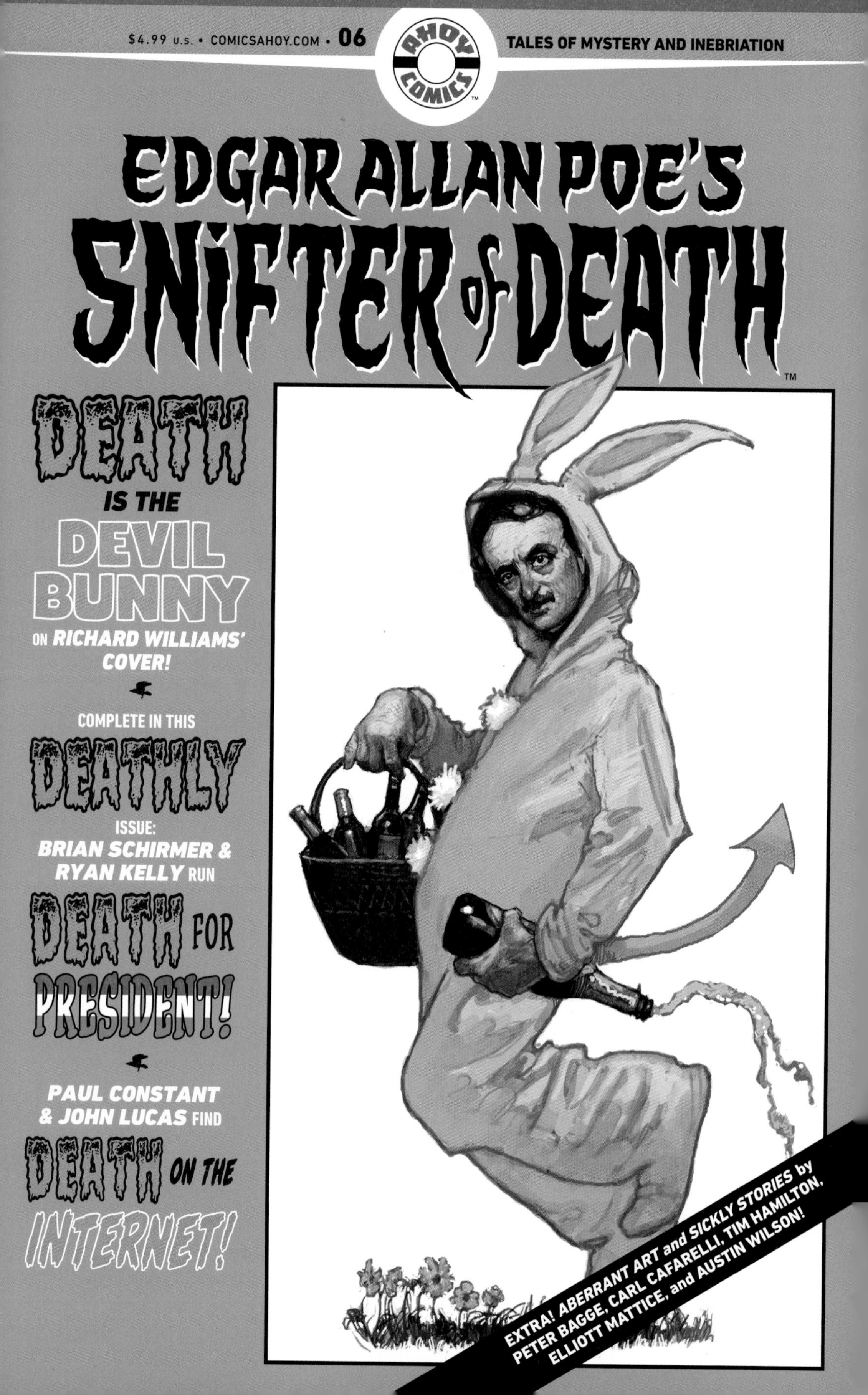
$4.99 U.S. • COMICSAHOY.COM • 06
AHOY COMICS
TALES OF MYSTERY AND INEBRIATION
EDGAR ALLAN POE'S
SNIFTER of DEATH
DEATH IS THE DEVIL BUNNY ON RICHARD WILLIAMS' COVER!
COMPLETE IN THIS DEATHLY ISSUE:
BRIAN SCHIRMER & RYAN KELLY RUN DEATH FOR PRESIDENT!
PAUL CONSTANT & JOHN LUCAS FIND DEATH ON THE INTERNET!
EXTRA! ABERRANT ART and SICKLY STORIES by PETER BAGGE, CARL CAFARELLI, TIM HAMILTON, ELLIOTT MATTICE, and AUSTIN WILSON!

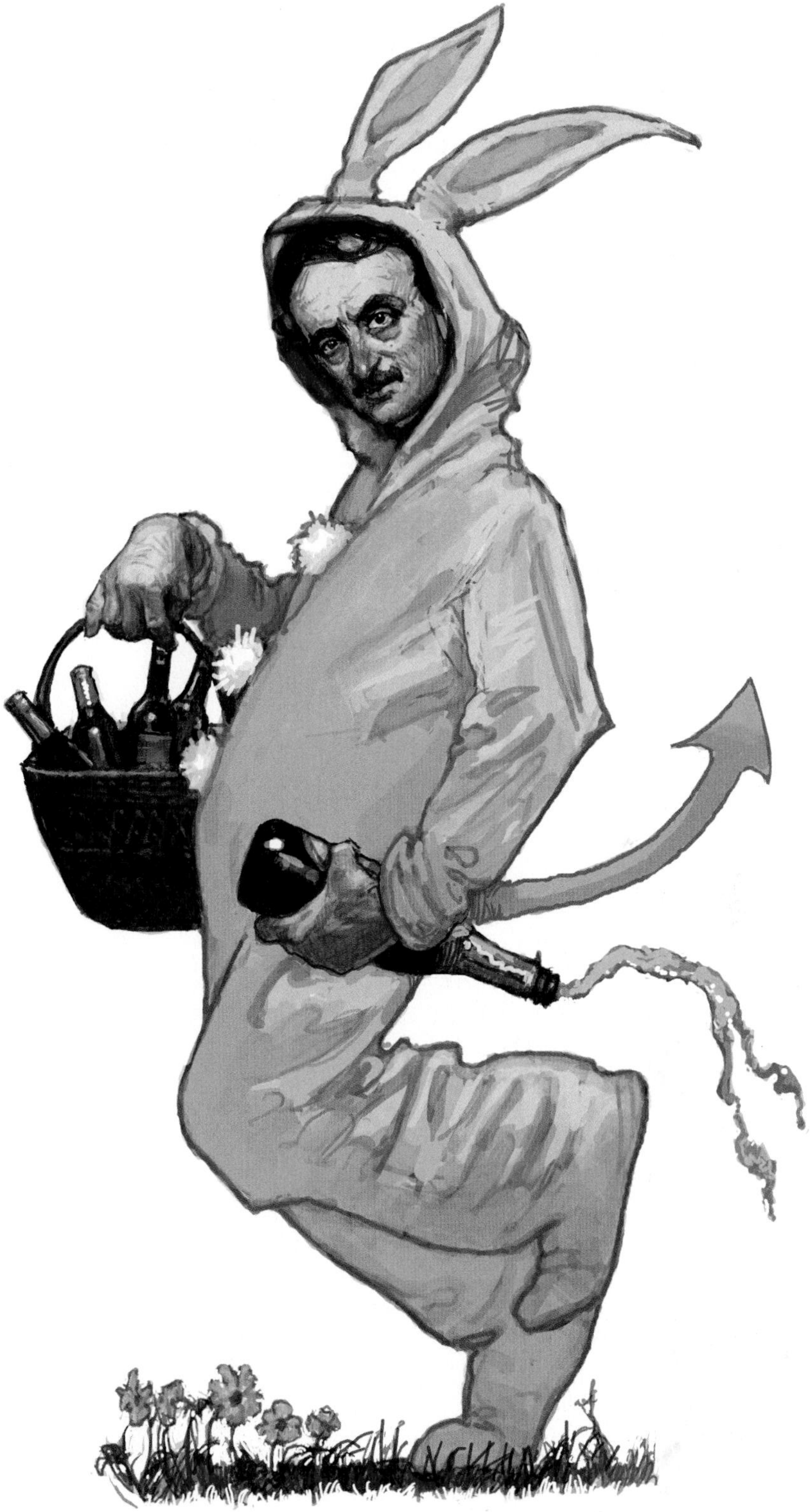

BIOGRAPHIES

BRYCE ABOOD is the fastest *Contra III* laser speedrunner in the world.

FRANK CAMMUSO creates brilliant graphic novels for children. The newest is the *Edison Beaker, Creature Seeker* series from Viking Books for Young Readers. Formerly, he was a political cartoonist for the Syracuse daily, *The Post-Standard*.

JUAN CASTRO, an inker and illustrator from Tijuana, Mexico, has been in the comics industry for over 10 years. He has worked on such titles as *Transformers, Halo: Escalation, Arrow, Aquaman, Grayson, Batgirl, Sensation Comics Featuring Wonder Woman*, and many more. He has been nominated for three Inkwell Awards.

PAUL CONSTANT has written journalism, criticism, and essays for the *Los Angeles Times, BuzzFeed*, the *Seattle Times, Business Insider, i09, Literary Hub*, and many other publications. His debut comic for AHOY with artist Alan Robinson, *PLANET OF THE NERDS*, was optioned for feature film development by Paramount Players. Find him online at paulconstant.com.

NORM FIELDS wrote 2,708 stories over a 40-year comics career. He is perhaps best remembered for "The Black Cat" (Blood of the Dead #19, Utility Periodicals, June 1953), "Edgar Allan Poe's The Black Cat" (Coffin of Bones #18, Radiogram Press, June 1953), and "Shriek of the Black Cat" (This Magazine Will Murder You #4, Wholesome Features, June 1953).

RICK GEARY has been a freelance cartoonist and illustrator for over 45 years. His illustrations and graphic stories have appeared in *National Lampoon, MAD, The New York Times, Heavy Metal, Disney Adventures*, and many other publications. His graphic novels include the biographies *J. Edgar Hoover* and *Trotsky* and the fictional murder mystery *Louise Brooks: Detective*. He has completed nine volumes in the series *A Treasury of Victorian Murder* and six volumes in *A Treasury of 20th Century Murder*, the latest of which is *Black Dahlia*. Rick and his wife Deborah live in Carrizozo, New Mexico.

Writer/actor/director **BRYCE INGMAN** is the only male writer living in Portland, Oregon without a beard. And it's not because he can't grow one. Because he totally can.

HOLLY INTERLANDI is a writer and editor of comics, fiction, articles, reviews, essays, interviews, and editorials (and poetry, but she hates saying that because it makes her sound like an obnoxious turd). She edited *Famous Monsters of Filmland* for nearly a decade and oversaw all of their comic releases, including *Lost in Space* and *Monster World*. She also wrote *Last Song* for Black Mask Studios. Holly lives in Los Angeles with her awesome dog.

RYAN KELLY is perhaps best known for the twelve-issue run of *Local* with writer, Brian Wood for Oni Press. Always a Mid-Westerner, Kelly received his art training at the Minneapolis College of Art and Design from which he graduated in 1998. There he studied under comic book artist, Peter Gross, with whom he worked on *The Books of Magic* and *Lucifer* for Vertigo. Ryan is on the MCAD staff, teaching classes for younger students and the occasional inking class as well. He has guest inked on *American Virgin* and drew the graphic novel *Giant Robot Warriors* as well as another Brian Wood project, Vertigo's *Northlanders*. Kelly has had various Minneapolis area exhibitions of his paintings. He has also done illustrations for *Rolling Stone* and *Time*, among others.

PAUL LITTLE is a Canadian colorist who has contributed hues to a bevy of titles from publishers including Image Comics (*Morning Glories, Five Weapons*), BOOM! Studios (*Sons of Anarchy, Palmiotti and Brady's The Big Con Job*), Joe Books (*Darkwing Duck, Disney Princess*), and many more. He lives in the honeymoon capital of the world and is one of the few people who can honestly claim to see Niagara Falls from his living room.

LEE LOUGHRIDGE is a color artist who has created award-winning work for Marvel, DC, Dark Horse and Image Comics throughout his 25-year career.

JOHN LUCAS is made entirely of popcorn and Karo syrup. It defies biology and common sense and has baffled the great minds of our times. Sadly, the judgements of big-brained muckity-mucks come at no small cost. So, John must toil away for the few odd coins a cartoonist's life will afford, that he may remain free of the chains of the debtors prison. John's work has appeared in funny books published by DC/Vertigo, Marvel, *MAD Magazine*, Dark Horse, Rebellion/2000AD, Image, Last Gasp, Top Cow, Insight, 1First and BOOM!, IDW, Dynamite, Kitchen Sink and, probably, a few others that have slipped my mind

STUART MOORE is a writer, a book editor, and an award-winning comics editor. His recent comics writing includes *Deadpool the Duck* (Marvel), *EGOs* (Image), and *HIGHBALL* (AHOY). His novels include three volumes of *The Zodiac Legacy*, a bestselling Disney Press series created and cowritten by Stan Lee, *Thanos: Death Sentence* (Marvel), and *Target: Kree* (Acontye). Stuart also handles Publishing Ops for AHOY on a freelance basis from his home in Brooklyn, New York, where he lives with two of the most spoiled cats on this or any other planet.

DEAN MOTTER, artist/writer and designer, is best known for the comics sensation *Mister X* (now in its 35th year). He has created works for *Superman*, *Batman* (most notably the award-winning "film noir" graphic novel, *Batman: Nine Lives*), *The Shadow*, *The Spirit*, *Mad Max: Fury Road*, *Spongebob Squarepants*, and *Wolverine*. His Vertigo series *Terminal City* was nominated for both Eisner and Kurtzman Awards. He is also known for the acclaimed graphic novel, *The Prisoner: Shattered Visage*, based on the '60s British TV series. Motter has also designed several award-winning album covers and book jackets. In the '90s Dean served on staff at both DC Comics and Byron Preiss Visual Publications as editorial art director, supervising graphic novel projects such as the works of *Ray Bradbury*, *Raymond Chandler* and *Harlan Ellison* as well as *The Hitchhiker's Guide to the Galaxy*. Motter has worked with the David S. Wyman Institute for Holocaust Studies and the Los Angeles Museum of the Holocaust illustrating the comic book accounts, *The Book Hitler Didn't Want You to Read*, and *Karski's Mission: To Stop the Holocaust*. Though he has spent most of his professional life in Toronto and Manhattan, he now resides and works tirelessly in Dixie.

SHANE OAKLEY became a freelance artist so he could get up late and not have to tuck in his shirt. He's been drawing comics for over 30 years for publishers both large and small. He's worked with Alan Moore, Neil Gaiman, Steve Niles and Alan Grant. He's normally not a name-dropper or braggart. He remembers newsstands full of monthly horror anthologies and never stops missing them. He likes Edgar Allan Poe very much.

JOEL OJEDA is a Mexican artist dabbling in moody, high power storytelling! He has lent his magic to companies such as UDON, Zenescope, DC comics, Heavy Metal and, now, proudly, AHOY!

TOM PEYER is cofounder and editor-in-chief of AHOY Comics. His recent writing projects include *THE WRONG EARTH*, *DRAGONFLY & DRAGONFLYMAN*, *PENULTIMAN*, *HASHTAG: DANGER*, and *HIGH HEAVEN*. In the before-time he wrote *Hourman* and *Legion of Super-Heroes* for DC Comics and was one of the original editors at Vertigo.

JON PROCTOR received his BFA from the Savannah College of Art and Design in 1997 and has since called the city home. In his early career, he worked primarily in the comic book industry. In addition to credits at Marvel and DC Comics, among others, Jon co-created the *Black Diamond* series with Larry Young at AIT/Planet Lar and more recently co-created *Gun Theory* with writer Daniel Way for Dark Horse. Jon has otherwise amassed an impressive client list for his illustration work in both editorial and commercial environments including The Wall Street Journal, Nike, Adidas, Amazon, and Cartoon Network. He has also worked for both mainstream and educational publishing houses, as well as local and regional press imprints. Away from the worktable, Jon enjoys travel both near and far—from trips to the local farmer's market to travels abroad.

MARK RUSSELL is the author of not one, but two, books about the Bible: *God Is Disappointed in You* and *Apocrypha Now*. In addition, he is the writer behind AHOY's *SECOND COMING*, *BILLIONAIRE ISLAND* and "The Monster Serials" in *EDGAR ALLAN POE'S SNIFTER OF TERROR*, as well as various DC comic books including *Prez*, *The Flintstones*, and *Exit Stage Left: The Snagglepuss Chronicles*. His series *Not All Robots*, co-created with Mike Deodato, won the Eisner Award for Best Humor Publication. He lives in obscurity with his family in Portland, Oregon.

BRIAN SCHIRMER writes comics like *Quests Aside* (Vault Comics), *Fairlady* and *Black Jack Ketchum* (both for Image Comics), and the self-published *Ultrasylvania*. In past lives, he's been a nightclub DJ, an improviser, a writer/director of zero-budget digital feature films, a vampire hunter, and a university professor. Only one of these is a lie.

GREG SCOTT is a comic book artist who pencils and inks his own work. He has drawn such titles as *X-Files*, *Black Hood*, *Steve McQueen*, and *Area 51*. He broke into comics through espionage: learning the time of day Marvel editors went outside for a cigarette break, he passed them art samples and was quickly given an assignment.

MADELINE SEELY is a multimedia artist and musician currently living and working in New York City. After receiving her BFA in painting from the Maryland Institute College of Art, she decided to pursue pretty much any creative outlet other than painting. Whether she's making heavy electronic music, weird videos, experimenting with new vehicles for eating hummus, or coloring for comic books, she's having fun and learning along the way.

PETER SNEJBJERG draws drawings for a living and has done so for many years. He has worked for a number of American and international comic book publishers. He lives in Copenhagen, Denmark.

FELIPE SOBREIRO is a Brazilian artist and colorist. He has worked for all major comic book publishers, including Marvel, DC, Image, Dark Horse, IDW, Heavy Metal and others.

ROB STEEN is the illustrator of *Flanimals*, the best-selling series of children's books written by Ricky Gervais, and *Erf*, a children's book written by Garth Ennis.

ANDY TROY has colored for Marvel Comics, DC Comics, Extreme Studios, and others, working on such characters as *Spawn*, *Batman*, *Captain America*, and *Iron Fist*. He lives and works in Huntsville, AL, where he used to play in the metal band Diamond White.

KIRK VANDERBEEK wrings words of wonder from thin air…or he just bangs his head solemnly, rhythmically, against the keyboard. It really depends upon the day. His fiction has appeared in *Falling Star Magazine*, *Cosmic Horror Monthly* and more, while his screenplays have earned accolades from a number of festivals and competitions and will surely (read this next part with desperation) make him rich one day. This anthology marks his comic writing debut.

RICHARD WILLIAMS' illustration work has appeared in many national magazines, most notably *MAD*, for which he was the cover artist during the 1980s. He has also illustrated children's books (*The Legend of the Christmas Rose*, *Lewis and Clark: Explorers of the American West*) and painted covers for many young adult books such as *Encyclopedia Brown*. His paintings have been purchased by Steven Spielberg, George Lucas, and Howard Stern and are in the collections of the Society of Illustrators and the Library of Congress.